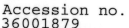

Irish Pastoral

Nostalgia and Twentieth-Century Irish Literature

OONA FRAWLEY
Queen's University, Belfast

IRISH ACADEMIC PRESS

DUBLIN • PORTLAND, OR

First published in 2005 by
IRISH ACADEMIC PRESS
44, Northumberland Road, Dublin 4, Ireland

and in the United States of America by
IRISH ACADEMIC PRESS
c/o ISBS, Suite 300, 920 NE 58th Avenue, Portland, Oregon 97213–3644

© Oona Frawley 2005

website: www.iap.ie

British Library Cataloguing in Publication Data
A catalogue entry is available on request

ISBN 0–7165–3321–9 (cloth)
ISBN 0–7165–3322–7 (paper)

Library of Congress Cataloguing-in-Publication Data
A catalog entry is available on request

Typeset in 11pt/13pt Sabon
by Carrigboy Typesetting Services, Co. Cork
Printed by in Great Britain by MPG Books Ltd, Bodmin, Cornwall

Contents

Acknowledgements

As is so often the case with studies that grew from the seeds of doctoral dissertations, this one owes a particular debt of gratitude to the advisor who offered insight and support. Catherine McKenna's wide-ranging knowledge and linguistic skill (and her patience with those like myself whose mastery of old Irish verb forms was often simply absent) have been an inspiration, as have her generosity, good humour and her consistently sharp editorial eye. For all of her work and effort, my warmest thanks. Clare Carroll and Joan Richardson, also at the Graduate Center, the City University of New York, were supportive and encouraging readers of the dissertation that gave way to this study, and their comments were tremendously useful in the preparation of this manuscript. Angus Fletcher's Graduate Center seminars provided the most fruitful ground for thoughts about nature, space, and about the sheer wonder of literature.

Several friends have generously read versions of various chapters. Particularly warm thanks to Lahney Preston-Matto, Spurgeon Thompson, Peter van de Kamp and Maggie Williams for their insightful commentaries, and their generosity in sharing their expertise, which has undoubtedly saved me many blunders. Any that remain are, needless to say, my own. A particular thanks to Lisa Hyde at Irish Academic Press, for all of her work on this book's behalf.

This book has been, fittingly, the work of two worlds: that of New York, and that of the Wicklow Mountains. My extraordinary fortune has not just been the experience of city and country, but to have had such love and support in both places. My mother, Maureen Frawley, who with my father, Bernard Frawley, introduced me to the long-distance idea of Ireland as well as to Ireland itself, has been involved with this subject matter for at least as long as I have been. For her willingness to listen to my excitement about all manner of literary and critical discoveries, and for unswayable support, I am most grateful. In Ireland, Donal Lenehan has provided far more than a set of willing ears; he has been unstinting in his support, understanding and love, and for all of these things I feel truly blessed. To my mother, to Donal, and to the memory of my father, this book is dedicated.

Irish Pastoral:
The Nostalgic Mode

Amongst scholars and writers, it has long been a commonplace to remark upon Irish literature's preoccupation with place, nature and landscape. From eighteenth-century antiquarians to Matthew Arnold, from William Butler Yeats to Seamus Heaney, the presence of nature and landscape in Irish literature has, over a period of several hundred years, consistently elicited attention. Too often, however, this attention has been limited to simple commentary when, instead, analysis was needed: the ways in which the representation of nature in Irish literature draws upon or deviates from classical and English pastoral models have not been considered.

As an exemplary probe into the development of Irish pastoral, this study offers an analysis of several Revival and twentieth-century texts, and attempts to situate these analyses in a wider Irish tradition of writing on nature and place. However, this book aims to go beyond the establishment of similarities or distinctions in representation, and starts from the premise that colonial and post-colonial cultures experience a fraught relationship with the nature and landscape of their homelands. The landscape of Ireland in, for example, the late nineteenth century, is both 'Irish' – in the sense that it is physically attached to the country – and not Irish – in that 'Ireland' does not exist as an independent nation; the tension between these two states manifests itself in the policy, law and debate of the time: but it is also manifested in literature. In literature, I argue, nature and landscape become signifiers, lenses through which it is possible to examine cultural and historical developments. Focusing attention on texts from the Revival as well as from the decades that follow Irish independence allows us to ascertain how cultural changes might be represented in depictions of nature and landscape. How, for example, does existence under a colonial government influence one's attitude towards the landscape?

How does the conception of nature and landscape change as a culture becomes an independent nation state? Do attitudes towards national space change as the nation ages? How do urbanization and increasing ties with Europe affect the representation of place and nature in Irish literature in the late twentieth century? How does an author's class and/or gender impact upon their representation of Irish place?

As these questions indicate, Irish literature's keen involvement with nature and place can be read as a verbal charting of not only the physical but also the social landscape. 'Landscape'[1] is itself always, as the art historian Simon Schama argues, a product of culture:

> Landscapes are culture before they are nature; constructs of the imagination projected onto wood and water and rock . . . But it should also be acknowledged that once a certain idea of landscape, a myth, a vision, establishes itself in an actual place, it has a peculiar way of muddling, categorizing, of making metaphors more real than their referents; of becoming, in fact, part of the scenery.[2]

Our ideas of landscape, in other words, settle over the land itself, forming ghostly fossils; it is thus possible to sample the strata, as it were, for the theme and development of nature and landscape in Irish literature.

Ireland's earliest literature demonstrates a marked preoccupation with place and the natural world, attested to by whole tracts dedicated to *dindshenchas* (a part of the larger *shenchas* of the Irish bard), or the lore of place.[3] This concern with the beauties of the external world and local narratives of place survives through the centuries, making itself apparent in medieval lyrics devoted to the praise of nature and God, in Finn and Cuchulain lore, and in bardic poetry. The tradition that the authors of these works were so conscious of is eventually inherited by the literature of the Revival, whose authors, in turn, after inhabiting the tradition, themselves pass it on. This engagement with a literary tradition is inevitably evolutionary: eighth-, twelfth-, sixteenth- and twentieth-century authors all write of nature and landscape differently. We might ask, then, whether some semblance of an 'original' tradition whispers from page to page, from generation to generation.

Irish literature demonstrates impulses to preserve both general nature and specific place; both strains consist of the commemoration of the physical landscape. Frequently such commemoration also memorializes loss – whether loss of the person for whom a place is named, or of the social system that witnessed the landscape described – and invokes nostalgia. Nature and nostalgia are thus intimately connected in Irish literature over many centuries, in that nature becomes a frequent site for nostalgia, a site from which to express the longing for lost culture.

The word 'nostalgia', from the Greek *nostos*, home, and *algos*, pain, was originally used in 1688 by a doctor to describe a condition of homesickness.[4] The word as it is used now, however, has expanded beyond its original definition: when we say that someone is feeling nostalgic,[5] we suggest that they are in a reverie-like state of remembrance for experiences which, as past, are unrecoverable.[6] The philosopher Gaston Bachelard has noted, however, that while memories represent the theoretically unrecoverable past,[7] 'the more securely they are fixed in space, the sounder they are'.[8] Bachelard's idea suggests a possible explanation for the intersection of particular, localized place and nature in Irish literature, and the theme of nostalgia. The more specific the description or setting for a poem or narrative, the more likely it will be to survive in the mind. This idea seems particularly important given that Irish literature – like many other literatures – is influenced by oral traditions of recitation and performance, to which memory was clearly of utmost significance.[9]

When nostalgia extends beyond the individual, it can become a sociological phenemenon that revolves around a longing for lost culture or theoretically unrecoverable past.[10] In this sense, nostalgia serves, quite effectively, as a safety mechanism designed to bridge past and present for cultures as they experience change. In post-colonial cultures, and in cultures that have experienced large scale emigration or social disruption, one would thus expect to find high levels of nostalgia, whether for the pre-colonial past, or for a time before emigration was economically and socially necessary. In Ireland, with its strange status as a western European former colony and its history of emigration, nostalgia has functioned at all of these levels.

Like the presence of nature and landscape in Irish literature, nostalgia has been much cited in relation to late-nineteenth- and twentieth-century Irish culture.[11] For many involved in Ireland's cultural Revival, and for many of the critics of this key period, the value of Irish culture lay in the past. So powerful was nostalgia as a sociological phenomenon in late-nineteenth- and early-twentieth-century Irish culture, in fact, that it established a stranglehold on culture and politics.[12] However, while studies of recent decades have offered revisionary critiques of the Revival for its overemphasis on nostalgia, there has been little attempt to analyse or trace the roots of the phenonenon.

Revivalists did not, in fact, invent the idea of looking towards the Irish past for cultural value; the conception of the Irish as a nostalgic, sentimental people has existed for centuries. 'Stereotypes', Terry Eagleton has written, 'are not to be confused with reality, and many of them are simply baseless; but they may occasionally provide clues to specific social conditions'.[13] The stereotype of the nostalgic and, from approximately the nineteenth century on, sentimental Irish is at once historically accurate and exaggerated. When it does exist, this sentiment and this nostalgia seem to derive from cultural instability: during times of unrest or insecurity, nostalgia functions to remind individuals, generations and entire cultures of times that, because of their distance from the unsettled present, seem safer and more stable. In other cases, though, the idea of the Irish as a nostalgic people is one imposed from without, based on Romantic and colonial ideology. In both cases – in the actual, manifested nostalgia within Ireland, and in the ideas imposed from without – a connection is forged between nostalgia and nature. So intimate are nature and nostalgia as themes, in fact, that Irish literature's use of nature is characterized by a continual heightening over time of the nostalgia present in the traditional pastoral mode derived from Theocritus and Virgil, resulting in what I will call the nostalgic mode,[14] or, more simply, Irish pastoral.

The traditional pastoral as developed by Theocritus and Virgil involves a seeming simplification and idealization of an existence in the natural world set against the mostly unwritten background of the court or city. Into this pastoral mode creeps a nostalgia for a simpler life and traditional virtues. By the time of the Renaissance, when the English pastoral bloomed under the twinned suns of Nature and Art, this literary convention had become a vehicle for philosophical and ideological debates, as the pastoral came to critique contemporary culture by comparing it to an imagined pure and simple existence of long ago. Thus what began as the 'simplest' of modes became one of the most complex and highly wrought, a set stage for sophisticated ideas and ideologies. William Empson's *Some Versions of Pastoral* and Raymond Williams's *The Country and the City* both explore and develop these ideas, demonstrating the endurance of the mode into modern English literature. While such studies have become cornerstones of the study of *English* pastoral, they do not account for the development of the *Irish* pastoral. Virgil and Theocritus's pastorals offered an idealization of a simple life in nature that implied a critique of their cultures; pastorals written under the rule of a colonial government about nature and landscape are necessarily different, and contain, as will become clear, not only idealizations of culture lost under colonial rule, but also critiques of that rule itself. Colonial pastorals are quite literally about 'homesickness'; the nostalgia contained in them is very real indeed.

In the chapters that follow, this study attempts a preliminary inquiry into 'Irish pastoral'. Harold Toliver introduced his study of 'pastoral forms and attitudes' by writing that 'Whether or not the texts examined here need all be considered "pastorals" is not as important as our discovering something in them through this lens that would be less noticeable through another'.[15] Like Toliver and Empson, I approach the texts examined in this study as 'versions' of a genre that is, in Ireland, necessarily hybrid, in the hope that something will indeed be revealed by huddling a diverse group of texts and authors under one umbrella. This assessment of the palimpsestic Irish pastoral begins with texts from the period of the Revival and moves through the late twentieth century, after offering a brief overview of the representation of nature in earlier Irish literature. Because this study presents itself as an exploratory one into largely uncharted territory, the focus has been limited to several major figures in Irish literature over the last century. While the inclusion of a wider range of authors would, of course, have been ideal, there is simply not the space within the present work to spread a wider net.

Situating Yeats and Synge against a backdrop of the earlier Irish literary treatment of nature and place offers the opportunity to reassess that which we think we know well. Scholarly analyses of major Revival figures such as Synge and Yeats have often begun with one or other of two things. First, there is the widely noted fact that the Ireland of which Yeats and Synge wrote drew upon earlier Irish literature for mythological stories or for character. Rarely, however, does scholarship note possible thematic or generic debts that Yeats and Synge might have had to early and medieval Irish literature. Second, there has been a general assumption that the idealizations of the nature and landscape of Ireland in Yeats's and Synge's respective works drew upon a European tradition of Romanticism and grew out of the need to create a self-consciously national literature. While in recent decades there have been many reconsiderations of the Revival, these axiomatic ideas have remained in place. When these premises are taken together, as they often are, an artificial divide arises between Revival literature and earlier Irish literature. Irish literature before the Revival becomes dissociative, out of sync, out of time: 'discovered' by Revival authors, raided only for plot or character, but not for theme, and certainly not for tone. While it is inarguable that Yeats and Synge wrote out of their own times and so reflect them, their immersion in and commitment to Irish literature and myth means that the break between medieval Irish literature and the Revival cannot be so sharp. There must, as well, be some continuity: by examining their work against a background of earlier Irish representations of nature, this study hopes to show a sense of thematic continuity. In seeking to demonstrate the endurance of a mode of Irish pastoral into the twentieth century, this study also challenges received ideas about Synge and particularly Yeats as representing nature and landscape in an exaggeratedly nostalgic and sentimental fashion, arguing that, on the contrary, both Yeats and Synge demonstrate the influence of an Irish pastoral tradition that goes beyond simple nostalgia and becomes political.

Another platitude about twentieth-century Irish literature is that authors like James Joyce and Samuel Beckett broke sharply from the literature of the Revival, writing against 'romanticized' views of nature as well as against nostalgia. While there is certainly truth in this idea, an insistence on it as absolute disallows the possibility of examining literature for a thematic such as nature and landscape. One strand of continuity between all of these authors is, I argue, a link between nature, landscape and place, and nostalgia. If Yeats's and Synge's representations of nature and place might be more fruitfully understood not solely in the context of Romanticism but also in the context of the Irish literary tradition, Joyce and Beckett's representations of nature and place might be more fruitfully understood as not simply a backlash against Revivalist sentiment and Romanticism, but as another way of making political commentary on Irish and, in Beckett's case, world politics.

This study draws to a close in examining two late twentieth-century authors whose work continues to shape the Irish pastoral mode. Seamus Heaney, perhaps the most exported of contemporary Irish writers, seems the obvious inheritor of a literary tradition preoccupied with place. Heaney's engagement with the tradition of Irish pastoral is complicated by the fact of Ireland's post-colonial status, by Northern Ireland's political crises, and by his own personal position as a Northern Catholic removed to the Republic. In his versions of pastoral, Heaney leaves unchallenged many of the tradition's tropes, so that it has been left to one of Ireland's most prominent women writers to offer a revisionary critique of what, up until recently, has been a largely male literary mode. As Ireland has become Europeanized and increasingly urban, the need for a reassessment of

Irish pastoral has become necessary, and Eavan Boland has been key in this process. Boland offers different perspectives on nature (traditionally, of course, associated with the feminine) and the landscape of Ireland (frequently personified as a woman) from her male counterparts, and offers a fitting conclusion to a study concerned with the direction of cultural traditions.

By examining the representation of nature in Irish literature from the Revival through the twentieth century, this study hopes to demonstrate the significance and, indeed, usefulness of nostalgia for Irish culture, and to encourage further study as to its role not only in the development of an Irish national literature, but in other cultures that have experienced extensive change, particularly other nations emerging or already emerged from the spectre of colonialism.

CHAPTER ONE

Nature in Irish Literature Before 1600: An Overview

As one begins to examine the representation of nature and place over the centuries, it becomes evident that Irish literature reflects multiple traditions of writing. Classical pastoral traditions, Irish language traditions, and English pastoral models are all significant influences on the literature of late nineteenth- and twentieth-century Ireland. What follows is a brief exploration of the ways in which nature and place were represented in secular[1] Irish literature prior to the period of this study. Far from attempting to be an exhaustive survey, it is but a contextualizing guide to the ways in which the function of nature and place in Irish literature has changed over time, and to the ways in which these three major traditions intertwined at different moments.

PASTORAL IN IRELAND'S EARLIEST LITERATURE

Ireland was exposed to the classical pastoral through Virgil, who was well known to Irish Christian scribes working in Latin. As early as the end of the seventh century, classical texts were being translated into Irish by scribes both in Ireland and on the continent; allusions to Virgil's works – *The Aeneid*, the *Eclogues* and the *Georgics* – in the poetry of such writers as Saint Columbanus and Sedulius Scottus attest to this exposure.[2] Irish literature was exposed to another form of pastoral through Christianity, which brought to Ireland its own image for the archetype of a perfect existence in nature in the story of Eden, and in the idea of God as creator of the world. However, while integrating significant elements of both the classical pastoral and the Christian story of a fall from pastoral perfection, Irish literature seems gradually to have developed a different representation of nature.

8

Because of their classical education, writers between approximately the seventh and tenth centuries were learned, and unlikely to produce either verse or prose uninformed by their education. While this seems obvious, the recognition that early Irish monastic writers were not only conscious of but schooled in literary models that employed pastoral and other poetic conceits challenges early scholarship on the 'nature poetry'[3] of the period. Many distinguished late-nineteenth- and early-twentieth-century critics described this early poetry as the product of a naive and innocent people given *naturally* to the task.[4] Early Irish lyric poets, critics believed, lived an ideal pastoral existence, and merely wrote true accounts of that life. There might, these critics admitted, be similarities between so-called 'hermit poetry' and the work of Theocritus, but, they concluded (providing no evidence but for belief in a widespread Irish eremitic tradition),[5] Irish hermit poetry was not imaginative, but genuine, by '"Simple Lifers" who really did live the simple life, and that in its simplest form'.[6] This critical attitude was shared by creative writers like Yeats and Synge, who wanted to believe in a primitive Irish culture untainted by artifice and pastoral conceit. Thus scholars of early Irish literature, like many Revival authors, read and critiqued with a nostalgic, idealizing gaze. Part of this nostalgic gaze was to believe that 'hermit poetry' was the product of actual hermits, rather than recognizing the classically pastoral devices at work.

The product of a monastic tradition that emphasized classical learning, 'hermit poetry' represents nature in a way that might be described as closer to the traditional pastoral mode than later medieval Irish literature. Rather than being written by actual hermits, this verse avails of a tradition that Maria Tymoczko calls 'a poetry of masks',[7] in which a well known figure is adopted by the author as the speaking 'voice' of the poem:[8] the recognizable persona of a hermit, for example, expresses gratitude for a simple, solitary life in nature, and praises nature's beauties. As a result of the frequency of personae like the hermit in the poetry, nature often appears within the framework of a conceit that could be described as classically pastoral: a 'simple' persona becomes the vehicle through which to express desire for a simpler life, which is directly contrasted with that of another persona (a king, for example), or implicitly contrasted with the more complex monastic existence of the silent author.[9]

An example is 'King and Hermit' ('A Marbáin, a díthrubaig'),[10] which offers a dialogue between the persona of Gúaire, a king known to have died in ca. 666 A.D., and his invented 'literary' half-brother

hermit Marbán.[11] These masks allow a comparison of two extremes
of existence; Marbán, for his part, praises the natural world in thirty-
three stanzas, resulting in an idealization in which bountiful nature is
a sign of God's munificence. In its focus on the difference between the
life of the country and the king's 'society', this poem owes much to
the pastoral tradition, not only in the conceit of the dialogue, but also
in the tautly wrought descriptions of nature which are used to cement
an argument, here for the value of projected eremitic life.

   From this and other of the earliest Irish poems, we receive a picture
of the natural world that appears relatively simplistic: natural cata-
logues (of trees, plants, crops and animals) are followed by thanks to
God for their production. Such sentiments, produced as we can now
assume them to have been by monastic authors with knowledge of
classical and Biblical literature, and couched within the framework of
conceits such as the mask and the dialogue, suggest that this representation is not, after all, so simple. Instead one could argue that early
Irish authors forged a Christianized pastoral, representing nature in
simple language that had as its inspiration not merely the literal
world of Ireland or the spiritual world of God that critics assumed to
be their only drive, but a complexity of literary sources. From classical
texts such as Virgil's, Irish scholars would have been familiar with the
ideal of the natural world as producing men who were simple, hard-
working and honest, and who lived in a generalized perfection devoid
of close-up detail that would mar that perfection. Knowledge of such
sources, when combined with a thorough comprehension of Biblical
books (particularly the Psalms) and exegesis, produced a literature
that credits God for the beauty of the natural world, and praises God
through the production of poetry. The adoption of eremitic masks
allowed poets to assume a familiarity with the natural world, and so,
by implication, to assume a familiarity with God.

   Hermit life was held up as an ideal within communal monastic life,
since so many monastary founders were reputed to have been
hermits. The adoption of eremitic masks suggests that, like Virgil and
Theocritus, the unknown authors of these poems are engaged in a
nostalgic exercise of imaginatively creating lives they have never lived.
This form of nostalgia is very different from the nostalgia present in
later Irish literature in that it does not mourn the loss of culture.
Instead, this body of poetry suggests a longing for a life unlived and
centred in an idealized nature through traditional pastoral conceits.

EARLY MEDIEVAL FENIAN LITERATURE.

If the treatment of nature in 'hermit poetry' is benign and serene, the portrait that we receive of nature in Fenian literature is reflective of a different ethos. A group of travelling, hunting warriors with royal pedigree, the *fían* were the focus of a wide selection of poems and prose tales,[12] which, like the Cuchulain Ulster cycle tales,[13] regained popularity during the period leading up to the Revival. Because a governing theme of the *fían* is the hunt, and because its members function on the periphery of society in nature, the natural world has traditionally been deemed significant in this literature. In the earliest *fían* literature of the ninth to the twelfth centuries, however, nature is in fact not prominent. While the hunt is a primary occupation of the *fían*, it is used as a mere frame for adventure and battle tales. Only in the handful of 'seasonal poems' ascribed to Finn Mac Cumhall does the natural world become a focus; in these nature is used as a seeming test of the persona's ability for second sight, or vision. As in the case of 'hermit poetry', early Finn literature, in its employment of literary devices, is not steeped in the nostalgia associated with later Irish literature that mourns the loss of culture: conventional descriptions of nature are dominant.

The *fían* is traditionally headed by Finn, whose childhood emphasized the natural world: women, stereotypically associated with nature, were his guardians in a wild environment. That a tree had been carved out for his protection, however, signals what Joseph Nagy has astutely observed is the transformation of a natural object into a cultural one. This, Nagy argues, indicates the *fían's* role: ushering youths from the world of nature into the world of culture by helping to secure land and property.[14] Finn's tree is also indicative of the ways in which the *fían* existed in nature. Unlike a figure like Sweeney, who, as we will shortly see, lives in a natural world largely devoid of cultural elements, the *fían* carve out of the natural world a culture that is, by all accounts, an established one.

The hunt can be seen as a primeval, basic way of life that existed primarily when humankind had not yet mastered settled agriculture. But what does the hunt become when it is a life chosen during a time when settled agriculture is, in fact, the norm? That the *fían* opt to exist in a more 'primitive' circle when all around them is evidence of the pattern of a more 'advanced' culture that has settled onto specific sites of land – they are, after all, involved in obtaining promised land – tells us that they are *consciously* attempting to create an existence in nature; this existence is not forced upon them. While youths who come to the *fían* for help as a last resort are forced into their positions outside of the culture for a time, the permanent members of the *fían* – such as Finn, Caílte and Oisín – have chosen this life and are unable (or unwilling) to undergo the rite of passage they perform for others. Further, the type of hunt in which these men indulge is not in fact primitive. The literature details the *fían*'s many hounds, horses, royal garments, precious metal spears and shields, and their accompaniment by family and musicians: their hunt is a royal endeavour reliant on cultural resources and domesticated and trained – not wild – animals. Thus while Finn and his men hunt voraciously, they are not living primitive lives, and this is the paradox of their existence. This paradox contributes to Finn's status as supreme outsider and insider; while he may hunt by day in the wildernesses of Ireland, by night he is taken in by kings and royal women, and enjoys all of the trappings of wealth and honour – in other words, the trappings of culture.

The earliest Finn lore tends to focus unanimously on heroic (and thus aristocratic) narratives of events such as battles, using the hunt – if at all – as a mere frame. While the *fían* do exist in nature in terms of their reliance on the hunt as an identity-forming activity, they are actively involved in culture, existing on a border between nature and culture and so creating lives that are fundamentally a combination of natural and cultural elements. 'The Quarrel between Finn and Oisín'[15] (eighth or ninth century) describes a reunion between Finn and Oisín after a quarrel and a year's separation: when Finn finds Oisín 'in a great wilderness',[16] they engage in a light-hearted verbal battle. Other than the initial reference to the wilderness, the natural world is not referenced; it serves as the backdrop to the tale, which itself serves as an example of the way in which nature is represented in Finn lore prior to the thirteenth-century *Acallam na Senórach*: it is given no special place, and remains in the background. In tales or poems, a forest or wilderness is the setting, but within that setting the poetic personae are concerned only with telling the tale of battle or heroism.[17]

Other pieces partake more specifically of the *dindshenchas* tradition of placelore. The tenth-century 'Almu'[18] details the history of the title place name (and will find its way into the *Acallam* in a version provided by Caílte), but while place frames the poem, it is quickly abandoned – as it is in the *Táin Bo Cúailnge*, as well – in favour of the tales of those involved in the naming. This, too, is typical: place is commemorated, but is not, as might seem at first to be the case, thematically central. Instead, cultural events that occur in a particular place are given centre stage.[19]

Seasonal poetry, a body of approximately ten poems within this earliest Fenian literature, does, however, focus more obviously on place and nature. Reflecting the early Irish recycling of particular mythological poetic figures, seasonal poetry presents a natural world that is the product of those figures' visionary capacity. In addition to vision, the Finn mask automatically draws upon a particular range of characteristics: heroism, prophecy, poesy, as well as a profound familiarity with elements of the natural world, ranging from hunting knowledge to knowledge of flora. The resulting overview of nature during a given season is both general and specific, covering many landscapes, as in the following example:

> I have tidings for you: the stag bells,
> winter pours, summer has gone;
>
> Wind is high and cold; the sun low,
> its course is short; the sea runs strongly;
>
> Bracken is very red; its shape has been hidden;
> the call of the barnacle goose has become usual;
>
> Cold has seized the wings of birds;
> season of ice, these are my tidings.[20]

These poems are, in effect, miniature natural histories of Ireland at particular times; they are not concerned with the persona's feelings about the natural world but with acute observation. Apart from this theme of vision in seasonal poems, *fían* literature shows a marked resemblance to other early Irish poems that centre on nature, and is not weighted down with the heightened nostalgia of later Irish literature – including later Finn lore.

LATE MEDIEVAL IRISH LITERATURE: *BUILE SUIBHNE* AND *ACALLAM NA SENÓRACH*

While by the twelfth and thirteenth centuries the traditional pastoral was gaining popularity across Europe, this form of pastoral was eclipsed in Ireland by the development of the nostalgic mode, due, it would seem, to changing social conditions: besides the momentous influence of Christianity on the period, there is the equally significant push of the Normans into Ireland. This period seems to represent a shift away from earlier Irish literary themes as, in addressing societal disruptions, the literature begins to develop the nostalgic mode, which engages nature as the *site* of nostalgia and longing. Since the nostalgic mode centres on mourning for a lost or changing culture, and situates its mourning in nature, the representation of nature comes to signify a loss of *culture*, and in this the nostalgic mode functions as a sub-genre of the traditional pastoral, which implies a lament for the loss of a *natural* world.

In medieval Irish literature the experience of nature is often associated with those on the margins of culture, and so it is appropriate that the earliest Irish 'nature poetry' often appears as scribal marginalia in manuscripts. This marginality, while witnessed in 'hermit poetry' or in early *fian* literature, is represented by no figure as clearly as Sweeney, whose story will serve to introduce the nostalgic mode, which provides the writing of the Revival with so many of its themes.

Upon hearing that a church is to be built in his territory, King Sweeney, reacting to a perceived threat to his land, goes angrily to the priest and throws the Psalter into a lake in protest; the priest, as punishment, curses him with madness. This madness takes the peculiar form of 'disgust with every place in which he used to be and desire for every place which he had not reached'.[21] Sweeney is condemned to flitting bird-like through the countryside, experiencing savage cold and an equally savage longing for his past life of splendorous, often *indoor* comfort, and yet able, as a result of madness, to compose poetry celebrating the *outdoor* beauty of nature. While the natural world of Ireland is lovely enough to seduce Sweeney into poems of extravagant praise, it is clear that his appreciation results from having been forced into nature: displacement brings the natural world into focus.

Both the Virgilian and Christian traditions offered Irish literature versions of the natural world that, at least in part, coincided with its own. All three visions of nature – whether Virgil's effortlessly green meadows, a retrospective longing for the Garden of Eden, or Sweeney's sky-down view of streams bordered by watercress – involve a longing for something lost. However, while the Edenic tradition laments the loss of the garden as man's natural state, and while the Virgilian tradition makes us aware that the pastoral life is under siege by a not too distant urbanism and the Roman equivalent of enclosure, Irish literature develops a different view: for it is the loss not of nature but of *culture* that is lamented, and the lament takes place within the context of the natural world that the other traditions mourn for its passing. Sweeney recognizes all of the contradictions of this fallen or displaced state when he says, 'This is a spot for a madman, but yet no place is it for corn or milk or food; it is an uncomfortable, unquiet place, nor has it shelter against storm or shower, though it is a lofty, beautiful place.'[22]

No matter how beautiful it may be at times, nature is far too real – whether cold, wet or uncomfortable – and far too threatening to be styled into traditional, pastoral artifice. Sweeney recognizes that nature is for those who are somehow outside of the social realm: for a madman, in this case, who, in his marginal status, is unable to obtain corn or milk – signs of cultivated and settled agriculture – and instead exists, uncomfortably, in nature's beauty. Sweeney's consignment to this 'unquiet' outdoor world signifies the mingling of cultures and times taking place: set in the seventh century, when Ireland had been Christian for at least two centuries, and redacted in the twelfth century (at the earliest) after the arrival of both the Vikings and the Normans, the tale collapses many centuries' worth of upheaval into one space. Nature becomes the site for expressing nostalgia for the past and Sweeney's disorientation at change. Sweeney eventually comes tentatively out of wilderness into a semi-settled life, establishes a tie to another priest and, at his self-prophesied death, thanks God for his life and repents any evil he has done. He undergoes, in effect, a rite of passage in which nature and nostalgia serve as the route to the acceptance of the new culture. That nature acts as the site for a rite of passage here as in Finn lore is also significant, since this further associates the natural world with cultural change in Irish literature.

Like *Buile Suibhne*, *Acallam na Senórach* involves an encounter between early Irish and Christian cultures, weaving a narrative out of an imagined meeting between members of the now languishing *fíana* and St Patrick with his entourage of bishops and clerics. The *Acallam* also marks the high point of placelore in Irish literature.[23] Many early Irish poems name specific places in Ireland; by the late middle ages, through figures like Cuchulain[24] and Sweeney, we see that more use is being made of – and more significance being given to – place. While Sweeney or the Ulster tales frequently name place through which they pass, though, Caílte, in the *Acallam*, structures his entire narrative around the history of place, creating a verbal map of Ireland in the process.

As with *Buile Suibhne*, nostalgia is built into this text composed in the thirteenth century, set in the fifth, and looking backwards from the fifth century to the mythological, pre-Christian era of the Fenians. Caílte's explanations of place names reveal that he is experiencing an overwhelming nostalgia in his roamings through the Irish wilderness. Like Sweeney, Caílte is haunted by a past that he cannot reclaim except through memory, which is fading. While Caílte would have existed in nature when the *fían* were at their height, that earlier existence was not marked by nostalgia in the natural world, as witnessed by the earliest *fían* literature. Thus we can speculate that Caílte's nostalgia, authored as it was in the thirteenth century, was created out of a social uncertainty that had not existed when the earlier literature was written.

Present in the text is a powerful reliance on the past to provide a sense of continuity that has been ruptured. Place becomes a particularly significant concept as a culture experiences change, functioning as a steadying force within an unsteady culture. It is not surprising, considering the changes underway in thirteenth-century Ireland, that placelore became so significant a part of the literary tradition: if other traditions (such as those tales revolving around pre- or non-Christian figures) were perceived as being on the verge of effectual extinction, a way of preserving that past was through the preservation of lore relating to the unchanging realm of the landscape.

If place names begin as a way of identifying and distinguishing peoples or clans, they turn rapidly into a modality that preserves those people's pasts. And when placelore becomes widespread enough to cover a great many individuals, what results is a mythological history of an entire people and culture. Out of the expansion of placelore, then, comes a text like the *Acallam*, which, through its heroes' all-Ireland exploits, manages to create a history of Ireland that can be constantly expanded simply by creating tales for any newly named site. The landscape, then, becomes a circular text that can be read beginning at any point in space.[25]

Caílte occasionally gives more than one possible history for a place, showing the adaptable nature of spatial (and orally inspired) narrative. In one instance, he relays the tale of Almu dying in childbirth.

> This green-surfaced mound was raised over her, and from her is the mound named. *It was previously called* the Mound of the Surveying. *Or* Alma was the name of the one who held it in the time of Neimed. *Or else* Nuadu Duri built a fort and stronghold there, and took a herd (*alma*) from the forest, so that it is called Alma after this.[26] (my emphasis)

Because we know from Patrick's guardian angels that Caílte's memory is faulty, it is possible to see his explanation as an indication of memory's demise. But it is also plausible that this versioning is part and parcel of the very idea of placelore, which seems governed by only one rule: if an event in the present and the person(s) involved are of consequence, the name of a site can be overridden (and over-written). As the example above shows, previous names or histories are not lost; they simply move further down the line, losing their top-of-the-page status in the palimpsestic text of the landscape. The literary text that results is one that necessarily includes these 'variants'[27] whose layering contributes to a mythology of place. The *fían* is the ideal organization for this type of exercise, functioning as it does in the natural world as a hunting party and so having such profound access to place. The *fíana* thus become not only masters of the natural world, but shapers of its history and mythology.

Like Sweeney's, Caílte's desperate sadness and nostalgia are situated in the natural world. Destined to roam Ireland across the *fían's* former haunts, Caílte is, though, unlike Sweeney, still situated in the places that he lived previously. What has changed for Caílte and Oisín and other *fían* survivors is the fact that the natural world is no longer the site of the cultural organization of the *fían*. For while the *fían* existed in the natural world, it was a world connected to culture: these men had constant interaction with settled society, and derived their fame from the kings and noblemen who required their assistance or against whom they fought. In the Patrician present, Caílte and his small band exist in the natural world without the comfort and aid of those cultural connections, and in this way they exist as Sweeney does, lamenting the lack of culture in their lives.

Caílte's powerful sorrow when he remembers the past indicates the extent to which such memories haunt and remind him, equally power-fully, of his present lack: the camaraderie and companionship – in other words the society – of the *fían*, in all of its former glory. To a man he encounters, he remarks that 'although you are hunting alone . . . I have seen you surrounded by many people, by fifteen hundred war-riors, fifteen hundred boys, and fifteen hundred women in the Ford of the Meeting of the Three Rivers to the South, where the Suir, the Nore, and the Barrow flow together'.[28] Caílte's nostalgia is not for a quiet life in the wilderness; what he longs for is in fact quite the oppo-site – a complete cultural organization of people living nomadically, moving to hunt, and bringing with them their own musicians, animals and families.

Caílte's story, like Sweeney's, records a rite of passage: he and his band of men become Christian, and, in exchange, their stories are recorded in writing, thus relieving Caílte of the responsibilities of

cultural memory and aligning him with the 'new' cultural organizations of Christian Ireland. Nature in this text is once again explicitly
connected to change and nostalgia, as Caílte mourns the loss of his
compatriots and their culture.

BARDIC POETRY

'The Frenzy of Sweeney' and 'The Meeting of the Ancients' reflect a
theme in medieval Irish literature – an existence in nature marked by
a nostalgia for a lost life. This theme can also be seen in Irish bardic
poetry, which flourished between approximately 1200 and 1700. As
'cultural guardians',[29] and in their concern with recording the glories
of patrons, bardic poets were automatically engaged in a nostalgic
exercise: the backward-looking tendencies of bardic poetry invited a
nostalgia for times past, which it was the duty of the bard to preserve
for future generations.[30] Bardic poets frequently composed poems of
place and employed certain natural imagery, but are not noted for
producing nature poetry. While nature was not among the most significant of themes for bardic poetry, however, its presence in the poetry
seems increasingly to indicate the transformation of the bardic order,
and coincides, particularly in later material, with the lament for that
order's waning significance. In this, bardic poetry, by the end of the late
sixteenth and early seventeenth centuries, demonstrates the preoccupation with nature and nostalgia that marks other Irish literature.
This preoccupation in bardic poetry seems due, in large part, to the
threat to territory – a theme familiar from Sweeney's tale and in the
fían's purpose – and the response of the poets to changing social and
political landscapes under a programme of English colonization.

After the arrival of the Normans, nostalgia begins to creep into bardic
language as the poetry explores 'pseudohistories' that explain the present
based on a creative reworking of the past, or prophecy a brighter future
that marks a return to past glories.[31] The Normans, however, did not
represent an immediate threat to the bardic order. Their presence in
Ireland offered the opportunity for further patronage, and inspired
bardic poets to rewrite Irish history[32] to include their new patrons,
just as, in the *Acallam*, the presence of Patrick and Christianity in
Ireland are explained retrospectively through a rewriting of the
Fenian tales. In this way, bardic poetry sanctioned authority.[33]

A 1256 poem of Giolla Brighde Mac Con Midhe's praises his
patron Gofraidh Ó Domhnaill's residence at Inis Saimhéar, warning
him in the process of the Norman presence at Sligo,[34] and offers a

catalogue of conventions and similes for praise drawn from the natural world. Ó Domhnaill's face is 'like the flower of the nut-tree',[35] and the bounty of his property – rivers teeming with fish, trees bursting into bud – is due to his own goodness and generosity; the natural world prospers due to proper leadership. Giolla Brighde closes the poem with a final simile: 'He will be like the sprouting of a seed in a springtime field'[36] that will not be routed by foreigners. Absent from this or other of his poems is a connection between nature and nostalgia. The natural world is one of many metaphoric vehicles through which to praise patrons, and serves primarily to sketch the symbiotic relationship between the natural world and governance.

Muireadhach Albanach's 'The Dead Wife', from the same period, is an unusual personal lament that employs similar language. His wife is a 'white comely blossom', 'her countenance like the white thorn', a 'tall fresh lithe-fingered branch', 'my smooth hazel-nut'.[37] Already similarities between these two thirteenth-century poets appear in the use of particular natural images: hazel-nuts, branches and blossoms seem to be part of established bardic convention, and demonstrate bards' ability to bend convention to a multiplicity of situations. These same natural metaphors are still evidenced in sixteenth-century poetry, as in Lochlainn Óg Ó Dálaigh's mid-century 'Great Expectations', which praises three sons of Thomond as 'fresh young seedlings', 'stately trees ever fruitful', 'fresh hazelnuts from the finest cluster'.[38] The recurrence of such metaphors over centuries suggests, William Gillies argues, 'consciously observed convention'[39] in which specific trees, animals and other natural images are part of a set of metaphors taught to, and so known by, all bards. By the mid-sixteenth century, however, these metaphors take on new meanings.

If the Normans were absorbed into bardic convention, the Tudors and their programme of colonization were to seriously disrupt it. From Lochlainn Óg Ó Dálaigh's time on, bardic poetry displays an increasing nostalgia and a desperation to keep tradition from being overwhelmed. As patrons gradually become involved in the political difficulties of the Tudor presence, and as these difficulties begin to gnaw at traditional governing structures, bards experience effects upon their own standing. Many late-sixteenth- and early-seventeenth-century poems thus describe very real – and not merely metaphoric – changes taking place within Irish society. During this period, the poetry begins to focus on its own significance within the culture, and to judge the state of that culture by the value placed on the role of the poet. As political and governmental change threaten the poet's role, bardic poetry laments the deaths of patrons and their relations, but also the threat to the bardic order itself.

Uncertainty about land titles, ownership and territorial governance had been increasing from the time of the Norman invasion, and was heightened by the arrival of the Tudor 'planters' into a society whose majority worked the land. The English system of legal deeds to indicate ownership often caused bewilderment, and resulted in an increasing anxiety over land. Native Irish attitudes towards land ownership had been largely based on the idea that a lord could extend his control by crossing into another lord's territory and seizing it by defeating him; 'hosting' was a common way by which control of land was asserted.[40] Initially, then, the planters' methods might not have seemed very different to those of the Irish lords.[41] Over the course of the sixteenth century, however, the sense of political and cultural crisis deepened and is reflected with increasing regularity, as Marc Caball's *Poets and Politics* demonstrates, in the bardic poetry of the period.

Gradually, the representation of nature begins to be tinged with nostalgia. Laoiseach Mac an Bhaird's mid-sixteenth-century poem 'On the Cutting Down of an Ancient Tree' addresses the crisis of the bardic order through a natural symbol. While the Irish maintained an attitude of veneration for trees, the Tudors viewed timber as the means to economic prowess and control of the seas. Laoiseach uses the bardic eulogy to lament not merely the loss of a tree, but an entire culture. Once a gathering place, the hill on which the tree stood is now bare and causes the poet deep distress: 'the cutting of the branch, my day of sorrow! the state of the land is baser thereafter'.[42] The natural state is inextricably bound to the human state: what happens to nature signifies what is happening to the population. Not only has the tree been cut down, but the hill has been taken over by outsiders, and it is with this image that the poem ends: 'The hill of the shoutings, torment of the schools, in the possession of enemies to-day! After its slopes sad to me is the fair hill that hath pierced my affection.'[43] The Irish tradition of inaugurating a chief or a king beneath a tree on a hill top lurks here; the loss of the tree, then, indicates cultural changes. Something has clearly altered between the thirteenth and sixteenth centuries in the way in which nature is represented in bardic poetry, and this poem serves as an early example of that change. Rather than serving as stock metaphors to praise leaders or mourn deaths, the set of natural images is now used to signify a nostalgia for a culture under seige.

Eochaidh Ó Heóghusa's poetry attests to this trend. As bard to three Maguires, the last of whom was Hugh Maguire who joined

Hugh O'Neill's Munster campaign, Ó Heóghusa's poetry inevitably leans toward lament for the crumbling of the culture by which he was formed. 'A Winter Campaign', written after his patron had joined the Munster rebellion, demonstrates the increased poetic presence of nature as a sign of cultural disturbance. 'Too cold I deem this night for Hugh', he begins.[44] Significantly, Hugh is out of doors, forced into an outdoor battle: as with Sweeney and Caílte, displacement and/or struggle against change means subjection to the natural world. Ó Heóghusa's description is of real events, however: and in fact Hugh Maguire would soon lose his life in service of the winter military campaign. As such political events are deemed unnatural, Ó Heóghusa depicts storms of extraordinary, unnatural power:

> To-night (it is venom to my heart) fiery showers are poured forth . . . Over the clouds' bosoms the flood-gates of heaven have been opened: it has turned small pools to seas; the firmament has spewed out its destruction.[45]

Nature has become apocalyptic; the historical forces at work are effecting terrible changes. His patron 'lies under the lurid glow of showering, flashing thunderbolts, beneath the fury of armed savage clouds'.[46] The English attack on Maguire and O'Neill's rebellion is also an attack by nature, and a sign that something has gone wrong. Because the leadership has been disrupted, the poet can no longer serve as what James Carney has referred to as an 'intermediary between the prince and the mysterious powers of nature'.[47] Ó Heóghusa's chilling description of Hugh extends until Hugh becomes part of nature, now being assaulted by the English: 'Grievous to me – it has wounded my heart – that the soft slope of his smooth comely side should be crushed in the wild sullen night . . .'[48] Like the tree in Mac an Bhaird's poem, Hugh becomes the symbol of an eroding culture pummelled by the natural world and by the foreigners; nature reflects the chaos of the culture.

Eoghan Ruadh Mac an Bhaird makes similar use of natural imagery to mourn the losses to Irish culture. Following the defeat of the earls at Kinsale (1601),[49] Eoghan Ruadh's patron, O'Donnell, sailed to the continent (1607)[50] with many others. 'Looking Towards Spain' depicts a nature upset by recent Irish events, and of which Eoghan Ruadh is suspicious. His patron has sailed 'over the gloomy raging sea',[51] and the poet asks 'the gods who blow blustering winds' to 'forsake their warlike apparel'.[52] Left behind in Ireland, the poet is

without a patron, and so without a livelihood; the result is a poem
that mourns the loss of his culture:

> There are others like me; I myself especially, O Aodh, am torn
> because of thy venture in the boiling wave of my mind.
>
> The sea does not stir without bewildering me, the wind rises not
> but that my mind starts, the tempest does not alter the note of the
> stream without bringing anguish upon me, now thou art gone.[53]

Once again we find that imagery of the natural world is inextricably
bound to a nostalgia for a lost culture: Eoghan Ruadh situates the
representative of that lost culture, his patron, in a natural world that
is changed and unreliable.

In Fearghal Óg Mac an Bhaird's 'Love of Ireland', the poet rather
than the patron is in exile. In this nostalgic look at the land that is no
longer his home, the nature of Ireland is emphasized. Fearghal Óg
writes of 'the melodious waterfalls', 'the tranquil fountains, that rich
fair level land of soft soil'.[54] Towards the close of the poem Fearghal
Óg includes several stanzas that are similar to earlier, ninth- and
tenth-century 'hermit poems' in their luxuriant praise of landscape:

> Green and flourishing is the grass of the island, thick are her nut-
> sweet woods, plentiful is choice fruit upon the dry smooth-sided
> hillocks.
> . . .
> The speech of her birds bright-feathered and ruddy is sleep music
> enough. O that I were to-day in that smooth land abounding in
> salmon: hail to the land of bright fountains![55]

Clearly this is an idealizing exercise, a nostalgic longing for a land of
pastoral perfection. It becomes clear, however, that Fearghal Óg is
lamenting the loss of more than Ireland's natural beauty: he sends
blessings to Leinster's host, to the women of Ireland, to 'the makers
of eulogies', and to 'those who unravel genealogical branches' as well
as to physicians, clerics and musicians.[56] The idealized presence of the
natural world of Ireland in this poem serves only to highlight a
nostalgia that mourns the loss of culture.

What these examples demonstrate is an increasing concern over the
centuries, and particularly from the mid-sixteenth century onwards,
with the demise of the bardic order, a demise often represented by the
same set of metaphors based in the natural world. Colonization and

conquest have so disrupted the social landscape, have resulted in such loss of life, and there has been such huge political change, that bardic poetry inevitably reflects these things. While this demise is, of course, represented as well in language that is more obviously political, or more obviously mournful, the fact that bardic poetry too unites nature and nostalgia adds further evidence that the nostalgic mode is part of Irish literary tradition, particularly during times of crisis.

The deepening sense of crisis from the mid-sixteenth century on seems to correspond with the increase in population of English and Scottish planters,[57] and the decrease in native Irish land ownership that was the result of the plantation schemes.[58] Native landowning Irish families could, of course, acquiesce to English authority in Ireland in order to obtain title deeds to land and solidify their position within the new political system. By the first half of the seventeenth century, there was a growing trend, as Irish landowners went into debt and were forced to part with some of their land or, in some cases, lost their land altogether.[59]

A major part of colonization was thus the disruption to traditional ways of governing land. Many of the bards' patrons found their lands confiscated or overrun; seemingly as a result, land, landscape and nature make an increasing appearance in bardic literature following the arrival of the Tudors, the bards being as concerned for their own welfare as for that of their patrons. Bardic culture depended upon the system of inherited land ownership in Ireland; interruption to this system led to a crisis within the aristocratic community since traditional family lands were suddenly threatened, in turn threatening the bardic community, which relied on the generosity of patrons for land. The concern with land ownership and with seeing landscapes of historical and mythological significance overrun by Tudor settlers was so disturbing that the bards were not to pay as much initial attention to the attempt at religious and linguistic reformation that the Tudors had as their goals as they were to the issue of land. Curiously, it would appear that it is ultimately the threat to land that sparks change within aristocratic Irish society: appealed to by those in exile on the continent and those actively involved in the counter-reformation movement, Irish landed families begin, by the time of James I's reign, to demonstrate a new awareness of the threat to their situation which is keenly portrayed in bardic poetry.

These changes in the political governance of land are crucial in seeking to understand the representation of nature in bardic poetry, particularly since one of the most significant of recurring tropes within bardic poetry from the twelfth to the seventeenth centuries is the representation of the lord being married to his land and the land, under right rule, prospering. This trope is, in effect, the Irish bardic version of the pathetic fallacy, in which, classically, the natural world mirrors emotions; here the natural world mirrors the state of governance and is feminized. The feminization of landscape and nature in later Irish literature seems to begin from this focus of the bards: deriving from Indo-European fertility rites,[60] the trope of rightful rule and the resulting prosperity of land was severely disrupted by the Tudor and Elizabethan conquests in Ireland, as witnessed in even the few examples above. The question of rightful rule and the prosperity of land became increasingly problematized in bardic poetry by the end of the sixteenth century, when the tropes, in one sense, have become something much more than that: the actual, physical landscape does indeed begin to reflect the inappropriate nature of the new leadership, as forests are felled to provide timber for the British naval fleet, castles are burned, and families evicted. The landscape thus indicates the very real decline of the lords, their families and the bards themselves. The bards and their patrons are sometimes literally pushed out into the natural world as Sweeney was; here nature again becomes the site of nostalgia, this time for the struggling bardic system and the culture that supported it. And as time went on, the trope of rightful rule and the land as female would feed into the *aisling*, and Ireland as personified woman would be the very sign of colonial defeat. Not for several hundred years would this stereotype of Ireland as forsaken, leaderless woman be challenged.

IRISH PASTORAL MEETS ENGLISH PASTORAL

While bardic poets were increasingly concerned with the transformation of their culture, in their midst was an English poet as interested in patronage and as preoccupied with charting Irish and English interaction. Edmund Spenser's career coincides with and serves to illuminate changes in Irish culture that would affect the presence of nature in Irish literature in the centuries to follow, since the Elizabethan era marks the transition from medieval to early modern, and Irish-language to English-language literatures, as well as from 'Irish Ireland' to colonized Ireland: the physical and political – and thus literary – landscapes of Ireland were changed permanently under Elizabeth's rule. While Spenser might seem a strange choice to end a discussion of medieval Irish literature, his work is, I argue, reflective of the collision between English and Irish ideas of nature, and their representation in literature.

By Spenser's time, English ideas of nature and landscape were as significant in Ireland as Irish ideas. Tudor and Elizabethan planters looked to nature as a potential economic resource; and trees, for a seafaring nation that relied on timber for ships, were particularly valuable. Irish forests could make the colony economically viable; but they also hid the 'wood-kernes' Spenser warned about in *A View of the Present State of Ireland*. For both of these reasons, Elizabeth I ordered the felling of the woods. Spenser was thus not only one of the last poets to witness Ireland before the major shift in political landscape after the battle of Kinsale and the flight of the earls to the continent, but also one of the last to witness a certain physical landscape, for after these events the English were able to begin in earnest both the process of clearing the forests that prevented the free movement of English travellers, and the correct mapping of Ireland.

Elizabeth had ordered not only that the trees be felled, but that the Irish landscape be mapped.[61] The new knowledge provided by exploration had led to a significant change in the perspective used to draw maps,[62] so that it was possible to grasp 'in a single instant the convexity of the terraqueous globe'.[63] The *mappa mundi*, the representation of an entire globe, was new to Spenser's time.[64] What I would suggest is that mapmaking ventures, the exploratory journeys that sparked them, and the resulting information about the physical world can all be seen as significant influences on Elizabethan narration: the cartographic mapping of empire becomes a metaphor for poetic, and epical, narration. The popularity of geography and cartography become, in Elizabethan prose and poetic works, a preoccupation with landscape and place, and the *mappa mundi* makes it possible to conceive of a totalizing narrative, one that encompasses not only the nation, but also the empire. This is in stark contrast to the preoccupation of bardic poetry of the same period, which tends to be concerned with local, familial narratives and smaller scale 'maps' of a culture. English and Irish ideas about nature and place during this period could not be more divergent.

In seeking to draw both paper and cultural maps of Ireland, the English relied upon outdated material to bolster their arguments for converting and controlling the Irish. The primary source on Ireland for those like Richard Beacon, Richard Stanihurst and Spenser – all of whom wrote prose tracts on the Irish situation – was Giraldus Cambrensis, Gerald of Wales, whose centuries-old claims in

Topographia Hiberniae provided justification for England's activity in Ireland. While admitting that the Irish had 'natural gifts', Giraldus concluded that they 'are so barbarous that they cannot be said to have any culture'.[65] This lack of culture and civility Giraldus tied directly to the pastoral: 'They are a wild and inhospitable people. They live on beasts only, and live like beasts. They have not progressed at all from the primitive habits of pastoral living.'[66] The Irish are *too natural*; and, despite attempts by Irishmen like Seathrún Céitinn to displace such ideas,[67] this medieval view remained firmly in the English imagination.

Elizabethans tended to view Ireland through the Christian myth of the fall and through the classical pastoral as it had been adopted by English writers, believing that Ireland had somehow fallen – regressed – into the undeveloped, uncultivated state of which Gerald wrote.[68] While the pastoral was celebrated as an ideal in Elizabethan poetry, though, it was an impossible reality to face in Ireland, where an actual pastoral economy existed.[69] While Ireland's pastoralism might have seemed the perfect 'foil' to the increasingly urban English court, Elizabethan writers resolved that Ireland must be reformed, and with force.

Analyses by Spenser and other planters repeatedly turned to landscape in their examination of the Irish problem. Sir John Davies's 1612 treatise, *A Discovery of the True Causes Why Ireland was Never Entirely Subdued*, identified as most objectionable Ireland's apparent disinterest in building and landscaping.[70] The uncivilized state that the Irish were believed to live in is closely aligned with the uncultivated state of the land;[71] the implication is, of course, that if the landscape were tamed so too would the people be. Such an attitude provided justification for policies aiming to reform.

Richard Beacon's argument that Ireland has regressed or fallen into a state of backwardness and barbarity is framed by pastoral metaphors and the language of England's burgeoning forest industry:

> like as the wilde olive and figge tree, by the continuall addressing of a skilfull husbandman, is made at the last kindely, profitable, and fruitfull, and not inferiour to the naturall braunches; so a commonwealth overgrowne with a generall corruption of manners, and thereby become savage, barbarous, and barren, like unto the wilde olive and figge tree may by the continuall pruning and addressing of a skilfull magistrate, be made obedient, civill, and profitable unto that prince, whom God hath constituted to be the labourer in that vineyearde.[72]

While some of Beacon's analogies draw upon classical sources,[73] they resemble contemporary analyses: Davies' descriptions of the governance necessary in Ireland employs similar conceits.[74] Such mappings of the Irish cultural landscape in prose assessments were typical: the English Protestant colonizer possessed civility, as well as a mandate to convert and reform the Irish.[75]

Spenser shares his contemporaries' beliefs: if his poetry celebrates the merits of a pastoral life, *A View* denigrates that life as primitive, savage; the pastoral 'can evidently figure as an ideal only within the conventions of poetry; the actual Irish cattle-based version posed too many problems'[76] for the English as they attempted to wield control. *A View's* prose is ferocious and Machiavellian in describing the steps that England should take in order to quell rebellions; to ensure that the Irish would not be able to retreat back into the woods for shelter, Irenius recommends 'that order were taken for the cutting and opening of all places through woods'.[77] While such attitudes have earned Spenser a notoriety, *A View* also allows for a celebration of Ireland as an ideal. The landscape that hid rebels and desperately needed reform was also 'a most beautifull and sweet countrey as any is under heaven'.[78] Without native inhabitants, Ireland is an ideal space: it is the people who are the chief problem.

These conflicting representations of Ireland would seem to indicate a contradiction in Spenser's positions as a poet (with loyalties to both antiquarian and pastoral traditions) and as a civil servant (with loyalties to the sovereign). Examined in the context of the Irish tradition that has been so briefly outlined here, Spenser's pastorals, seen by so many as the height of the genre in English, reflect not only this famously uneasy and ambiguous relationship with Ireland, but also the way in which an interaction with the Irish landscape might have influenced his conception of pastoral. *Colin Clouts Come Home Againe*, a late work, from 1595, displays what may be the influence of the Irish view of nature as represented by a figure like Sweeney. While there are indications that Spenser had a certain familiarity with Irish literature[79] and intended to write on it, I do not claim that he was aware of texts such as 'Sweeney' and the thematic treatment of nature; what I suggest, however, is that by 1595, after so many years in Ireland, Spenser had undoubtedly gained a sense of the realities of the landscape, experiencing, in effect, some of the realities of nature which are present in Irish literature. These realities – exposure to the elements of which Sweeney complains, the bewildering labyrinth of the forests – have made their way into the poet's vocabulary. Over the

tropes of pastoral, Spenser lays a 'real' pastoral drama – the story of
a genuine journey between court and countryside. Colin's fictional
journey and Spenser's real one (his visit to London to present the first
half of his epic) result in a poem that embodies classical and Irish
pastoral tendencies, one that serves to remind us that from the
Elizabethan period onwards, Irish and English literary forms are
inextricably intertwined.

Situated in a supposedly ideal pastoral world, Colin – like Sweeney –
expresses a complicated longing for the past (in the form of Cynthia's
court) as well as a quite bitter disdain for the corruptions traditionally
associated with the court in the pastoral mode: drawn to the court,
which has 'no griesly famine, nor no raging swerd' (ll. 314), he is also
repelled by it, at least in part because it is responsible for his exile
'into that waste, where I was quite forgot' (ll. 183).[80] Rather than
presenting a 'simple pastorall', Spenser has written a poem made
complex by the realities of English and Irish political landscapes. By
opting to tell his pastoral tale of a journey across land and sea,
between country and city, Spenser has created a 'map' of the English
and Irish situations, unknowingly drawing attention to gaps between
English and Irish experience. Like early English paper maps of
Ireland, this 'map' is inherently unstable, since Spenser relies upon
only his own and not a native perspective of Ireland and, on his
return to London, finds it equally disorienting, as many an immigrant
or colonial servant has found similar returns 'home'.

After Colin describes Cynthia's glorious court, he is asked by a
shepherd why he

> . . . back returnedst to this barrein soyle,
> Where cold and care and penury do dwell:
> Here to keepe sheepe, with hunger and with toyle,
> Most wretched he, that is and cannot tell.[81] (ll. 656–9)

This passage is illustrative of the contradictions of the poem: the ideal
pastoral place has been intruded upon by the present realities of the
natural world. The earth, rather than producing all that the shepherds
might need, is barren; the shepherds are thus transformed into hard-
working farmers threatened with hunger and poverty of a kind
usually associated with later, mid-nineteenth-century Ireland.[82] As in
Buile Suibhne, the actualities of a life in nature make it impossible to
idealize that life. And, most interestingly, the shepherds are condemned to silence about the actual conditions of their lives – 'Most

wretched he, that is and cannot tell' – since the pastoral mode would shatter under the burden of such truths.

Colin's lament resembles contemporaneous bardic poetry; his displacement results in a mournful pathos that centres on the natural world, which mirrors his feelings of displacement by becoming barren. Interestingly, and ironically, if one views Spenser's poem in the context of Irish bardic tropes, the barrenness of the land reflects the misrule and improper leadership of the English: something has gone very wrong in Colin's world. While the poem attempts to reassume the traditional pastoral mode following such intrusions of reality, the attempt is unconvincing. Colin, like Sweeney and other Irish literary figures, experiences nature because he is a marginal figure: he is outside the realm of the court, and, while he is able to recognize advantages such as his removal from courtly corruptions and deceits, for the most part his tone is one of resignation and reluctant acceptance of his marginal position. As an outsider, Colin sees the realities – and not merely the surface glitter – of the court, and in this too Colin resembles Sweeney, who is also forced to recognize the negative aspects of settled, more 'urban' culture. If, however, Colin recognizes some beauty in the Irish landscape, it is, again like Sweeney's, a forced recognition. Spenser's failure to simply idealize the landscape in the poem thus puts him in line with an Irish literary tradition.

Colin Clouts Come Home Againe is also, in its bewildered mixing of classical, Irish and English pastoral modes, an apt example of the cultural confusion of empire. Colin's ambivalences – his sense of exile, longing to return to Cynthia's court, longing to leave the court's corruptions, and the confused sense of the word 'home' in the title – show him to be in the new-to-the-era position of having to grapple with dual and duelling allegiances: thus classical and English pastoral conventions and the realities of the natural world vie in the poem in indication of a complex political situation for which little precedent existed. Importing the classical and English pastoral forms in full regalia into the Irish landscape and the Irish pastoral economy at the end of the sixteenth century, Spenser evidently found that this pastoral needed to undergo fundamental changes. The classical pastoral's tendency to idealize the natural world was not as effective when applied to a non-imaginary landscape overrun with rebels and soldiers and real shepherds struggling to make a living in unstable conditions. While classical and English pastorals had traditionally been written from urban space about a relatively distant – and unknown – countryside, Spenser's pastoral eclogue was written from within rural space looking towards the distant court, inevitably altering his conception of pastoral, and ultimately making it an impossible reality.

In *The Faerie Queene*, these ambiguities are present whenever Ireland is mentioned and it is, in fact, in attempting to address the space of Ireland that the poem abruptly ends. When its first installment appeared in 1590, *The Faerie Queene* was prefaced by the following dedication: 'To the most mightie and magnificent empresse Elizabeth, by the grace of God Queene of England, France, and Ireland defender of the Faith &c.' Spenser significantly grants Elizabeth the title 'empresse' before 'queene', and goes on to identify her in terms of place and geography. This association is extended in the edition that appeared six years later: by 1596, Elizabeth is not merely a 'mightie and magnificent empresse', but is 'renowned for pietie, vertue, and all gratious government', and, like a skilled Monopoly player, has added to her properties the colony of Virginia.[83] Based upon these changes, one senses that the 'et cetera' – 'defender of the Faith &c' – refers to the multiple, and expanding, roles Elizabeth must play as an acquirer of empire: she must now defend much more than the faith that her father swore to uphold. It would seem that the term 'et cetera', then, can refer as well to any as yet untaken, unconquered or 'undiscovered' territories; 'et cetera' becomes the ultimate colonial motto, a description of the responsibilities and expectations of empire. These dedications, and the association of Elizabeth with place, are of particular interest when one considers that Spenser's English epic was written in Ireland and makes significant use of the Irish landscape. *The Faerie Queene* is considered by many to be the first great *English* epic; but this epic attempts to create a national, verbal map – attempts to chart a culture through time just as a geographical map charts space – while engaging a landscape other than its own.

Writing a national epic outside of the realm of the nation proper is a strange task, an exercise in nostalgia and the consecration of memory as opposed to a celebration of a present-day, lived experience of place.[84] The England invoked in *The Faerie Queene* was necessarily an England of the past, a glorification of that which had already occurred; Spenser's decision to write in what was, in his day, an already archaic form of English reinforces this sense of the presence of the past. The sense of archaic time could only have been enforced for Spenser by the continuing dominance of the Irish language over English, and the seemingly archaic English used in Ireland.[85]

In order to construct a narrative set in an almost mythological past, Spenser required the distance from England that a position in Ireland provided him with. The antiquarian, Susan Stewart writes, 'seeks to both distance and appropriate the past. In order to entertain an antiquarian sensibility, a rupture in historical consciousness must have occurred, creating a sense that one can make one's own culture *other* – distant and discontinuous'.[86] Clearly Spenser experienced this 'rupture': being in Ireland, he was physically and intellectually at one remove from the centre of the expanding empire; while still preoccupied with court activities, he was freed from the quotidian politics of London. In addition, rather than being settled in the Pale of Dublin, the centre of colonial Ireland, Spenser was stationed instead in Cork, at a rural outpost still hard to reach without car, compass and waterproof boots. Twice marginalized, Spenser lived surrounded by forest and a way of life that might well have seemed archaic to a middle-class man eager to move up through the court ranks.

Angus Fletcher has argued that *The Faerie Queene* is not so much a story as a map, and of an *imagined* geographical space.[87] If one begins with this premise, it is interesting to consider the fascination with the labyrinth that Spenser demonstrates in his epic. The labyrinth is, by definition, unmappable, a directionless place in which the compass ceases to be of help, a space over which it is impossible to gain perspective. In this the labyrinths of *The Faerie Queene* resemble the Irish forests so objectionable to Elizabethan colonizers: the forests, like labyrinths, are sites over which no control can be exerted. Significantly, Spenser's English epic begins in such a labyrinthine forest, in the Den of Errour. Forest is space that is veiled to us and yet we can move through it; such movement proves perilous in the first book of *The Faerie Queene*, as characters literally lose sight of truth in the guise of the character Una as they wend their way through the woods.

Movement through a wilderness or an unmapped landscape necessarily means that that landscape is altered; the unknown becomes known, and gradually it becomes possible to trace a path, and to return to it – to recover truth, in the context of Book One. In Book One the knight is forced to negotiate the labyrinth of the forest; the poet Spenser was clearly engaged, if not enchanted, by the idea of a wandering wood. Spenser the planter and colonial servant, however, could only recommend that the bewildering forests be cleared. It is thus appropriate that Spenser begins *The Faerie Queene* in a forest much like the ones known to have covered a still substantial portion of Ireland at the midpoint of the sixteenth century, and ends it with a very different map of the Irish landscape in the *Mutabilitie Cantos*, one that has been cleared not merely of trees but also of prosperity and significance. In these final cantos, Spenser engages the Irish landscape not as an economic prospect but mythologically, and so charts a fallen and forgotten landscape.[88]

The representation of Arlo Hill as an Edenic retreat gone wrong – an abandoned meeting place of the gods – goes beyond pastoral ideal-ization of landscape and moves towards the creation of myth. This mythologizing of landscape recalls the *dindshenchas* tradition; Spenser seems to have absorbed some of the Irish tendency to commemorate through place, a tendency which would have dovetailed with his preoccupation with etymology. Rather than engaging the Irish landscape as a problematized space that must be tamed to be of use to the English, or as a pastoral trope, Spenser maps out a mytho-logical history that explains the 'present state of Ireland' and provides justification for the English presence, just as in the *dindshenchas* tradition there is a layering of history in the discussion of a procession of names over time.

After informing us that Nature will meet the pantheon and the upstart Mutabilitie atop this hill, Spenser famously poses the paren-thetical question: 'Who knows not Arlo-Hill?' (VI.36).[89] Few, of course, know it: maps of the period did not include Arlo Hill, a rather small peak in the Galtee Mountains. The projected reader's ignorance allows Spenser his digression into the Faunus episode: it becomes necessary to give the history of the place that was of old 'the best and fairest Hill/ That was in all this holy-Islands hights' (VI.37). So ideal was this location that the gods chose to adjourn there for what Spenser describes as 'pleasure and rest' (VI.38) – here is the ideal pastoral landscape that proved impossible to depict in *Colin Clouts Come Home Againe*. The concentration on place gives way to the myth itself, of Faunus spying on Diana while she bathes in what becomes a 'guilty brooke' (VI.47), and of the ensuing chase. The result of Faunus's spying is not merely Diana's displeasure, however, and the mock hunt – the incident allows Spenser to create a myth that acts as a prophecy of the destruction of Ireland, that points, in other words, to the Ireland of *A View*.

Diana abandons the landscape, and issues her curse over the land. In creating a myth of Ireland's fall from a state of pastoral perfection due to the 'foolish' god Faunus, Spenser justifies the Elizabethan quest to redeem Ireland, to drive away the wolves, to rout out thieves. It initially appears extraordinary that, in his English epic, Spenser chooses to situate the classical pantheon atop what in reality is a rather small peak visible from 'his' castle at Kilcolman. It is this positioning, however, that allows him to explain the English presence in Ireland, and to situate himself on the map of Ireland and on the map of Elizabeth's empire. In mythologizing, appropriating, and so mapping this place in the Irish landscape, Spenser acts as an agent of empire, acquiring, in Elizabeth's name, another territory that can be listed under the term 'et cetera'. *The Faerie Queene* ends on this famously indeterminate note, leaving us with an epic as incomplete as the young empire to whose queen Spenser devoted his epic, leaving us – explorers, cartographers – to imagine the space he has been unable to chart.[90]

The traditional literary pastoral upon which Spenser drew had transformed itself in his writings. Rather than writing from an urban space about a largely unfamiliar rurality, Spenser found himself, by virtue of his position as a colonial administrator, writing about the rural from a firsthand knowledge. Pastoral nostalgia, under these conditions, is also changed: Spenser's personal nostalgia for London court society becomes emphasized at times, making him into a figure who, like Sweeney or Caílte, longs for culture while situated in nature. *Colin Clouts Come Home Againe* absorbs this type of nostalgia that is much more typical of Irish literature than of the traditional pastoral forms in which Spenser was grounded, suggesting that, over time in Ireland, Spenser absorbed something of the Irish tradition that expressed longing for the loss of culture while in nature. His experience also suggests that classical and English pastoral forms were not only urban but explicitly upper class in their removal from nature and landscape's realities. As a middle-class man who 'earned' his land in a grant from the queen, Spenser has a very different experience of nature than those who inherited estates and did not need to look to Ireland or other colonies for potential prosperity.

Spenser's most obvious influence on Irish literature would not make itself felt for several centuries, when he would be taken up by Yeats, and later by Heaney. In another sense, though, Spenser's influence on Irish literature – and on the topic of nature in Irish literature – was felt much more quickly. Since Spenser wrote in English, in Ireland, he marks the beginning of a new era in Irish literature, which, following the battle of Kinsale, turns to the English language far more than in previous centuries. In turning to the English language, Irish literature was to engage again some of the more traditional pastoral forms that had so influenced sixteenth-century English writing, including Spenser's, and that had been present in the literature of the ninth and tenth centuries. As Ireland came under tighter colonial control, and as English became the dominant and dominating language, pastoral themes would re-emerge in a way that they hadn't since the earliest Irish literature, and would culminate in the period of the Revival.

CHAPTER TWO

The Roots of the New
Irish Pastoral

As a practice, colonialism involves the movement and subsequent settlement of people in lands not their own; as an ideology, one might say, it involves the movement and subsequent settlement of ideas. One result of both the practice and ideology of colonialism in Ireland after the era of the planters is the increasing difficulty in separating 'English' and 'Irish' conceptions of nature and landscape in Irish literature. This already complex interaction is made more so by the widely felt influence of European Romanticism: itself, it would seem, a product of colonial attitudes towards 'primitive' cultures. For Irish literature from the late-sixteenth to late-nineteenth centuries, the result of this mingling of ideas would be a new strain of pastoralism that would dictate, in part, the tenor of the Revival.

If the map is an appropriate signifier of Tudor and Elizabethan attempts to control Ireland during the sixteenth century, the museum, by the beginnings of the eighteenth century, becomes a signifier of European attitudes towards both the natural and cultural world. Indeed, since the Renaissance's 'cabinet of curiosities' is 'the commonly accepted prototype of the modern museum' and 'emerged contemporaneously with the age of discovery and exploration'[1], the map itself gives way metaphorically to the museum, the two dimensional representation to the three dimensional. Museums also tend, as anthropologists attest, to display the cultural objects of 'others', and thus – like Elizabethan maps – implicitly involve the notion of colonization and ownership.[2]

The eighteenth-century European attempt to classify and systematize all things natural resulted in an interest in displaying the findings of scientific study; this led to the establishment of natural history museums in Ireland as elsewhere. The interest in collecting and

35

displaying is in itself part of colonialism, since 'exotic' specimens from farflung colonies were highly prized and themselves became signifiers of the wealth required to travel, or of one's connection with colonial administration. For those who remained at home, the rise in numbers of societies and museums attested to the profound drawing-room interest in the past.[3] More than this, however, the establishment of museums 'at home' in Ireland would contribute to what has been referred to as a process of 'internal colonialism'[4] in which a country encloses in a museum its own cultural objects that are perceived as having passed from use and become obsolete. Irish museums, in other words, would testify to a certain defeat of elements of Irish culture and would admit to the passing of certain Irish cultural forms. The very idea of the museum in a colonial setting would encourage the belief that 'native' traditions were 'past', and would also provide a specious sense of comfort in that the lost culture was 'preserved' for all to see behind the glass cases of the museum.

In Ireland, these developments, along with the influence of the Picturesque and early Romanticism, led to a form of Irish anti-quarianism that began to flourish amongst Anglo-Irish writers at the end of the eighteenth century.[5] The Picturesque and early Romantic interest in the ruin as a sign of antiquity was well suited to Ireland, which had ruined landscapes enough to occupy numerous budding archaeologists, painters and tourists. But the ruin was a signifier of more than just 'antiquity':

> A ruin in traditional Picturesque terms is both a sumptuous formal exercise for the painter and, for the sentimental tourist, a focus for vague nostalgic reverie. It is obsolete. Because it serves no contemporary vital function, as a building is designed to do, it now works as a means of imaginatively releasing the spectator from the present. And if one is predisposed anyway to feel alienated from many aspects of contemporary culture, then a 'pensive ruin' is just the right emblematic trigger.[6]

In this sense, the Picturesque becomes the painterly version of pastoral, the visual embodiment of cultural nostalgia: there is no doubt that the English Picturesque grew out of an intense upper- and middle-class dissatisfaction or 'alienation' in the face of the massive cultural effects of industrialization and of enclosure,[7] just as pastoral reflects a dissatisfaction with the complexities of urban existence. English Picturesque did not, however, signify the rupturing of cultural connections as it did in Ireland, where the ruin connoted a hidden – and largely unremembered – past.

The rise in tourism[8] that coincided with the rise of the Picturesque and Romanticism meant that many more visitors were exposed to Ireland,[9] resulting in a new awareness of the Irish landscape and of the past as it was represented by that landscape. The resultant new views stand in stark contrast to those of the Elizabethans, held only two hundred years earlier. Where the Elizabethans saw ruination as a sign of rebellion, 'wild' landscape[10] as a sign of incivility and lack of culture, these antiquarians and early Romantics saw – some no doubt through their Claude-glasses[11] – inspired beauty and mystery, and the remains of ancient culture. Astonishingly, wildness in landscape comes to be perceived as a sign of *good* government.[12] That Ireland appeared to have been so thoroughly colonized, of course, allowed such ideas to flourish: remains of Irish culture were, after all, merely remains, and not a threat. The Irish landscape began to be perceived as a 'natural' museum of ancient Irish history that could tell tales display cases could not, and in a far more melodramatic setting. Removed from the museum's supposed display of 'fact' as well as 'science', landscape could be interpreted more freely and beyond the bounds of what were often seen as English establishments. And, significantly, these perceptions would contribute – even if unintentionally – to an early nationalism.

JAMES MACPHERSON

In Ireland the early Romantic emphasis on the possibility of viewing elided culture through landscape owed much, however, to the influence of a Scotsman who was to have one of the most significant influences upon Irish and European Romanticism generally, and who directly inspired the work of – or at least provoked a response in – a handful of prominent Irish antiquarians. Beginning with James Macpherson's notorious forgeries of *Ossian* between 1760 and 1765,[13] the Celt and Irish and Scottish mythology and literature gained popularity across Europe. While believing himself to have been working with a Scottish tradition, Macpherson was, of course, actually working with a shared Gaelic heritage of Scotland and Ireland; Macpherson did not write in Ireland, and did not intend to write on Irish material, which he claimed was not as old as the Scottish literary tradition. In Ireland, Macpherson was thus almost immediately regarded as having hijacked Irish material, and so came to have a profound impact on the conception of Irish literature, sparking Irish scholars to stake their own claims for *Ossian* and its medieval sources.

Macpherson took as his subject the Finn tales, rewriting them and claiming that he had discovered ancient Scottish manuscripts which, coincidentally, dovetailed with his own day's sensibilities about nature. While Macpherson did embark on copious research, it was clear – almost immediately to many – that the texts were not mere translations but the creative work of a contemporary poet. In his creation of a 'real' medieval figure, Macpherson managed to capture the spirit of an age that was increasingly looking to nature and an imagined simpler life that contrasted sharply with an increasingly complex and urban European culture.

Macpherson's emphasis on tradition and on the antiquity of his texts created a melancholy, nostalgic mood in his characters that did much to associate the Celt with such sentiments. Macpherson is, in fact, accurate in portraying Oisín (Ossian or Oscian, in his texts) as experiencing nostalgia, although Macpherson's version incorporates elements of the traditional literary pastoral, complete with pathetic fallacy and an idealization of a lost natural world:

> My eyes are blind with tears; but memory beams on my heart. [. . .] He fell as the moon in a storm; as the sun from the midst of his course, when clouds rise from the water of the waves, when the blackness of the storm inwraps the rocks of Ardannider. I, like an ancient oak on Morven, I moulder alone in my place.
>
> . . .
>
> It is night; and I am alone, forlorn on the hill of storms. The wind is heard in the mountain. The torrent shrieks down the rock. No hut receives me from the rain; forlorn on the hill of winds.[14]

The similarities between Macpherson's version and the thirteenth-century *Acallam na Senórach* are immediately apparent. Ossian, like his medieval counterpart, laments his position as the sole survivor of his clan, and is presented as living in the natural world as a result of having lost his position in society. However, the difference here is in the representation of nature. In Macpherson's version, nature mirrors Ossian's emotions and reflects his state of mind; in the *Acallam*, there is no sense that the natural world in which Oisín finds himself reflects the change in his own status: in fact, there is every sense that the landscape has remained unchanged. Unlike in the *Acallam*, nature in Macpherson becomes the site of antiquity, a symbol of a lost time and a lost ideal in which man and nature lived in harmony. From early *fían* literature, it is clear that the relationship between man and nature in thirteenth-century Ireland was not so simple, in that the *fían* were defined not only by their existence in nature but in culture as well; but Macpherson's texts, saturated with contemporary idealizations of nature, were far more appealing than the medieval realities.

As the view of nature is different in Macpherson's text, so is the nostalgia. As forgeries, Macpherson's versions of the Finn tales contain a classically pastoral nostalgia for a life in nature that has never been lived; they do not contain nostalgia for lost culture but only for an imagined, idealized existence in nature. The past that is longed for is thus not a part of an organic tradition, but an invented one. And this invented pastoral was to have enormous effect.

Macpherson had taken the shell of a medieval story and had imbued it with the sensibilities of his own time, sensibilities influenced by increasing tourism and fascination with the unknown aspects of the natural world, and with 'primitive' cultures and civilizations. Stories of Finn and Oisín were not, in their original medieval forms, simple romanticizations of the natural world; Macpherson's version chose to ignore this fact and offered instead an idealized and senti- mental version not only of Ossian and his life, but of the world in which he lived. Macpherson recognizes this idealization – and also makes a crucial bid for the 'reality' of his texts – in an introduction to the first edition of *Fingal* (1761/62), where he writes that his characters' 'virtues remain, but the vices, which were once blended with their virtues, have died with themselves'.[15]

Over a period of several hundred years, the idea of nature and landscape had changed dramatically in Europe, becoming something alternately (and sometimes both) sublime and beautiful, rather than merely symbolic of the state of man after a fall from Eden.[16] Macpherson occupies a key place in this story as an author who attempted to pass off his European touristic, colonial and Romantic sensibilities as authentically Celtic, an author who, in other words, represented the change in attitudes towards the natural world. Macpherson's insistence that his stories were reflective of a reality consciously asserts the Romantic belief that earlier times and cultures were defined by an existence in nature marked by simplicity and, by extension, simple joys: Macpherson created, in effect, a new European pastoral for his age, one that astutely tapped into changing attitudes towards the natural world, and one that would provide a remarkably inspirational ground to poets from Goethe to Arnold. Beyond his influence on the young Romantics and thus an entire school of European poetics, Macpherson's legacy would eventually dictate the early tenor of the Irish Revival, at least in part because of the response to Macpherson by writers in Ireland, who, in their own 'recoveries' of Irish culture, began to adopt Macpherson's tone.

Within a short period of Macpherson's publications, studies such as Sylvester O'Halloran's *An Introduction to the Study of the History and Antiquities of Ireland* (1772), Joseph Cooper Walker's *Historical Memoirs of the Irish Bards* (1786), Charlotte Brooke's *Reliques of Irish Poetry* (1789) and Edward Bunting's *General Collection of the Ancient Music of Ireland* (1796) demonstrated a new awareness of Ireland's ancient culture. Crucially, however, the recovery of ancient culture was, in these Irish authors' work, linked to nationalism, so that the texts become, in a sense, early critiques of colonialism in their determination to reclaim a particular culture as belonging to a particular group of people. The attempt to retrieve the Irish past and translate it into the present was seen as a necessary action: as Charlotte Brooke notes in her introduction to *Reliques of Irish Poetry*, 'I trust that I am doing an acceptable service to my country, while I endeavour to rescue from oblivion a few of the invaluable reliques of her ancient genius'.[17]

However much such authors worked to establish the 'invaluable' nature of Ireland's ancient culture, and to wrest from Macpherson his claim for the Finn material as Scottish, Macpherson's tone was extraordinarily influential. Walker, for example, in *Historical Memoirs of the Irish Bards* (1786), stresses melancholia, so that his interpretation of the bards reads like Macpherson's interpretation of Ossian:

> Such was the sensibility of the Bards, such was their tender affection for their country, that the subjection to which the kingdom was reduced, affected them with the heaviest sadness. Sinking beneath this weight of sympathetic sorrow, they became a prey to melancholy. Hence the plaintiveness of their music: For the ideas that arise in the mind are always congenial to, and receive a tincture from, the influencing passion. Another cause might have concurred with the one just mentioned, in promoting a change in the style of our music. The Bards, often driven, together with their patrons, by the sword of Oppression from the busy haunts of men, were obliged to lie concealed in marshes, in gloomy forests, amongst rugged mountains, and in glyns and vallies [sic] resounding with the noise of falling waters, or filled with portentous echoes. Such scenes as these, by throwing a gloom over the fancy, must have considerably increased their settled melancholy.[18]

This passage might well have been written by Macpherson: phrases such as 'heaviest sadness', 'sympathetic sorrow', 'influencing passion', and words like 'gloomy' demonstrate the impact of Macpherson's style and the pervasive ideology of the period. As in Macpherson's version of the Finn material, there is a certain amount of accuracy in Walker's description: for the bards often were pushed out into the world and did indeed mourn for the loss of their cultural position, as we have seen. And, curiously, Walker does recognize that some significant change occurred within the tone of bardic poetry as a result of 'the subjection to which the kingdom was reduced'. However, the language of this passage – like many others – throws a blanket of romantic ideology over the political situation encountered by the bards in the late-sixteenth and early-seventeenth centuries, emphasizing instead a kind of racial categorization: that the Irish experienced a 'settled melancholy' due to their 'sensibility'.[19]

Several decades later, James Hardiman's *Irish Minstrelsy or Bardic Remains of Ireland* (1831) vehemently and candidly objects to Macpherson's claims to Irish material, expressing a discontent felt by many, and lamenting that such work has produced 'succeeding authors, unable or unwilling to separate the truth from the fable':[20]

> it has long been a subject of regret, with the writer, that the remains of our national bards, of those men who, according to James Macpherson, 'have displayed a genius worthy of any age or nation', should be consigned to obscurity at home, while a neighbouring nation derived so much literary fame from a few of those remains, boldly claimed and published as its own.[21]

Hardiman laments that Macpherson's forgeries have proven so influential as to produce 'contented copyists',[22] and yet despite this, and despite his objections to what he perceives as Mapherson's misuse of Irish material, Hardiman, like the very 'copyists' he critiques, makes use of a language and of ideas that derive directly from Macpherson:

> Sentiments of virtuous love were never more delicately or fervently expressed than in the ancient relics of the pastoral muse of Ireland. The language in which they are conveyed is chaste, elegant, and pure, and the imagery which they present, is a faithful delineation of the most captivating features of natural scenery and rural beauty. The blossom bloom and fragrance of the flowery ornaments of the garden and field – the charming verdure of our island green – the murmur of the

waterfall – the sparkling of the dew – the plumage of the swan, and the mildness of the dove – the sweet notes of the cuckoo, the black-bird, and the thrush, and the liquid gold of the bee, perpetually occur, and continue to heighten the rich description of female beauty contained in these rural effusions.

. . .

In the rich, but imperfectly explored, mine of Irish poetry, which teems with brilliant gems of national genius, the elegaic vein is that most likely to attract and reward attention. The mildly chastened and exquisitely tender specimens of this captivating species of poetry are innumerable. The feelings of a people, broken down by long ages of oppression, and the sweetly expressive language of the land, were alike favourable to the elegaic muse.[23]

Like Walker, Hardiman makes a passing reference to the notion that 'long ages of oppression' might have influenced or contributed to what he calls the 'elegaic vein': but the reference is not developed or explored; instead, what stands out is the highly romanticized language used to describe the landscape found in early Irish poetry, and Hardiman's efforts to subtly refute certain stereotypes by employing words such as 'virtuous', 'chaste', and phrases like 'mildly chastened' – the Irish, far from being wild or uncivil, are well behaved and 'broken down'. Despite suggesting opposition to these negative ideas about the Irish, Hardiman is, however, eager to occupy other stereotypes that have become popularly associated with the Celt as sentimental, nostalgic and connected to nature. In their attempts to reclaim Irish literature from Macpherson, figures like Walker and Hardiman create their own form of Celtic Romanticism by stepping into and occupying such stereotypes. By affirming that the Irish tradition was in fact 'elegaic' and inspired by a 'pastoral muse', antiquarians unknowingly encouraged later writers like Yeats and Synge to employ conceits that, far from being peculiarly 'Irish' or 'Celtic', were in fact representative of the blending together of many ideas over hundreds of years. And these ideas and conceits owed much to the presence of a colonizer in Ireland.

While the sort of Irish Romanticism employed by figures from Brooke to Hardiman expressed interest in the ruin and in wild landscape, it differed from English Romanticism, and was certainly not as widespread a phenomenon. For the Irish, and particularly for those who were politically or socially active, the Act of Union (1800), which tightened English governance of Ireland and moved parliamentary control to London, had implications for landscape that could not be covered by Wordsworth's lyricism alone. Absentee landlords, high rents, enclosure, the difficulty in obtaining land to rent and uncertainty about fixity of tenure had been problems for decades, but the Act of Union was to worsen these crises. As a result, *English* Romanticism did not take hold in Ireland to a comparable extent, relying as it did upon a leisured class who had time to observe the natural world from a detached position.[24] One always feels that Wordsworth writes his lyrics from an interior space, observing himself, in retrospect, in the natural world.[25] In Ireland, that distance did not exist by impossibility: 'Nature in Ireland', as Terry Eagleton has put it, 'is too stubbornly social and material a category, too much a matter of rent, conacre, pigs and potatoes for it to be distanced, stylized and subjectivated'.[26]

Within the general Irish population was, in fact, what Luke Gibbons has deemed a resistance to the romanticization of nature that had taken place in England.[27] A part of the agenda of Irish Romanticism was to assert difference from England, and to find evidence for the existence of a pre-colonial culture, as witnessed by even the few excerpts cited above. Demonstrating that that culture was not one of the wilderness, of wild nature, was an unconscious part of the goal. The wilderness, in English Romanticism, was the site of primitive, pre-industrial, undeveloped culture; for the Irish, who had for so long been charged with primitivism by the English, Romanticism was thus very different. As a result, books of the period such as O'Halloran's and Brooke's tended to emphasize the *cultural* aspects of the Irish past: O'Halloran and Hardiman might occupy stereotypes of the Irish as sentimental and possessed by landscape, but they do so within the context of a written literary tradition of many centuries, thus insisting, as J.W. Foster has noted, 'that the ruined landscape bore witness to a dignified pre-conquest culture'.[28] The land of Ireland becomes, then, a museum, a preserver of a past which might otherwise have been forgotten.

And, strangely, as a preserver of history and culture, the landscape itself begins to personify nostalgia, the trait assigned to those medieval Irish figures who had existed in it. This is intertwined, of course, with the fact that from Cromwell's time onwards the Irish Catholic majority were largely forbidden or prevented from engagement in trade or commerce: the only employment generally available was the land, even after Catholic Emancipation in the 1820s. Even an otherwise typically biased 1889 English tract on *The History of Land Tenure in Ireland* recognizes that

Land, by the fatal policy of England, was made the vital necessity of
the Celtic race. Half the land hunger of the Irish peasantry has its root
in the transmitted idea that the possession of land is an essential of
existence. The legislation which for a century deliberately shut the door
to the growth of Irish commerce, and which systematically laboured to
reduce to subjection the native race, bound them to the land by barring
all other means not only of wealth but of bare subsistence.[29]

As a result of its colonial status, Ireland during the rise of English
Romanticism simply could not experience the same sense of worship
for the simplicity of a life in nature, since, under English legislation,
the 'simplicity' of a life in nature was largely the only life available.
The land thus became a signifier of enormous weight and power: the
only way of surviving, the site of exploitative rents and land laws that
favoured landlords even in their absence, and, since it could not be
owned, a sign of all that was unjust about English colonial control.

Far from producing a bevy of poets in line with Wordsworth,
Coleridge and Shelley, Ireland during the Romantic period was preoccupied with other issues removed from purely aesthetic concerns;
the absence of industrialization in Ireland further eclipsed the
possibility of a distance from nature that might have allowed for its
widescale romanticization. Irish writers recognized the association of
Romanticism with liberty, and, as a result, some of the writings of the
period are concerned with addressing the political implication of
English (mis)rule as well as with glorifying the ancient Irish past as
one unmarked by the presence of colonizers like the English. The best
known pieces of writing from this era, though, because they were
produced by Anglo-Irish writers, tend to avoid addressing the
political situation too directly.

THE FAMINE

The Celtic-Romantic literary form was thus to pass from Macpherson,
Walker and Hardiman's hands into the eager palms of several generations of scholars and writers, but only after one of the most stark
periods of Irish history, a period that went against the grain of the
idea of Romantic nature. Progress within Ireland on literary and
cultural matters was largely halted by two factors. Before the cata-
strophe of the famine years, additional British troops arrived in
Ireland to quell a rise in nationalism – which was largely the result of
the intolerable conditions of tenants and farmers; the result, in other

words, of an issue of nature and landscape – and also to aid in the Ordnance Survey, which would further alter the idea of landscape in Ireland. The Survey, which set out to map the entire island of Ireland in the 1830s, represented an assertion of colonial control over Ireland that sent teams of both British soldiers and Irish intellectuals into previously neglected areas to record (but in practice often alter) place names as well as charting the landscape.[30] That this was a determined colonial move is evidenced by the fact that Britain undertook a similarly intensive survey only in India, another long-term colony. While the detailed mapping of the Irish landscape sought to exert colonial control, though, it also provided archaeological evidence that would later be picked up by those seeking liberation from England. Daniel O'Connell's movement towards independence and Catholic Emancipation relied, in part, on the ideas brought to life by this colonial endeavour.[31] The outbreak of famine, however, would bring such nationalist movements abruptly to their knees.

It is a cruel irony that shortly after the height of Romanticism in England, Ireland was engaged in a fatal battle with nature. If the Irish had maintained a close relationship to the natural world through working the land, that relationship seemed severed by the events of the Famine. Nature could no longer be seen as a neutral force; instead, it was a force that betrayed arbitrarily, weighing life and death lightly. Documentation of the number of deaths during the years 1840–50 is well known; but during this period the landscape, as well as the people, was dramatically impacted. Post-Famine Ireland resembled a war zone: land was in utter devastation; fields were unrecognizably blackened; much of the remainder of forest had been cut down for fuel; whole villages had been deserted due to death, starvation and eviction; the countryside was awash with men, women and children searching for food and shelter. The landscape became cleared of people, with the result that additional areas of the country were 'picturesque', even though '[t]he 'beauty' of its landscape came at the cost of this unthinkable human misery'.[32] The physical and psychic disruption to the Irish landscape was enormous. If England had a gentle relationship with nature during the period, the Irish had what can be described as a volatile, violent relationship.[33] The trust in nature, if it had been firmly in place in the years before the Famine, was now shattered: the Famine was the literal failure of the pastoral. As Sean Lysaght puts it,

> The Famine, the long memory of deprivation of the land, and the loss of names for nature, all combine to stifle that more romanticized view

of the natural world that we get in England. We can express the problem as a series of stereotypes: English culture has given prominence to a sentimental, pastoral view of nature and countryside based on continuity, belonging, and fruition; Irish experience has been marked by the opposites: discontinuity, exile, and sterility.[34]

The sense of 'discontinuity, exile, and sterility' was everywhere in evidence. Between the uncountable deaths and emigrations that took place during the 1840s and 1850s, the Irish population had dwindled to its lowest level in several hundred years. It is from this period, though, that Ireland's movement for independence derives. The phrase 'God brought the blight, but the English caused the Famine' is telling of the attitudes that arose out of that decade: resentment of the colonizer had grown to an alarming height, and was to fuel the movements that began the process of nation building. Given the severity of Famine conditions, it might appear a surprisingly short time before pastoral ideas began to creep into the rhetoric of the nation. However, if one considers that Famine conditions were aggravated by evictions of tenants who simply could not pay rent,[35] and by the consolidation of small farm holdings into larger ones due to the death or emigration of tenants, the Famine can be seen as the trigger of a further nostalgia for land and for the right to own one's own homeland.

MATTHEW ARNOLD

In the immediate aftermath of the Famine, much of the scholarship about Ireland was taking place outside of the country. Of post-Famine, Victorian scholars, Matthew Arnold is particularly significant, and his lecture and essay 'On the Study of Celtic Literature' (1867) influenced almost every author involved in the Revival, besides having considerable influence on opinion outside of Ireland about the Irish. Despite its title, the essay is not in fact about literature, but is instead an obvious product of Romantic and post-Romantic interests in philology and racial classifications as they arose out of Romantic nationalism. Besides these pseudo-scientific influences, Arnold is also strongly influenced by new movements in legitimate science, particularly Darwin's theories,[36] and sees the eventual merging of races within England, Scotland, Wales and Ireland as 'a consummation to which the natural course of things irresistibly tends'.[37]

While Arnold's colonial biases are obvious – undoubtedly he is imagining that the Scots, the Welsh and the Irish will become in some way more English, and not the other way round – he is, in his own eyes at least, attempting to eliminate hostile difference.[38] Arnold argues that elements of the Celtic exist in other European groups, and this makes ironic sense, since those 'Celtic' characteristics that he goes on to describe were assigned and created, in many cases, by non-Celts, and describe general human characteristics instead of racially specific ones – although critics of the time were not to see this so clearly.

After outlining this futuristic meshing of cultures into one larger, pan-British Isles culture, Arnold goes on to describe characteristics specific to the Celt, drawing upon Renan's earlier essay on Celtic poetry,[39] but arguing with his description of the Celt and furthering it. This idea of the Celt being endowed with a sentimental character – an idea descending directly from Macpherson's Ossian – becomes Arnold's main thesis, one which he develops relentlessly:

> Sentimental – *always ready to react against the despotism of fact* . . .
> Balance, measure, and patience, these are the eternal conditions, even supposing the happiest temperament to start with, of high success; and balance, measure, and patience are just what the Celt has never had.[40]
> [Arnold's emphasis]

By this point, 'sentimental' has become one of several key words to describe the Irish, and encompasses both 'nostalgia' and 'melancholy', as well as hinting, I would argue, at the state of being colonized. Arnold offers here a justification of the Irish situation that relies upon a description of a national character.[41] In the same way that Spenser's description of the Irish situation blames the Irish for the ruination of a landscape that was, in fact, largely destroyed by the planters, and in the same way that Walker's description of the bards as innately melancholic avoids the politics behind the expression of nostalgia in late-sixteenth- and early-seventeenth-century bardic poetry, Arnold's description removes English political responsibility from the equation.[42] As a result of such a justification, 'Irish identity was reduced to a cultural imaginary, in a restricted aesthetic sense, all the more to remove it from more quotidian matters of power and self-determination.'[43] The Irish could not achieve 'success' since they were endowed with such characteristics.

Beyond the direct political implications of such a move, Arnold, like Renan before him, connects his belief in the Celt as sentimental to an involvement with the natural world: 'The forest of trees and the forest of rocks, not hewn timber and carved stones, suits [the Celtic people's] aspirations for something not to be bounded or expressed.'[44] Arnold perceives sentiment as being inextricably bound to landscape. As we have seen, though, the link between such sentiment and landscape is a different one in original medieval material to the one described here. Rather than perceiving the fact that, in medieval Irish literature, nature frequently becomes the site for nostalgia because of severed cultural connections, Arnold superimposes the post-Macpherson and post-Romantic, urban conception of the natural world as connected to a primitive and more 'magical'[45] culture on to Celtic character. The world of the Celt, as Arnold sees it, is wild and untamed – 'not hewn timber and carved rocks' – and thus more 'natural'. The nostalgic and 'sentimental' character of the Celt thus allows him to perceive the natural world in a way that is somehow unavailable to more advanced (and less sentimental) cultures. This is a clear demonstration of the influence of pastoral on Arnold's thinking.

IRISH SCHOLARSHIP: STANDISH JAMES O'GRADY

Arnold's ideas were immensely influential throughout Europe in determining and re-inforcing a stereotype of the Irish. These ideas were not, of course, limited to scholarship and writing outside of Ireland, but were also integrated into the internal scholarship of the forming nation. Of Irish scholars who influenced creative writers of the Revival, Standish James O'Grady (1846–1928) is undoubtedly the most significant. O'Grady's course of study propelled him into a lifetime career[46] on the subjects of Irish history, myth and culture, using as his sources medieval texts: annals, *Lebor na hUidre*, the Book of Leinster, and the Book of Lismore, amongst others.[47] Like others before him, O'Grady was sparked to his task by the reading not only of O'Halloran's *Antiquaries of Ireland*, but of Macpherson, who had 'stolen' Ireland's literature for his own purposes:

> Poor Ireland, with her hundred ancient epics, standing at the door of the temple of fame, or, indeed, quite behind the vestibule out of the way! To see the Swabian enter in, crowned, to a flourish of somewhat barbarous music, was indeed bad enough, but Mr MacPherson![48]

O'Grady's response to Macpherson's forgeries of ancient Irish literature was to attempt to redress what he saw as an affront to Irish literature. The result was that O'Grady was to become to the Revival what Macpherson had been to the Romantics, a figure who paved a path that was to bear the tread of all those to follow. Like Macpherson too – despite his reaction to Macpherson's mode of scholarship – O'Grady took liberties with Irish material, although for a different purpose.

O'Grady recognized that his subject did not have mass appeal and was inaccessible even to those who spoke or read modern Irish; he aimed to create such an appeal by modernizing Irish history through an editing process that made use of a dated English that aspired to seem antiquated. 'The true method', he wrote, 'would certainly be to print it exactly as it is without excision or condensation';[49] this method he deemed impossible due to the volume of material he was dealing with, but also because he recognized that the early Irish language and the early Irish mores that the texts represented were too 'foreign' to be acceptable in their original form.

> I desire to make this heroic period once again a portion of the imagination of the country, and its chief characters as familiar in the minds of our people as they once were. As mere history, and treated in the method in which history is generally written at the present day, a work dealing with the early Irish kings and heroes would certainly not secure an audience. Those who demand such a treatment forget that there is not in the country an interest on the subject to which to appeal . . . On the other hand Irishmen are as ready as others to feel an interest in a human character, having themselves the ordinary instincts, passions, and curiosities of human nature. If I can awake an interest in the career of even a single ancient Irish king, I shall establish a train of thoughts, which will advance from thence to the state of society in which he lived, and the kings and heroes who surrounded, preceded, or followed him. Attention and interest once fully aroused, concerning even one feature of the landscape of ancient history, could be easily widened and extended in its scope.[50]

O'Grady's explanation for his procedure is fascinating, for if we read carefully here we catch glimpses of a tone that will prevail in major writers like Yeats and Synge. O'Grady emphasizes that the past is an 'heroic period', implying not only that the Irish past is in sharp contrast with a present full of defeat and resignation, but that there is an ancient aristocracy to be found in Irish history.[51] Also significant is that O'Grady stresses not the traits peculiar to the Celt or the Irishman; instead he goes out of his way to emphasize that the Irish have 'ordinary . . . human natures'. And, finally, O'Grady makes it plain that his approach necessitates the creation of a mythologized version of Irish history. There were, of course, political reasons for the 'deception', since, as one critic describes it, 'To present the sagas in their original form and detail would have been to offer substance for accusations of crudeness and immorality.'[52] The effect, however, was that, in creating a fictionalized history of Ireland, the scholarship that preceded and coincided with the Revival followed Macpherson's lead.[53]

Writing in 1879, a year after the first volume of his *History of Ireland* appeared, O'Grady outlined his theoretical approach to Irish history, claiming that he had committed an error in the first volume: 'that I did not permit it to be seen with sufficient clearness that the characters and chief events of the tale are absolutely historic'.[54] This claim to historicity indicates the contradiction of his work: fact and fiction mingling without differentiation. O'Grady's choice to create a real and at once imagined history of Ireland through literature – itself an imaginative presentation of the world – was to prove enormously successful, however.

As with Arnold's essay, O'Grady's material shows the infiltration of post-Romantic sensibilities and ideals, as well as the more complicated ideal and goal of Irish nationhood.[55] The 'new myth'[56] that O'Grady created certainly became a north star to which writers and thinkers in Ireland turned for bearings. Not only was Ireland's historical status as a place of ancient literature almost instantly revived through O'Grady's work; inspiration was also drawn from the idea of an ancient culture independent of England's. Thus Ireland's potential for independence was highlighted through O'Grady's translations:

> When the study of Irish literary records is revived, as it certainly will be revived, the old history of each of these raths and cromlechs will be brought again into the light, and one new interest of a beautiful and edifying nature attached to the landscape, and affecting wholly for good the minds of our people.[57]

That O'Grady chooses to focus upon this image of the landscape as representing the Irish past – as well as the possibilities for the Irish future – is telling, and confirms the attitude that was in the air: the landscape itself was a museum of the past. The prominence of the Irish landscape becomes a way of 'confer[ring] permanence on the legacy of the heroic age',[58] an age that was *naturally* aristocratic. O'Grady's focus on not merely the past, but on an aristocratic past, was to exert enormous influence.[59]

O'Grady translated and interpreted medieval Irish material, and chose to cast the translations in an archaic English that emphasized the literature's antiquity, and by direct extension, the antiquity of Irish culture generally. Like Spenser's use of an English idiom that was already archaic in his time, O'Grady's use of dated English forms demonstrated a conscious preoccupation with the past, and in Ireland the past had, to a large extent, gone unexplored and had not penetrated the nation-to-be's consciousness. J.W. Foster's description of such work as 'going backwards, however vaguely, in order to go forwards'[60] is fitting: in order to establish the idea of Ireland as a nation, few things would be as important as the ancient culture to which authors and scholars alike turned. O'Grady's language was a bid for the historical authenticity that he realized was necessary to re-establish that ancient culture.

Through O'Grady's publications, which were in many ways a response to Macpherson and to Arnold, the Irish, Seamus Deane notes, 'who had shown a marked inclination toward this view of themselves, finally took possession of the stereotype, modified the Celt into the Gael, and began that new interpretation of themselves known as the Irish literary revival'.[61] While I have argued that this process had occurred earlier – with the likes of Walker and Hardiman and not just with O'Grady – O'Grady's work did indeed encourage the firm reclamation of stereotypes that were a part of the colonial heritage, and an emphasis on an idealized vision of the Irish past. Significantly, though, this vision of the past engaged place and landscape as the site of the 'real' Ireland,[62] and it was this new mythology that was to take hold of the nation-to-be's consciousness.

The fact that the Revival is known by that name immediately indicates that this period of cultural development involved looking back to earlier traditions and literatures in Ireland: unlike a 'renaissance' – a rebirth – a 'revival' looks to put life back into something which has died, and suggests a religious zeal for doing so. Revival authors and scholars produced a body of work that consciously called upon Irish traditions eclipsed by years of colonialism, creating, in the process, the idea of a self-consciously nationalist Irish literature, but one which, ironically, inhabited colonial stereotypes. This process was visible not only in the work of literary figures, though; the reclamation of stereotypes and the rewriting of history also fell into line with a nationalist view of Ireland. The politicians of the Revival period tended to focus relentlessly, as scholars did, on recovery of a glorious past. Political nostalgia, like the Revivalists' literary nostalgia, chose to emphasize the connection of the Irish to landscape and countryside, despite the urban roots of many of the age's political movements. The use by scholars such as O'Grady of edited versions of the past was paralleled by edited versions of history that politicians like Collins and DeValera chose to highlight: and these versions of the past often emphasized rurality and used rural images to create the idea of the nation.[63] The result was that for scholars, poets and politicians, rurality became a sign of Ireland's past, and the symbol of the goals of the Irish present: a psychological return to the land.

This goal was, of course, working in tandem with another, which was the actual recovery of land. In the post-Famine years, the land issue, which had for so many centuries been a debate of quiet furor in Ireland, became more pressing than ever. Decades of laws had been seen as 'too little too late', but the establishment of the Land League in 1879 and its rapid seguing into a Home Rule movement forced the British government to respond. Following agitation by figures as different as James Fintan Lalor, Isaac Butt,[64] Michael Davitt and Charles Stuart Parnell, the British government finally seemed prepared to address the issue with definitive acts of Parliament. As recent studies on the 'Land Wars' have demonstrated, the land had become, in a breathtakingly short time, a metaphor for nationality, since 'the wider political objective was grafted onto the agrarian one'.[65] After relatively ineffectual acts like those of 1860 and 1870, the institution of such laws as the Ashbourne Act (1885) and the Wyndham Act (1903) allowed tenants to buy out farms with money provided by the Treasury. The impact of these laws on land ownership in Ireland was enormous. The *idea* of land was democratized in an unprecendented manner; for the first time in several hundred years, Irishmen were encouraged by standing law to purchase land. The result was twofold: first, the demesne and the power of the Anglo-Irish Ascendancy went into decline, resulting eventually in a power vacuum that early nationalists and an emerging Catholic elite would be only too eager to fill; and second, within a decade of the Wyndham Act, a majority of former tenants had purchased their land,[66] making it possible to imagine Ireland as an Irish owned space: in other words, a nation.

It is not surprising to find that in the literature leading up to Irish independence, there is a conscious reclamation of the Irish landscape through a process of verbal mapping, as well as in the reclamation of the Irish language and Irish place names. This mapping, often in the form of detailed observation of the land and its natural beauties, as well as in a self-conscious return to nature themes of early Irish literature, is an identity-forming process that the Irish are not alone in undergoing – a half century earlier, in attempting a conscious shaping of an American identity, Emerson, Thoreau and others turned to the land and an aesthetic of nature. It would appear that in fashioning a modern nation, then, there is a dependence, at least in part, upon an invented, and inventing, pastoral; when the forming nation is emerging from a colonial heritage, the process is necessarily complicated, however. The tradition of Irish literature's involvement with place, nature and landscape offered such an invented and inventing myth to writers like Yeats and Synge, who sought to regain in their works what amounted to an impossible, Darwinian origin of Ireland.

The loss of the Irish language seems to have significantly contributed to the nostalgia that arose around nature and landscape, at least in part because of the loss of words to describe that world.[67] This mode of nostalgia can certainly be seen in the literature of the Revival, a period during which the overwhelming majority of authors wrote in English, and were frequently unfamiliar with either modern or old Irish. The ability to invoke place names that did survive in Irish and had been translated into English became an important, if indirect, way of recovering the past, in Yeats for example, just as the recovery of tales in Irish – by the likes of Lady Gregory and Synge – comes to signify the direct inheritance of the Irish language, and, consequently, of the past.

While tenant farmers who purchased land had reason to be economically and practically hard-headed about it, a mystique of the land began to blossom amongst non-rural inhabitants who sentimentalized this 'return to the land' by 'natives'. The adaptation of (and return to) a traditional pastoral nostalgia within Irish culture corresponds, unsurprisingly, to the development of an urban society that, prior to the era of the Revival, was relatively small. Institutions like the Land League, the Irish National League and the United Irish League – all of which focused relentlessly on the issue of *rural* land within their political schemes – were largely urban-based.[68] Yeats, Synge and others involved in the cultural movement of the Revival relied upon often sophisticated urban concepts of nature: their very distance from the practicalities of working the land allowed them to engage in idealizations that led to the construction of the idea of the Irish nation as rural, traditional and, quite consciously, not English. Such urban sentiments about nature, landscape and rurality, inherited as they were, in part, from non-Irish sources, encouraged a form of national pastoral that ignored natural realities such as the ones that had occurred during the Famine, as well as the less physically catastrophic, but still devastating, realities to be described later in the century by writers such as Patrick Kavanagh. In many ways, this is unsurprising: given that political institutions in Ireland throughout the nineteenth century took as their aim the recovery of land tenure and ownership, and given the consequently inseparable nature of the land question and nationalism, even the passing of the Wyndham Act could not dispel what had, in effect, become a new mythology; there was, as Philip Bull notes, an 'inability of the political culture to free itself from the habits of mind and action created by the land issue'.[69]

This new mythology was put into effect with a breathtaking rapidity: only fifty years after the Famine, when such a rupture had occurred between the Irish people and the natural world, politics and literature managed to reforge a bond based on the principles of the pastoral.

The Abbey Theatre, as a prominent cultural vehicle for these ideas of pastoral, cultural nationalism, subscribed heavily to the ideal of the landscape as the site of the glorious Irish past in its production of 'peasant plays', and the peasant became the icon of real Ireland. That most of the leading figures in the Revival were not only urban-based, but Anglo-Irish, contributed to the perception of the peasant as child-like, uncomplicated, inherently 'natural', and, in a significant way, antique. The 'new' was thus linked inextricably to the 'old', quite consciously. The Abbey, with its determinedly rural canon, attempted to tap into pastoral myths, subtly transforming the idea of the present into an inheritance of the heroic past.

This is not to suggest that the Revival was a rude movement in which the past was systematically raided to fit into some schema of the present; it was, in fact, a highly complex interpretation of the past that relied heavily on pastoral reminiscence to provide a sense of continuity and stability. The use by Revivalist authors of older Irish material was not simple; for authors such as Synge and Yeats, arguably the two most prominent writers of the period, the Revival was a process of translation in the broadest sense of the word. Not only did many writers, including Yeats,[70] rely upon translations into English; they also made their own 'translations' of tales and myths, transforming them into works that, like O'Grady's, were aligned with contemporary mores and ideals.[71] The process, then, was like an assembly line of ideas, leading from the original sources of Irish history and literature to English language translations, ideologies of nationhood, an influx of pastoral thinking as it had filtered down via Romanticism and nationalist thinking, and finally to the authors of the Revival itself.

The influence of these forms of nostalgia is evident not only on the creative writers of the period, but also on the scholarship to follow in its wake. One has only to glance over Kenneth Jackson's analysis of Celtic nature poetry to see the ways in which Arnold's romantic determinations of nationalisms and O'Grady's turn to the Irish past impacted scholarship on early Irish writing, both in Ireland and outside of it; and Jackson is not alone in showing these influences.[72] Most authors of the Revival and those to follow – whether scholars or artists – demonstrate a tendency to turn to the Irish past for inspiration, but an Irish past thoroughly imbued with the spirit of European Romanticism. The enduring impact of Macpherson, Arnold and O'Grady might have peaked during the period of the Revival, but certainly did not disappear; the past, and the idea of the backward look, were to remain tremendously significant within the study of Irish material.[73]

As an aesthetic modality, nostalgia centres upon a preservation of the past and the longing for lost culture, as in the case of the medieval Irish literature examined in the previous chapter; by the time we reach the era of the Revival, this nostalgic mode shifts its focus to the preservation of a past that the authors have themselves not experienced. In this sense, by the late-nineteenth and early-twentieth centuries, the nostalgic mode and the Irish pastoral have absorbed something more of the pastoral as it developed in English literature, arguably as a result of the increasing intertwining of English and Irish culture after colonization and the influence of English language and literary forms on Irish sensibilities.

What evolved consequently during the period of the Revival was a new use of memory in literature, for what these authors did – whether scholars such as Arnold, O'Grady, Jackson or Flower or writers like Yeats and Synge – was to make use of non-living memory. That is, they managed to leap from the realm of actual, self-experienced memory to a realm of imaginative memory that was nostalgia.

> To participate in the existentialism of the poetic, one must reinforce the union of imagination and memory. To do that, it is necessary to rid oneself of the historian's memory which imposes its ideative prerogatives. It is no living memory which runs along the scale of dates without staying long enough at the site of memory. Memory-Imagination makes us live non-event situations in an existentialism of the poetic.[74]

Revival authors engaged in this process by choosing to make connections between their own time and the literature of the Irish middle ages, finding resemblances or connections that did not rely upon what Bachelard refers to above as 'living memory'. In 'On the Sublime', Burke deems such resemblances food for the imagination: 'Hence it is, that men are much more naturally inclined to belief than incredulity.'[75] Revivalists, searching out these resemblances, found inspiration in the past, experiencing as a result a nostalgia for a time during which they did not live; the question became, by the modern age, whether or not they were capable of belief, for, as Bachelard notes, 'reverie extends history precisely to the limits of the unreal'.[76]

Given the tendency of the Revival to look to the past for literary inspiration, it is unsurprising that nostalgia flourished as a literary form. The sociologist Fred Davis's identification of three types of nostalgia is helpful here. The first type he calls Simple Nostalgia, 'that subjective state which harbors the largely unexamined belief that things were better (more beautiful) (healthier) (happier) (more civilized) (more exciting) *then* than *now*'.[77] The second category is Reflexive Nostalgia, which is Simple Nostalgia plus the voice of a 'Truth Squad or remonstrating Greek Chorus wanting to deflate, correct, and remind'.[78] The final type is Interpreted Nostalgia, which 'moves beyond issues of the historical accuracy or felicity of the nostalgic claim on the past and, even as the reaction unfolds, questions and, potentially at least, renders problematic the very reaction itself'.[79]

In these three categories can be seen the development of the Revival as a movement. Initially authors like Yeats and Synge exercised something remarkably similar to Simple Nostalgia, before gradually moving towards a Reflexive Nostalgia in which they began to see facts of the past as well as idealizations. The third category of Interpreted Nostalgia is perhaps the most significant, as it divides, initially, as we will see, an author like Yeats from one like Synge. Where Yeats remained in a state of Reflexive Nostalgia for the Irish past for a longer period of time, Synge moved swiftly towards Interpretive Nostalgia, coming to a critique of his own idealization of, for example, the Aran Islands.

Whichever category of nostalgia we are confronting in these authors' works, however, nostalgia in a general sense allowed writers of this period to imagine and thus to posit a form of continuous identity for the Irish and the soon-to-be Irish nation. By turning to historical facts or mythological figures specific to Ireland, authors of the Revival period were able to bridge the past and present effectively, allowing for a continuity that glossed over and made easier a present highlighted by political and social uncertainty. Sociologically speaking, then, nostalgia was a phenomenon that made artistic and political sense for the period; what was surprising was the extent to which authors like Synge and Yeats unknowingly inserted themselves into a tradition that connected this nostalgia with nature.

CHAPTER THREE

Yeats: Mapping the New Ireland of the Mind

Few poets are as associated with place as William Butler Yeats, whose name has become so intimately connected with Sligo that poetry readers worldwide know the region as 'Yeats Country'.[1] Yeats cultivated romantic images in his early poetry, and Irish Tourist Board promotions have popularized a self-consciously romantic and nostalgic image of Yeats as connected to Sligo and select other places throughout Ireland. Scholarship has, in certain ways, added to the romantic aura that surrounds Ireland's first Nobel Prize winner, with wonderfully mysterious and evocative titles such as *The Man and the Masks* and, more recently, *The Apprentice Mage*.[2] While Yeats's romanticisms have been addressed by critics, relatively little scholarly work has considered his use of place and nature. This critical neglect seems to have resulted from a general, and vague, acceptance of the notion that Yeats's representations of nature and place segue with popular representations of his poetry and the mood of the Revival as merely twilit and full of 'purple glows':[3] the prevailing attitude seems smugly to suggest that we understand all there is to be understood about this aspect of Yeats's poetry. To see Yeats as writing about place and nature in merely a Romantic tradition or classical pastoral form easy to reconcile with such popular representations is too simplistic, however; for while Yeats's earliest poetry does demonstrate the influence of a variety of Romantic and pastoral nostalgias, his writing gradually develops a very different representation of nature, increasingly realistic and made complex by visions, infused with a new pastoral nostalgia for an Ireland of the imagination. By comparing even a handful of Yeats's early poems with some of his later pieces, it becomes clear that when it comes to his writings on nature, Yeats ends up being far from a poet of 'simple' nostalgia, in the sociologist Fred Davis's terms.[4] Yeats's poetry reflects not only the influence of

European Romanticism, but also partakes of the larger Irish tradition of writing about place as a way of memorializing – and so reviving – lost culture. When considered in these terms, the nostalgia popularly associated with Yeats's work is not meritricious, but a pointed political tool that allows him to recover Irish traditions eclipsed by years of colonialism and, eventually, to offer a critique of his own memorials.[5]

In his autobiographies, Yeats describes his first poetic attempts as pastorals 'in imitation of Shelley and Edmund Spenser'.[6] These influences, when combined with that of Blake, a profoundly mystical poet cum prophet, go far in illuminating early Yeatsian poetics and philosophy.[7] From the beginning of his poetic career, Yeats is attracted to poets for whom nature, mysticism and vision are paramount. Interestingly, these three elements are also fundamental to some early Irish poetics, particularly 'seasonal poetry':[8] from early on, Yeats is, even if unknowingly, engaging with an Irish tradition. This engagement would, of course, become conscious and pronounced, and lead Yeats to new perspectives on his early poetic inspirations. Spenser, Yeats concluded,

> the first poet struck with remorse, the first poet who gave his heart to the State, saw nothing but disorder, where the mouths that have spoken all the fables of the poets had not yet become silent. All about him were shepherds and shepherdesses still living the life that made Theocritus and Virgil think of shepherd and poet as the one thing; but though he dreamed of Virgil's shepherds he wrote a book to advise, among many things, the harrying of all that followed flocks upon the hills, and of all the 'wandering companies that keep the wood'.[9]

Yeats comes to see Spenser as not merely a national poet but a poet whose loyalties extended too far; Yeats himself was to attempt to become a national poet 'Bound neither to Cause nor to State' ('The Tower' III.9)[10] – and, indeed, the attempt was begun long before there was officially an Irish state to which to give one's heart. Besides Spenser's state loyalties, though, what Yeats objects to is Spenser's inability as a pastoral poet to accept pastoral 'realities'. Through Virgil and Theocritus, Yeats invokes the classical pastoral mode, idealizing and positing a time in the Irish past when shepherd and poet were 'one thing' – conveniently denying the existence of 'native' class structures in Ireland (bards were, after all, part of an aristocratic class) and attempting to flatten the Irish cultural past into a simple, naive, naturally and innately poetic one. This denial of class systems allows Yeats – taking a cue from Standish James O'Grady – to emphasize the universalism of the heroic and aristocratic in Irish myth and history: the shepherd-poet becomes the aristocratic hero; the peasantry have royal pedigree. Yeats's manoeuvring resembles Synge's, as we will see, although with Yeats there is something more personal at work, perhaps: not only does the equation of the shepherd or peasant with the aristocrat recall the marginalization and life in nature of aristocratic Irish literary figures like Sweeney, Finn and Oisín, as well as numerous bards of the late-sixteenth and early-seventeenth centuries; the equation also suggests a defensive analysis of the 'marginalization' of Anglo-Irish Ascendancy families like Yeats's own. Yeats's sense of his family's economic decline provided a contemporary basis for the imaginative linking of the peasant with the aristocrat. That Spenser refused to make this imaginative leap before him is one of the reasons for Yeats's turning away from his influence.

Three centuries removed from the Elizabethans, a product of the many changes in attitude towards landscape and nature in Ireland and in Europe that romanticize a life in nature, and with his own particular tendencies to idealize antiquity, Yeats easily sidesteps the attitude that the Elizabethans could not, in effect quarrelling with Spenser for not taking pastoral modes far enough. If Spenser found it impossible to reconcile 'actual' pastoral with poetic pastoral idealizations, Yeats did not; where Spenser denigrated the Irish as wild, uncivil and uncultured, Yeats would move to the other extreme and celebrate 'natural' Irish culture to forge a new, *politicized* pastoral. Pastoral forms necessarily imply a critique, since creating an ideal world highlights the rupture of ideals in some present world. Yeats's new Irish pastoral might well be described as anti-colonial: in its defiant celebration of ties to the landscape and to pastoral living, it pits itself against London and city life, against the attempts by English colonizers over many centuries to 'civilize' the Irish and to erase Irish culture, and so critiques Ireland's colonial situation in the late-nineteenth and early-twentieth centuries. Yeats learned, in other words, more than poetic forms from a poet like Spenser: he was also learning politics.

Besides partially eclipsing the influence of Spenser on his work, Yeats's nationalist tendencies resulted in his encounter with Irish authors – including O'Grady – who changed his perception of what he might do as a poet. Despite a sense that the early Revival authors he read were not as gifted as his favourite Romantic poets, Yeats found himself particularly fascinated by one aspect of work by writers like James Callanan:[11] he was drawn to these writers in part

because they described places with which he could connect, which
were of significance to a sense of *national* space. Place was, after this
reading, to become a recurring theme in Yeats's work. In Irish folklore the entrance to the otherworld is found in the actual, physical
landscape; for Yeats, place and nature similarly become entrées into
another world of Ireland that he longed for – a world that he
associated particularly with his Sligo childhood – and that, in his
early poetry, is itself otherworldly because so idealized.

If Elizabethan cartographic and prose maps attempted to assert
control over Ireland through the demonstration of intimate knowledge
of the country, Yeats's project is, in a sense, similar: the insistence on
Irish place in his poetry would also claim the country, this time in
service of a new forming nation. By imaginatively 'mapping' his
Ireland of the mind Yeats could, like early Revival authors, contribute
to the creation of a modern Irish national literature through his
retrieval of Irish place. In this sense, Yeats, in Edward Said's words,
'belongs to a tradition not usually considered his, that of the colonial
world ruled by European imperialism'.[12] The literature of a cultural
and political movement like the Revival, Said argues,

> develops quite consciously out of desire to distance the native African,
> Indian, or Irish individual from the British, French or (later) American
> master. Before this can be done, however, there is a pressing need for the
> recovery of the land that, because of the presence of the colonizing
> outsider, is recoverable at first only through the imagination. Now if there
> is anything that radically distinguishes the imagination of anti-imperialism
> it is the primacy of the geographical in it. Imperialism after all is an act of
> geographical violence through which virtually every space in the world is
> explored, charted, and finally brought under control. For the native, the
> history of his or her colonial servitude is inaugurated by the loss to an
> outsider of the local place, whose concrete geographical identity must
> thereafter be searched for and somehow restored.[13]

Yeats's slight swerve away from the English influences so important
to his early imaginative life and his subsequent invocation of localized, specific Irish place in his poetry can be seen as a part of such a
movement towards reclamation: for he attempts to restore, imaginatively, an ancient geography of mythological Ireland as well as the
Ireland of his own day. What Said refers to as this 'cartographic'
impulse results in the creation, charting, or discovery of national
space 'not pristine and prehistorical ("Romantic Ireland's dead and
gone", says Yeats) but one that derives historically and abductively

from the deprivations of the present'.[14] The sense of lack in the present must lead to an imaginative reworking of that present based on the past; in such an exercise, nostalgia is key. Yeats's nostalgia for his Ireland of the mind is initially as personal an exercise as it is political, since he and other Ascendancy figures are aware of their waning significance in Irish society. This personal and political nostalgia and his imaginative work in reclaiming that Ireland go far in creating a space that is, as we will see, increasingly realistic and less sentimentalized: a space that moves, in other words, beyond the merely nostalgic, and becomes not simply about relieving homesickness, but about creating a home. This process of 'cartographic' reclamation did not happen overnight; it takes many years, in fact, for Yeats's poetry to create a cultural map of Ireland, and for his representations of place and nature to change: at the beginning, 'Romantic Ireland' is thriving. Gradually, however, that Ireland disappears, and we find that it has been replaced by a more concrete, 'real' Ireland in which Yeats increasingly offers critiques of his own nostalgia.

'THE WANDERINGS OF OISIN'

It is instructive to examine the representation of nature and place in 'The Wanderings of Oisin' since, as Yeats's first poetic success, it is amongst his earliest expressions of nature and place and so gives us a sense of his beginnings. It is also interesting because it takes as its inspiration the Finn tales – it is yet another response, in other words, to Macpherson's claim over Irish material: Yeats's first major poem is itself an act of *political* reclamation. Interestingly, while Yeats's use of Irish source material for the poem indicates his commitment to the continuation of a national literature even at this stage, and while he is already engaged by Irish authors and so already aware of the potential significance of place to Irish literature, nature and landscape are remarkably indistinct in this poem published in 1889.

This indistinction and distance from a reality of nature is due, for some critics, to Yeats's distance from his original sources for the poem. Rather than turning to the *Acallam na Senórach* itself for inspiration, Yeats turned to translations, notably Michael Comyn's mid-nineteenth- century version, 'The Lay of Oisin in the Land of Youth', and to translations of the Ossianic Society (which, of course, was itself a response to Macpherson's publications). Harold Bloom has criticized Yeats for reading 'a version of a version' and for being 'so far from mythology, and indeed in every sense so far from Ireland, that we need not be surprised to discover that his poem, despite its Celtic colorings, is in the centre of English Romantic tradition'.[15] While Yeats certainly is distanced from his sources and from the Irish language, he is not, I would argue, so removed from Ireland itself – despite his frequent physical absence from the country – for Yeats exists adamantly in an Ireland of the mind, similar to the way in which Joyce might be described as imaginatively inhabiting Dublin, despite decades of living abroad and only a handful of returns to Ireland. Ironically, in his removal from the actual space of Ireland – in his 'homesickness' and nostalgia – Yeats's situation also bears resemblance to Spenser's, whose distance from London propelled him into the writing of an epic celebrating precisely that from which he was removed. Yeats's absence from Ireland allows him to imagine an abstract and idealized country that contributes to the creation of a new Irish pastoralism in literature: even at this stage, Yeats is showing signs of moving beyond Romantic forms.

'The Wanderings of Oisin' is an early manifestation of Yeats's Ireland of the mind, and is a combination of themes from medieval Irish literature that engaged Yeats: the otherworld, the Fenian life in nature, and the collision between Irish and Christian cultures. Although Yeats models his 'Oisin' on dialogic versions of the *Acallam*, itself a dialogue, his poem is not an exchange in any meaningful way: Oisin is so deep in reverie for his past that he frequently ignores (or at least fails to hear) Patrick's very occasional comments or questions. The poem is less concerned with the actual interaction between a purportedly pre-Christian Irish figure like Oisin and Patrick than with Oisin's memories; Yeats idealizes pre-Christian Ireland, in a sense, merely by marginalizing Patrick as he does here. This idealization, of course, relies on the belief, common amongst Yeats and his contemporaries, that pre-Christian Ireland was the vestige of 'original', untainted Irish culture.[16] Oisin's reveries thus often revolve around the life of the Fenians, their hunting, their successes, their battles. But because Yeats focuses his poem on Oisin's adventures with Niamh, the memories of Fenian life are secondary to the haunting memories of his time with her in the land of youth.

Opting to set his poem largely in this otherworld allows Yeats to produce, at first, a romanticized, idealized nature that is unspecific and vague (much, it would seem, like his own projected remembrances of the 'lost' Ireland of his childhood). The language of this (un)natural world is as rich and gorgeous as Spenser's tapestry-like description of the Bower of Bliss: phrases such as Niamh's 'O Oisin, mount by me and ride / To shores by the wash of the tremulous tide' (I ll. 80–1) or Oisin's description of galloping over a 'glossy sea' (I l. 132) evoke a perfection in nature that is of the imagination, and not very different from the imaginary world created in early Irish voyage literature, which also seems an influence here.[17] But, like Spenser's Bower of Bliss, and like the unknown space of the sea that threatens early Irish voyagers, this world has a sinister undercurrent that leads eventually to Oisin and Niamh's sadnesses on the three islands. By Book II, the 'glossy sea' has become 'the sea's waste/shaking and waving' (II ll. 163–4); the experience of the otherworld, which negates Oisin's memories of his past life with the Fenians, is not all pleasurable. If we begin with an idealized world, we are rapidly shown into one that is far more difficult to negotiate; Oisin, in the otherworld, is an outsider, and his outsider status, and his displacement from the world of the Fenians, suggests a 'cause' for this disintegration of the ideal. This is not a simple imitation of Romantic nature; even here Yeats's attitudes towards nature have their roots in intellectual develpments of the post-Romantic era, as we will see.

Like the *Acallam's* Oisín, and like Macpherson's Ossian, Yeats's Oisin is nostalgic – 'Remembrance, lifting her leanness, keened in the gates of my heart' (III l. 152) – for a time before Ireland was Christianized, for a time before his friends were mere memories. (This is quite possibly a reflection of Yeats's own nostalgia for a time when the Ascendancy's place in Ireland was politically assured.) And, like the medieval Oisín, Yeats's Oisin experiences his nostalgia while wandering Ireland, although we do not, in this version, receive specific descriptions of place. Instead, Oisin's memory functions at an imagistic level, recalling pictures of landscapes of earlier times that are general: fingers of waves upon the shore, plains blown by wind, trees, the experience of the sea. This practice allows Yeats to develop a representation of nature that goes beyond Romanticism in its emphasis on the 'tension between mind and images';[18] Yeats's Oisin, unlike Macpherson's, is not surrounded by a natural world that reflects his own pathos. In fact, nature is so heedless of Oisin's situations that an utter separation between man and nature is suggested by the poem; nature, as image, lacks the consciousness suggested by many of Yeats's Romantic predecessors.

This imagistic nature is appropriate to Yeats's early nationalist goals, in many ways. Because Yeats is imagining characters removed from him by a space of many centuries, as well as by linguistic difference, and because the landscape of medieval Ireland is obviously unknown to him, creating images instead of specificities allows for a cultural retrieval that is, in its vagueness, entirely recognizable: knowable images bridge past and present by allowing the reader to think, for example, 'this is the same sea on which Oisin gazed'. The use of vague place in the poem thus offers a sort of grounding to the reader by allowing for a connection to be made between the landscape of Irish mythology and the landscape of the present. It was only a short time, however, before Yeats would realize that specificity of place would serve his aims far more effectively.

THE POST-DARWIN PASTORAL: FROM NATURE TO PLACE

Ireland and its history, literature, folklore and landscape would prevent Yeats from falling into the usage of typical Romantic forms, in part since to consistently invoke actual place was to insist on a kind of reality that Romanticism did not often suggest.[19] Yeats avoids what David Daiches calls the 'excesses'[20] of Romantic poetry in part because he adds to his understanding of pastoral and Romantic modes his knowledge of the Irish tradition, but also because, in Darwin's wake, it did not seem possible any longer to believe that nature was entirely knowable and connected so intimately to human needs and wants. In his autobiographies, Yeats described being 'deprived by Huxley and Tyndall, whom I detested, of the simple-minded religion of my childhood'.[21] The crisis of faith induced by science led Yeats to turn increasingly to the study of folktales, folklore, mythology and 'a new religion, almost an infallible Church of poetic tradition' that, he believed, 'may be the nearest I can go to truth'.[22] The encounter with scientists who disturbed belief in historical Edens was traumatic enough for Yeats that it eliminated the possibility of 'simple' belief, and marked the beginnings, one could argue, of Yeats's belief in art over nature: for from an early stage, art became the seat of Yeats's faith.

For the man who identified himself as an 'evolutionist' while at school,[23] and who – like many of his generation – underwent the trauma of the loss of 'simple faith' in nature after reading Darwin, nature is thus also a betrayer and the site of marginalization in his early poetry. Besides in 'Oisin', this is reflected in an early poem such as 'The Madness of King Goll' (composed 1884), in which nature is a site of displacement along very similar lines to *Buile Suibhne*.[24] The intensity with which King Goll experiences the natural world and his sense of displacement in existing in nature suggests that Yeats is making use of the medieval tale of Suibhne Geilt; King Goll, like Sweeney, 'must wander wood and hill / Through summer's heat and winter's cold' (ll. 70–1). Yeats is also presenting us, however, with a landscape that, in the post-Famine and post-Darwinian era, cannot function as an Edenic, pastoral place. The natural world itself here provides the refrain that drives the king mad, with its refusal to 'hush' and its constant noise, movement and change: 'the leaves a-flutter round me, the beech leaves old'. King Goll's outsider status and his madness in nature reflect medieval Irish themes, and force us to consider Oisin's displacement within this context, as well as Yeats's disillusionment at the hands of Huxley, Tyndall and Darwin: nature, Oisin learns, is unreliable. Place, Yeats would decide, was not.

This type of disillusionment and the gradual displacement of the classical pastoral form are in increasing evidence in much of Yeats's early work. In 'The Song of the Happy Shepherd' (composed 1885), Yeats begins by declaring that 'The woods of Arcady are dead,/ And over is their antique joy;/ Of old the world on dreaming fed;/ Grey Truth is now her painted toy' (ll. 1–4). The lament in these lines is explicit; the poetic persona mourns the loss of the possibility of dreaming as a source of inspiration and delight; instead, modernity has forced the poet into accepting truths about the world that utterly contradict the traditional pastoral dreamworld of the shepherd. The highly stylized pastoral form at use by Yeats here is also an 'antique joy', as he was to realize shortly; for it was not long after this period in Yeats's development that he began to move away from such already created imaginative worlds like 'Arcady' to the creation of his own.

BRIDGING PAST AND PRESENT

'The Wanderings of Oisin' and other early poems such as 'The Madness of King Goll' and 'The Song of the Happy Shepherd' suggest a natural world that is the site of displacement, the realm of outsiders, whether because of divinity or madness or simply the passage of time that makes the Fenian or the shepherd's way of life seem literally outmoded. Since a faith in an actual, historical Eden was no longer possible, Yeats would go on to create his own Edens beyond the real, in the realm of imagination. Having lost his faith in nature, Yeats turns to the Irish past and Irish literature. Yeats's notebooks, which demonstrate this increasing commitment to Irish literature, are filled, R.F. Foster notes, with 'evocations and correspondences. The holiness of Irish landscape, in keeping with the old bardic doctrine of *dindshenchas*, was stressed'.[25] Landscape, unlike nature, Yeats discovered, *was* reliable; such 'correspondences' between the world of old Ireland and the Ireland that Yeats sought to revive in the present aimed to create a nationalist literature by bridging past and present. By forcing the realization that there were 'correspondences' between past and present Yeats argues, in effect, for the idea of an independent Ireland in the present.

These attempts to bridge past and present on a national, cultural level were also, of course, attempts to bridge his own present and past; Yeats binds himself not only to the memory of his family's former status, but to the memories of childhood in the Sligo landscape. Yeats's identification with and idealization of the landscape of Sligo came in large part through explorations of his childhood world and the influence of another type of 'pastoral' writer, Henry David Thoreau:

> . . . I was nursing a new ambition. My father had read to me some passage out of *Walden*, and I planned to live some day in a cottage on a little island called Innisfree, and Innisfree was opposite Slish Wood where I meant to sleep [on an overnight trip].
>
> I thought that having conquered bodily desire and the inclination of my mind towards women and love, I should live, as Thoreau lived, seeking wisdom.[26]

It is telling that the boy Yeats finds the American essayist inspiring. Thoreau, with *Walden*, had followed Emerson's lead in attaching the ideal of American independence and thoughtfulness to nature, and so had done much to create a nation out of words, carved, as it were, out of tree and stone and canyon and clay. Thoreau was, significantly, not only a writer of poetic merit; he was also a political activist, and his texts epitomized the idea of writing itself as a political act.[27] Thoreau's example might thus be described as quite appropriate to Yeats's own career, involved as he was in literary, cultural and political movements.[28] The idea of Thoreau's experiment at Walden remained with Yeats, and the childhood dream of living like Thoreau produced one of his most famous early poems. 'The Lake Isle of Innisfree', among the first of Yeats's poems to specify place and generate its images from this specification, was composed in late 1888, only an approximate year and a half after the completion of 'The Wanderings of Oisin'. The difference between the two poems' representations of nature is subtle, but significant. Yeats's account of the poem's genesis continues to reward examination:

> I still had the ambition, formed in Sligo in my teens, of living in imitation of Thoreau on Innisfree, a little island in Lough Gill, and when walking through Fleet Street very homesick I heard a little tinkle of water and saw a fountain in a shop-window which balanced a little ball upon its jet, and began to remember lake water. From the sudden remembrance came my poem *Innisfree*, my first lyric with anything in its rhythm of my own music.[29]

Yeats had nurtured the ideal of living like Thoreau, but ended up in London instead: as a result, a poem like 'The Lake Isle of Innisfree' arises out of a nostalgia – Yeats himself refers to his 'homesickness' – for something that Yeats has only in part experienced himself. The sound of water from an electrically powered fountain triggers the memory of something he once imagined but has not experienced; the poem that results is a nostalgia for a time in Sligo when such an experience was still possible. Like ninth- and tenth-century Irish poems that posited an imaginary, perfect future, 'Innisfree' turns towards an unexperienced pastoral dream. In this imagined future, the poet will live a life that is almost directly an imitation of Thoreau's:

> I will arise and go now, and go to Innisfree,
> And a small cabin build there, of clay and wattles made:
> Nine bean-rows will I have there, a hive for the honey-bee,
> And live alone in the bee-loud glade. (ll. 1–4)

While the images of a cabin for one and bean-rows are clearly derivative of Thoreau, other images are peculiarly Yeatsian, and particularly Irish in setting, resembling early Irish monastic poems centred on an imagined, ideal future in a private cell and the pastoral dream of raising crops to live on. This famous poem does not, in other words, derive only from an English Romantic tradition; Thoreau offered Yeats the example of pastoral living as a political act, and the resemblance to early Irish 'hermit' poems is striking. Yeats's specification of place here is also significant in its continuation of the *dindshenchas* tradition: this is not simply a poem about the desire for peace, but peace in a particular Irish spot, associated in Yeats's mind with the quiet, steady reverie of childhood. The profound dreaminess of Oisin's descriptions of land and seascapes comes literally to earth here; as a real space, 'Innisfree' stands up to idealization in ways that unspecified and merely imagined landscapes cannot. Yeats has planted the seed of Thoreau's experience and it grows into an Irish one, imagined from the space of the 'pavements grey' (l. 11) of London.

THE STABILITY OF PLACE

'Innisfree' becomes a centrepiece of the Yeats canon, for it is with this poem that Yeats asserts his determination to write a personalized, while nationalized, poetry, rooted in the place and nature of Ireland. Yeats seeks to literally and figuratively ground his writing in the landscape most familiar, most known to him. The *literal* grounding allows for what Yeats himself refers to as a 'stability':

> Though I went to Sligo every summer, I was compelled to live out of Ireland the greater part of every year, and was but keeping my mind upon what I knew must be the subject matter of my poetry. I believed that if Morris had set his stories amid the scenery of his own Wales, . . . that if Shelley had nailed his Prometheus, or some equal symbol, upon some Welsh or Scottish rock, their art would have entered more intimately, more microscopically, as it were, into our thought and given perhaps to modern poetry a breadth and stability like that of ancient poetry.[30]

In part because of his absence from Ireland, Yeats calls upon the relative stability of place, which allows him to retain a 'claim' to Ireland, in effect. It also allows the creation of a stable identity for not only himself but for the Irish nation as it is forming in his and his contemporaries' minds: for, as recent historical research demonstrates, the question of the land had become inextricably bound with the question of nationality and Irish identity.[31] And, as Yeats makes clear, the more stable the poetic image in terms of place, the more likely that image was, conversely, to reach a broad audience, which implies that the attachment to place was a phenomenon that Yeats expected to stretch beyond the realm of Ireland.

The sense of place was to become the touchstone to which Yeats would return in order to ground his poetry: 'all my art theories depend upon just this – rooting of mythology in the earth'.[32] The use by Yeats in his poetry of well known places in Ireland allows him to act within a specifically Irish tradition of recording the story of place, whether by the anonymous compilers of the *dindshenchas* or by the bardic poets; to this tradition Yeats adds the places significant to him on a personal level – such as Innisfree, Coole Park, Ben Bulben – resulting in a poetry in which place is paramount. In choosing names to include in his works Yeats, one critic writes, performed 'the role of the ancient Irish *fili* (bardic poets) whose task it was to perpetuate in the memory, men and heroic acts; as Homer has made the names of Ithaca, Chois and Troy places of imagination for generations who never visited Greece'.[33] Yeats approaches his task, in other words, with a consciousness of what would happen to his chosen placenames were his poetic ambitions to succeed: for the generations who had been separated from Irish culture, Yeats would connect past and present.

Declan Kiberd has pointed out, however, that 'there was undeniably something strained'[34] in Yeats, Synge and Lady Gregory's use of the *dindshenchas* tradition: the distance that they and other Revival authors experienced from the natural world of Ireland, with its traditional tales of place, and their lives as urban or demesne-based middle- and upper-class Anglo-Irish was exacerbated, in Yeats's case at least, by ignorance of the Irish language. That there is a strain is reflective not merely of Yeats's ignorance of the Irish language or the realities of Irish Catholic experience, however, but of colonialism itself: the strain is a result of an historical rupture far beyond Yeats's personal relationship to Ireland. The recognition that in order to create a national Irish literature the distance needed to be bridged, *despite* the strain of doing so, is evident in Yeats's writing.

> Might I not, with health and good luck to aid me, create some new *Prometheus Unbound*; Patrick or Columcille, Oisin or Finn, in Prometheus's stead; and, instead of Caucasus, Cro-Patrick or Ben Bulben? Have not all races had their first unity from a mythology that marries them to rock and hill?[35]

Yeats recognizes, again and again, the significance of place and landscape within national literatures – since place and landscape are, inevitably, specific to a country. He also recognizes that, in order to create a literature both contemporary and national, he can bind himself to landscape and so bridge a seemingly unbridgeable gap between himself and the past, between Ireland in the present and Ireland of long ago. Considering that following the Famine there had been an increasing connection between the question of land and of nationality, Yeats's insistence on Irish place in his poetry is unsurprising: in setting out to write a national literature, and as one not merely aware of but involved in contemporary political movements, Yeats makes use of the one thing that he knows to stir passion in so much of the population: the Irish landscape. The binding of self to nature and landscape is not merely a sentimental exercise, or an intellectual one – although it is these things as well; this is a political act that insists, regardless of Yeats's own particular relationship to the soil or the land, on the right of the Irish to Ireland.

Unlike Arnold and countless other critics, Yeats does not presume that the Irish relationship to nature is closer than other cultures'; all cultures are formed, he claims, and all myths created, out of a connection between a people and a landscape.

> All literatures are full of these or like imaginations . . . I do not think [Arnold] understood that our 'natural magic' is but the ancient religion of the world, the ancient worship of Nature and that troubled ecstasy before her, that certainty of all beautiful places being haunted, which it brought into men's minds.[36]

While Yeats, unlike Arnold, recognizes what amounts to an international reverence for place, he has evidently absorbed something of Arnold's argument. He does not connect a familiarity with nature to a peculiarly Celtic sentimentality, but instead connects it with 'ancient' (and primitive) culture, and implies what appears to be a more general sentimentality: the 'troubled ecstasy' of nature (which recalls Walker's century-old description of the 'settled melancholy' of the bardic poets) and the fact that place is 'haunted' suggest that Yeats perceives a quite complex relationship between man and the natural world. This inevitably Darwinian relationship, one that he would address in his more mature poetry, is overtly sentimentalized in the manner of Macpherson, Arnold, O'Grady and many others: while the Irish might not be alone in their relationship with nature, that relationship, Yeats believes, exists because of a certain primitivism. Yeats is thus attempting a complicated juggling act, weaving together Irish traditions regarding landscape and place in literature and the more recent development in Irish political circles that connected land with nationality, as well as contemporary European Romantic attitudes and ideas that idealize nature as the site of primitive, unevolved culture.

Yeats's claim that all cultures in their early evolutions were somehow bound to nature is, in his mind, a part of a general primitivism that has disappeared in all but folk literature, which 'has a passion whose like is not in modern literature and music and art, except where it has come by some straight or crooked way out of ancient times'.[37] In his autobiographies and essays, Yeats describes his attempts to marry that 'passion' and connection to nature from folk literature with his sophisticated European sensibility. No matter how embellished or lovely, Yeats declares, he does not wish to create a poetry that lacks these primitive elements. Keats, Shakespeare and Virgil, Yeats believes, lacked this primitivism, and

looked at Nature without ecstasy, but with the affection a man feels for
the garden where he has walked daily and thought pleasant thoughts.
They looked at nature in the modern way, the way of people who are
poetical, but are more interested in one another than in a nature which
has faded to be but friendly and pleasant, the way of people who have
forgotten the ancient religion.[38]

Having grown up on Romantic writing and on a poet such as Spenser,
and having spent such time imitating English pastorals, Yeats is well
aware of the distance involved in such an exercise. Significantly, while
Yeats recognizes – and seems to deplore – this distance in Keats,
Shakespeare and Virgil's writing, it is precisely that distance which
produces a poem like 'Innisfree': for it is a poem written in retrospect,
a poem derived from an urban situation that reminds the poet of a
more rural, and more peaceful, existence – and one that, in all like-
liness, did not exist. Despite his dislike of the distances between classical
pastoral and reality, Yeats was to fall back on pastoral metaphors with
a certain consistency,[39] has a background in traditional and English
pastoral forms not easily shaken; and he has, in fact, precisely the
relationship with Coole Park that he deplores in Shakespeare and
Keats: he feels affection for it in large part because of its familiarity
and the thoughts he has experienced in it. So while he disparages
distance, he feels it nonetheless; hence in his writings of nature, an
element of pastoral nostalgia is inevitably present. This nostalgia
functions, however, in the service of the particular goal that Yeats
attempts to reach: the retrieval of ancient Irish culture. By submitting
himself to nostalgia in his writing, Yeats performs a task necessary to
the reclamation of culture and the establishment of the nation,
demonstrating, in effect, how past and present are linked and continuous. For stretching – or perhaps one could say more appropriately
longing – oneself imaginatively over time results, ultimately, in a bridge.

THE NEW IRISH PASTORAL

Yeats's early poetry reflects the minglings of these ideas so far under
discussion: the influence of traditional and English modes of pastoral
(particularly via Spenser); that of Romantic poetry (through Blake
and Shelley) and its Macpherson-inspired beginnings; the very
different ideal of political pastoral offered by Thoreau's actual life in
the woods;[40] a general late-Victorian European sensibility regarding
the natural world (through Tyndall, Huxley and Darwin); Yeats's

personal sense of displacement from Ireland and his sense of the loss of family standing within Ireland; and the very significant influence of Irish literature and Irish political attitudes towards land. These influences intertwine in Yeats's poetry to create what amounts to a new Irish pastoral heavily reliant upon the conception of landscape as one of the only available mechanisms that can bridge the present and past, while still representing the rupture between them.

While Yeats's use of Irish place in his poetry is quite specific in a poem like 'The Lake Isle of Innisfree', in other poems of the early 1890s, nature often appears as symbol, as a backdrop to other action. There is a sense in which 'Innisfree' represents one arc of his poetics, in which the idea and image of Ireland is made physical, made concrete, made, in effect, real; in other poems, though, such as 'The Two Trees' and in the poems in which he employs the symbol of the rose, Yeats demonstrates that his preoccupations as a poet go far beyond the *merely* national or concrete: representative of Maud Gonne, of the goal of Irish nationhood, the rose becomes an aggregate symbol, a symbol of the symbolic itself. Yeats is drawn in two directions: towards the abstract and the concrete at once.

By the end of the 1890s, however, another movement had begun. By this point, it is clear that Yeats, like those to whom Niamh calls in 'The Hosting of the Sidhe', is being called away: the Irish literary past has established a firmer grip on his imagination. Like Lady Gregory, Yeats found himself increasingly interested in resurrecting the idea of a glorious Irish past through the inspiration of material from earlier Irish literature and from living people whose way of life seemed fast to be disappearing; this belief that a reservoir of energy is to be found in mythology and its living symbols is reflected in a collection like *The Wind Among the Reeds* (1899), and undoubtedly grows out of his experience of accompanying Lady Gregory as she gathered folklore.

By this stage it is clear that, for Yeats, the representation of the natural world is a part of a collection of images which are the driving force of his poetics. These images, many of them recurring, frequently rely upon the memory of the past, or on imagined memories of historical pasts.[41] Within the space of these imagined, projected memories, place becomes increasingly significant, and seems to correlate with Yeats's increasing interest in the occult – which, of course, also allowed him communion with various pasts. Yeats thus begins increasingly to associate place[42] with ghostly apparitions, visitations and memories of the past. As he wrote to Katherine Tynan, Sligo 'to me is the loneliest place in the world. Going for a walk is a continual meeting with ghosts for Sligo for me has no flesh and blood attractions – only memories and sentimentalities accumulated here as a child making it more dear than any other place.'[43] Landscape, particularly the Irish landscape, is, in fact, the past. Yeats has thus gradually developed a way in which to reconcile the competing tendencies in his work towards both the abstract and the concrete: place and landscape can serve as a physical grounding even to the mystical and the visionary.

Coole Park became a repository for a particular part of Yeats, for it was there – in what was already a significant space for him – that Yeats first experienced visions that were to become so vital to his poetics:

> I was crossing a little stream near Inchy wood and actually in the middle of a stride from bank to bank, when an emotion never experienced before swept down upon me. I said, 'That is what the devout Christian feels, that is how he surrenders his will to the will of God.' I felt an extreme surprise, for my whole imagination was preoccupied with the pagan mythology of ancient Ireland, I was marking in red ink, upon a large map, every sacred mountain.[44]

Yeats's surprise may not be shared by the reader; having spent a good deal of his childhood and early adulthood reading Spenser, Shelley and Blake, all poets preoccupied with the prophetic and with the natural world, it seems in fact unsurprising that, having immersed himself in the space of prophecy, he should have come to the visionary. As he writes himself of his first vision, he was at the time preoccupied with ancient Ireland. While other legends and other literatures dealt in foreign lands, 'the Irish legends move among known woods and seas'.[45] Yeats, escaping from the city to the countryside of Lady Gregory's retreat, also moved 'among known woods', and it was out of this movement that his visionary poetry grew, much as 'seasonal poetry' attributed to Finn amounted to vision of the natural world known to him. Yeats's knowledge of Finn lore certainly extended to this knowledge of Finn's visionary capacity and vision as an inspiration for poetry; in discovering his own capacity for vision he has succeeded, it would seem, in connecting with the 'primitive'. Yeats's interest in vision produces, even in early poetry, a complicated representation of the natural world as the site of vision; nature remains the liminal space in Yeats's poetry that it was in medieval Irish literature.[46]

By 1926–7, when he composes 'Sailing to Byzantium', Yeats is still concerned with vision, but the image of the imagined perfect (and so pastoral) world has changed: 'Romantic Ireland' has suffered a death

in the intervening years. Denis Donoghue begins a 1980 essay on
'Romantic Ireland' with an enquiry into this very phrase,[47] and goes
on to provide a keen analysis – perhaps the keenest available – of
Yeats's relationship to the idea. Using Schiller's distinctions between
the naive mode of poetry (in which the poet is nature) and sentimental poetry (in which the poet *seeks* nature), Donoghue makes the
following assessment of Yeats's work:

> What then do we find in Yeats, if not a sentimental poet trying to
> persuade himself, to begin with, and his readers, thereafter, that a naive
> relationship to nature is possible? For what else is Romantic Ireland
> but the assertion that a naive relation to an original or aboriginal
> Ireland is indeed possible?[48]

As we have seen, early poems do attempt to convince both speaker
and reader that the naive relationship with nature can be achieved:
even the syntax of 'Innisfree' ('I will arise and go now') suggests that
the achievement of such a state is only a matter of will and conse-
quential action. But this belief was unsustainable, even from its
inception: Yeats is too much a product of his time, too much a man
of the post-Romantic, post-Darwin and post-Victorian ages to be able
to insist too long upon such a notion. Donoghue recognizes that even
after its demise as a possibility, the idea of a romanticized Ireland
based on primitive relationships with nature is invoked by Yeats to
some purpose; 'that is, he continued to use it for its ideological
force'.[49] Donoghue's argument is one with which I am in agreement;
but what I would take further is just this use by Yeats of the nostalgic
image of Ireland as an *ideological tool*. A canny self-promotor, and a
canny promotor of ideologies that people would attune to, Yeats
recognized early, I have been arguing, the power of nostalgia to take
root in people's imaginations and lead them to projections of
idealities into the present, with the Irish nation itself as that ultimate
projection. If 'Romantic Ireland' was 'dead and gone' for Yeats
himself, he was too astute to recognize that it was not for other
people. Denis Donoghue describes 'Romantic Ireland' as a 'set of
values espoused, promoted, bought and sold in the market-place,
subjected to an adversary rhetoric from Joyce to Austin Clarke,
endlessly deconstructed, and yet, even now, not entirely annulled.
Sequestered, rather.'[50] I would argue that Yeats himself begins the
process of deconstructing the image of which he was a final key
architect: the architect whose task it is to complete the externalities
of a structure that has been in the making for several centuries. And

once the structure is completed, Yeats stands back and begins to undo some of his own work.

The leap in Yeats's representation of nature and landscape is stark when one considers the otherworld of 'The Wanderings of Oisin' next to the also otherworldly Byzantium: and this leap, interestingly, takes place over the years in which Ireland as a modern state is created, formed and fought over. The nostalgia with which Yeats wrote in his early poetry was a pastoral sentiment for his vision of Ireland's lost past: and Yeats seemed to write nostalgically as a way of creating a present-day Ireland that had *not* experienced a rupture from its own past and its own traditions. As the reality of the state takes shape, and as violence erupts, Yeats's nostalgia is shaken:[51] in July of 1919 he wrote to John Quinn in New York that the country was 'reeling back into the middle ages without growing more picturesque'.[52] It is at this stage that his nostalgia becomes more pronounced, in a way, because he realizes the folly of unreflexive, simple nostalgia, and seems to long for the time before this disillusionment set in. And yet what happens for Yeats poetically after this is most interesting: by the time he comes to write a poem like 'The Second Coming', Yeats's nostalgia is quite consciously for an Eden that he has created, one that escapes the nets of historically linear narrative and thinking, as nostalgias do. Yeats would go on to create, in Byzantium, an imagined ideal world in an ahistorical past, one not linked with the linear historical development of the actual world. And, strangely enough, this imagined ideal is an urban pastoral, an artificial construction.[53]

In 'The Second Coming' (composed 1919), much as in the later 'Sailing to Byzantium' (composed 1926–7), Yeats, as one critic describes it, 'adopts the stance of a seer, and what he describes is not an actual landscape but a metaphoric one: we do not feel that a falcon flies before his eyes any more than that he literally sees a blood-dimmed tide'.[54] By turning the poetic persona into a visionary speaker, Yeats exercises a nostalgia for the visionary abilities that earlier Irish poets were reputed to have; but the vision here is bleak and dictated by events both in Europe and in Ireland. 'The Second Coming' represents an anti-Eden, an anti-Byzantium: the poetic mask is concerned with the start of another cycle of history, this one marked by the 'rough beast, its hour come round at last' that 'Slouches towards Bethlemen to be born' (ll. 21–2). This poem, one of Yeats's best known, is not

– save for the final line's invocation of the religiously weighted place of Bethlehem – connected to a known landscape, let alone an Irish one; the preoccupation with vision has eclipsed the possibilities of such a connection. It is almost as if, when the poet's sight is 'troubled' by images such as the ones of the poem, a concrete connection to an actual world is impossible. The nostalgia present in the poem is for 'the ceremony of innocence . . . drowned' (l. 4). Yeats has gone far beyond his Romantic influences: the presented world is clearly *unnatural*, somehow centreless and broken. This sense of the natural world as entirely chaotic (ordered only by the careful language but pointedly not reined in by rhyme) marks an enormous change in Yeats's representations of landscapes: if in his early poetry he was aware of the threats of the natural world – as in 'Oisin' – he still managed a degree of idealization. But by the time he comes to write this poem, that idealization is not possible, although Yeats continues to attempt it, as Denis Donoghue described: he tries several years later to make Byzantium a paradise, but it is a paradise beyond him, of which he loses all but linguistic control. The increasing challenge to belief in the existence of historical paradises coincided, of course, not only with the shock of violence that announced the Irish republic, but also with the international violence of the First World War.[55] Yeats's profound difficulty with reconciling his need of the past – witnessed in his preoccupation with Irish mythology and literature, in his selective interest in certain moments in Irish history, and too in his faithfulness to the memories of his Irish childhood – with the impossibility of recovering that past ends in his creation of a place like Byzantium, out of time, out of nature, and yet somehow reliant on all of his previous experience.

'That is no country for old men' (l.1), Yeats begins 'Sailing to Byzantium', seeming to allude to the mythical and timeless Tir na nOg; immediately the poem is outside of time, outside of the natural world, in an imagined universe. As such, Byzantium becomes a pastoral place, a pastoral reverie, born out of Yeats's nostalgia for a universal pastoralism, and not merely an Irish one.[56] Yeats's inclination to believe in universal connections is bound inextricably to his use of vision, which plays constantly upon an international memory and recurring themes and symbols. The poem closes:

> Once out of nature I shall never take
> My bodily form from any natural thing,
> But such a form as Grecian goldsmiths make

> Of hammered gold and gold enamelling
> To keep a drowsy Emperor awake;
> Or set upon a golden bough to sing
> To lords and ladies of Byzantium
> Of what is past, or passing, or to come. (IV ll.1–8)

Yeats recognizes that this imaginative paradise is in some ways unnatural, perhaps in part because of its urbanity; the final stanza reflects a (Spenserian) preoccupation with the conflict and opposition between nature and art, and Yeats comes down firmly on the side of art and the role of the poet. Like his medieval forbears, Yeats has become skilled in the poetry of masks. The poetic persona, he who will entertain, is also he who will speak of the world as it was, is, will be: time has become something flat in this Byzantium, capable of being read by the poetic persona regardless of his own position within time frames; in this the persona's abilities resemble those of Finn in medieval Irish lyrics, as well as seeming to encompass those abilities traditionally assigned to the Irish bard. In this new Irish pastoral that links together many traditions, Yeats has moved beyond the tradition of a natural setting and has created a modern, urban space that is timeless and perfect,[57] and seemingly informed by the imperfections of the realities Yeats has so pointedly left behind.

'Sailing to Byzantium' is not, of course, a 'popular' poem in the manner of 'Innisfree'. Reflective of Yeats's mature style, it is a far more 'difficult' poem, which perhaps explains its lack of currency within the popular cultural domain of Yeatsian promotion. But 'difficulty' is not, it would seem, the reason for the popular neglect of this poem; it is not 'popular', I would suggest, because the poem does not conform to the image of Yeats as the writer of rural Irish romance. R.F. Foster notes several times that in later life Yeats often refused to recite his early poetry, and 'remained resentfully conscious of the fact that his early work continued to sell best, and that this was where his popular audience remained':[58] by the time of a 1925 Swiss lecture, Yeats had to recite 'Innisfree' 'with an air of suppressed loathing'.[59] Yeats had turned away from his own idealizations, criticizing the 'element of sentimentality' in his early work;[60] 'Sailing to Byzantium' lacks that sentimentality and so can be read as Yeats's response to his own constructions of rural place. Byzantium is, crucially, not only a city, but a 'foreign' city – there is no possibility of the Tourist Board including it on a 'Yeats Country' map, or, indeed, on any present-day map. Byzantium exists as a representation not of the 'Romantic Irish' (or indeed merely Romantic) relationship between man and nature; instead, Yeats explores the opposition between them. Of course, this dichotomy of nature and man was but one of many oppositions to occupy Yeats throughout his lifetime; I do not suggest that this particular one is somehow the most significant. Certainly, though, nature was a key in the symbolic order that came to compose Yeats's poetics. Byzantium, as an *urbanized* Eden of the mind, is a solid example of that order, and represents clearly the change in Yeats's representations of nature and place.

RECOVERING THE UNRECOVERABLE

Yeats does make a return to the past, however, in a move that allows him to recover it as fully as possible. The way in which he does this is to rely upon the speech of peasants, fishermen and other figures generally representative of the Irish people as he imagines them to exist. The far more naturalized speech is immediately less formal; and yet, ironically, it is in this less formalized speech that Yeats makes a solid return to more traditional pastoral forms and overlays them on an Irish experience. Poems such as 'The Fisherman' (composed 1914) and 'Shepherd and Goatherd' (composed 1918) offer a new Yeatsian language that moves further towards the rootedness that Yeats had sought from early on by employing simple language. These are pastoral poems, employing personae to express a commitment to a belief in a simpler and more profound existence that is not only unavailable but never actually was, for the personae are 'but a dream' (l. 36) and '[do] not exist' (l. 35). Yeats's recognition that traditional pastorals are in fact literary exercises that ignore the realities of the world is itself not often recognized; it is easier, of course, to accept the popular image of Yeats as the devout sentimentalist who never repents or relents in his nostalgia for the perfections of the lost past. Yeats's own poetry, however, contradicts this interpretation again and again, as do his lectures, essays and interviews: on tour in the United States in 1932–33, he told a Boston reporter that a genuine Irish literature would develop as 'Irishmen begin to hate and to love Ireland', rather than simply nursing illusions; Joyce, he thought, 'came to hate the illusory Ireland and so he went into exile'.[61] Yeats had not exiled himself as permanently as had Joyce, but his critique was no less severe. Towards the end of his life, Yeats offers an explicit critique of his own earlier, unchecked nostalgia and idealizations, in 'The Municipal Gallery Re-visited' (composed 1937):

John Synge, I and Augusta Gregory, thought
All that we did, all that we said or sang
Must come from contact with the soil, from that
Contact everything Antaeus-like grew strong.
We three alone in modern times had brought
Everything down to that sole test again,
Dream of the noble and the beggarman. (VI ll. 2–8)

The impossibility of recovering the past is often Yeats's theme: the loss of the pastoral age, the loss of the very *possibility* of the pastoral age, and finally the realization that these themes ultimately rested upon the expression of that impossibility, which, ironically, managed to preserve something – if only the sense of loss – of that lost past. 'All one's life', he wrote, 'one struggled toward reality, finding always but new veils. One knows everything in one's mind. It is the words, children of the occasion, that betray.'[62]

Yeats, over the course of his life, changed drastically the way in which he portrayed landscape and the natural world of Ireland. In his early poems, nature and landscape are unspecific, vaguely romantic, and it is not until Yeats comes to his reading of Irish literature that his poetry becomes grounded, rooted, in the placenames of his Sligo childhood and in the Ireland of his adult life. In this changeover one finds the roots of the pastoral tradition, but also the Irish tradition of *dindshenchas*. While the invocation of place in Yeats is often a part of a backward-looking longing for some past, it is also an invocation that merely grounds what is an unstable present by connecting that present to the past. It is in these early and middle phases of his poetry that Yeats is the most 'sentimental' and 'nostalgic' in popular terms: his use of figures such as Oisin offer a romantic and nationalist Ireland, one in which the beauty of wild nature is ever-present.

It is not until the reality of present-day Ireland was revealed to him – primarily, it would seem, through the violence of the Easter Rising – that the poetry shifts into a much more concrete and sturdy representation of Ireland. 'Romantic Ireland' being dead and gone, Yeats's nostalgia is tempered, refined and opened up to images beyond those offered to him by Irish literature alone. Poems such as 'The Second Coming' and 'Sailing to Byzantium' represent this shift: no longer is Yeats turning to images of the Irish past in a specifically Irish place for his lost Eden, which is, by the time of 'The Second Coming', all but impossible. Instead, Yeats creates an imaginative pastoral place that combines all of his interests – in the spirit world, in the visionary, in the past, in mythology. The failure of the actual memory of the past to provide comfort and inspiration moves Yeats, as it does Synge, beyond the realm of lived memory into the memory of an unlived, unexperienced past. Where in his early poetry Yeats would have attempted the futile reconstruction of the perfect world of his Sligo childhood, in his later works he recognizes the impossibility of such a reconstruction:

> I thought: 'There is a waterfall
> Upon Ben Bulben side
> That all my childhood counted dear;
> Were I to travel far and wide
> I could not find a thing so dear.'
> My memories had magnified
> So many times a childish delight.
> I would have touched it like a child
> But knew my finger could but have touched
> Cold stone and water.
>
> ('Towards Break of Day' (1920) p. 233 ll. 5–14)

Were it possible for us as readers to 'travel far and wide' through the spaces represented by Yeats in his poetry, we would be on a strange tour indeed. This imagined tour might begin in the exictement of a journey with Oisin across a fantastically idealized land and seascape; it might continue in the almost eroticized light that is permanently settled in 'Innisfree'. Just as we would become used to this romantic space of Ireland, however, it would be swept away from us and we would find ourselves bewildered tourists indeed, lost in an unrecognizably artificial paradise called Byzantium. Were this imaginary tour possible, the Irish Tourist Board would certainly not be as earnest in its marketing of this 'alternative' Yeats Country, which might begin as some edenic journey, but would end in a Dantesque descent into the unknown, into the 'foul rag and bone shop of the heart' ('The Circus Animals' Desertion' (1939) III l.8), which might peddle souvenirs that the tourist would likely as not wish to forget: parodies of the very paradise from which we had come.

CHAPTER FOUR

Synge, The Aran Islands, *and the Movement Towards Realism*

Synge shared with Yeats not only a commitment to Irish literary and cultural traditions, but also a profound preoccupation with Irish landscape. The Aran Islands, Kerry and Wicklow haunted Synge's memory and imagination and inspired his writing. All of these places were, quite literally, beyond the pale, removed from the hub of political activity that was Dublin at the beginnings of the twentieth century – and Synge was removed for the most part as well from obvious hubs of cultural activity like Lady Gregory's estate that might arguably be perceived as urban outposts. Synge's experience of Irish place was, in this sense, rural in a way that Yeats's was only infrequently following childhood; the resulting representations of Irish place and landscape are, not unexpectedly, also very different.

The differences in Yeats and Synge's representations of place and landscape are predicated, it would seem, in their other commitments: Yeats made himself into the consummate 'public man' and insider, while Synge appeared to make himself marginal to the political committees and organizations that so defined Ireland of the period. Undoubtedly influenced by his position as part of an Anglo-Irish family whose wealth had not deteriorated to the extent that Yeats's family's had,[1] Synge seemed to edge away from the overt political involvement by which Yeats in part defined himself and his creative work: not subject to the social displacement that Yeats felt himself to be, Synge distanced himself from the Anglo-Irish Ascendancy's historical role as the governing class in Ireland. This distancing should not, however, be read as a disavowal of politics. The tendency has been to see Synge as strictly apolitical, based in large part on Yeats's and Lady Gregory's reminiscences, which of course had their own agendas. These literary takes on Synge have been echoed by critics; Nicholas Grene, for example, writes that Synge had an unusual 'capacity to leave aside the problems of his class'.[2] More recent assessements have attempted to balance the scales: P.J. Mathews's *Revival* has argued that Synge's publication of articles on Irish culture and literature 'mediate developments in Ireland to a wider European audience',[3] marking Synge as a participant in what Mathews refers to as the 'self-help' movement of the Revival. Not a 'joiner' in the way that Yeats was all his life, Synge demonstrates political involvement in other ways: writing itself is a political act.

Synge's seeming political self-marginalization is most clearly evidenced in his decision to make himself physically marginal by journeying to the Aran Islands.[4] The Aran Islands had come to be seen by Revivalists as an outpost of 'pure' Irish culture, largely because the Irish language remained the primary tongue for communication. And since for many the Irish language functioned as a sign of a pre-conquest and even pre-Christian past, the islands rooted off of Ireland's western coast consequently became the site where the past might be visited, a geographical space of cultural memories: the Aran Islands were, in effect, deemed a museum.

> In general, objects preserved in museums come from out of the past, so that the observer experiencing them in three-dimensional space must somehow also cross a barrier of change in time. Paradoxically, however, these objects are at the same time *timeless – removed from history in the very process of embodying it*, by curators seeking . . . to preserve objects in the original form. Removed, however, from their original contexts in space and time, and recontextualized in others that may or may not seek to recreate them, the meaning of the material forms preserved in museums must always be acutely problematic.[5] (my emphasis)

While the Aran Islands could not be removed from their spatial situation, Revival attitudes towards them still served to 'recontextualize' them in a crucial way; so crucially, in fact, that we might better describe the process as a 'decontextualization'. The Revivalist idea of the Aran Islands ignores time altogether, so that the islanders themselves seem to become objects whose function it is to be subject to the gaze (whether pseudo-anthropological or touristic is a matter of debate here) and 'embody' Irish history. Aran and the west of Ireland more generally thus formed a 'timeless' space in which historical cycles were frozen: it was as if the islands and their inhabitants were oblivious to what had occurred in Irish history over the last several hundred years. The oblivion to historical processes accorded to the islands suggested not only the recontextualization that takes place in museums, but also a child-like ignorance and simplicity that appealed to the Revival's notion of 'pure' Irish culture as being untouched. The islands were also, though, a space in which the natural world played a dominant role, and which became a repository for ideas of what the 'real' Ireland had been: not only simple and pure, but natural. This 'natural' state of Aran existence would become key in Synge's interpretation of the islands.

Despite their presence in the popular Revival imagination, the islands remained a relatively unusual destination, for both Irish and foreign tourists;[6] Synge's trips were even more unusual because of the extended nature of his stays away from the 'mainland'. Henry David Thoreau's move from the 'mainland' to Walden Pond has been described by Stanley Cavell as a re-enactment of the Puritan mission of the transcendental act, 'an attempt to live the idea'.[7] I would suggest that Synge's annual visits to the Aran Islands are similarly transcendental, attempts to live an idea that, one senses, Synge is to discover: not only in the language of the peasants as it floats up to his room, but in the tongues of the taunting sea and the moaning wind. The life that Synge attempts to re-enact is one that he has read of, but not experienced directly; it is a life of the distant past, and Synge attempts to recover that past by imagining himself as existing in it. Even Synge's first trip to Aran is, one feels, in some way a return,[8] for Synge attempts to return to and recover a lost Irish culture.

Thoreau's Walden experience was founded upon what Emerson had called 'self-reliance', and took as its inspiration another of Emerson's creeds, turning away from English forms in order to create an American literary, artistic and aesthetic tradition. Synge's journey to Aran was based on different principles:[9] the Revivalists' concern with the west was as a site of lost culture and so not the invention of a new tradition, but the recovery of old ones eclipsed by colonial occupation. Synge's journey to Aran is thus transcendental as a nostalgic act, in its attempt to move beyond experienced time and recapture a lost past. But it is transcendental in another way as well: as an attempt to move beyond the self. As Luke Gibbons has noted, 'the recourse to the west in Ireland is impelled by a search for community, a desire to escape the isolation of the self and to immerse oneself in the company of others'.[10] In removing himself from a largely urban life, Synge is actually attaching himself, purposefully, to a community the likes of which he has been unable to find in modern urban Dublin culture, in an attempt to live out the ideal of communal inter-reliance as Revivalists have imagined it to exist in the Ireland of

the past. This attempt marks Synge as very different from Yeats and
other Revivalists; Synge did actually remove himself from the mostly
urban political organizations of the period to immerse himself in a
more natural environment.[11]

In journeying to the Aran Islands, Synge is searching, self-consciously,
for some 'primitive' (to use his word) Irish culture that he and Yeats
and others of the Revivalists need to provide them with a bridge to
the past. The Revival is characterized by this tremendous nostalgia
for the past, and its reliance on past myths and metaphors to ascribe
meaning to contemporary Irish culture. In Synge's case, as frequently
in Yeats's, the nostalgia is situated in the nature and landscape of
Ireland: for the lost culture being sought is intrinsically natural. 'I
cannot say it too often', Synge writes in a notebook, 'the supreme
interest of the island lies in the strange concord that exists between
the people and the impersonal limited but powerful impulses of the
nature that is round them'.[12] By immersing himself in the landscape
of the Aran Islands, Synge will, he hopes, somehow gain access to this
'concord' with nature, which is not to be found elsewhere in the
modern world.

Synge saw his task on Aran as multifold. He would immerse
himself in the Irish language, which he had been studying for some
time, and would thus immerse himself in the ancient culture to which
that language allowed him entry. As an Irish speaker, Synge worked
in both English and Irish, thus ignoring a division observed by many
others. Besides allowing him a linguistic space that was, outside of
Aran and other specific regions of Ireland, immensely private,[13] Irish
gave Synge a subject matter that he felt connected him to the remote
past, allowing him to exercise the nostalgic desire to bring that past
into the present. Synge's 'surprise', in *The Aran Islands*, at 'the abun-
dance and fluency of the foreign tongue'[14] of English on Aran registers
this nostalgia. Synge's hopes for Aran are clear: to find a civilization
untouched by the historical and political currents of several centuries.

These hopes were founded in large part upon Synge's study of Irish
literature. Like Yeats, Synge found his discovery of Irish literature
overwhelming – but Synge, as Declan Kiberd's *Synge and the Irish
Language* demonstrates, committed himself to a systematic study of
both Irish literature *and* the Irish language,[15] and the wider social
goal of writing and circulating essays on the literary traditions of that
language. His immersion in the Irish literature and culture of centuries before was driven by a desire to unveil a hidden past and pull
it into the currents of the present – driven, in other words, by a

nostalgia for that past. The manifestation of that nostalgia and that desire was to be the writing of *The Aran Islands*.

Synge's childhood love of the natural world recorded in his auto-biography[16] developed into his adult habit of walking through various regions of Ireland in order to know people and landscape. Synge attributed his attachment to nature as having been awakened

> by a prolonged unsatisfied desire . . . Perhaps the modern feeling for the beauty of nature as a particular quality – an expression of divine ecstasy rather than a mere decoration of the world – arose when men began to look on everything about them with the unsatisfied longing which has its proper analogue in puberty.[17]

What Synge describes here is the beginnings of pastoral longing: having been separated from a life in nature and from the practical usefulness of the natural world, men of the upper-middle and upper-classes begin to recognize its beauty, in part because they are at leisure to do so, and also because they have the necessary funds to travel and so examine landscape for merely aesthetic qualities. This sense of separation was heightened, for Synge, by his pubescent confrontation with Darwin. Synge experienced a far more traumatic loss of faith than Yeats; in no small part because of exposure to Darwin and science, Synge abandoned the idea of a career in the Church.[18] Synge eventually came to terms with the dilemma by creating for himself an 'incredulous belief that illuminated nature',[19] much as Yeats turned to art in the wake of similar revelations. Unable to sustain a belief in human beings as the unique focus of the universe, and unable any longer to believe in a God, Synge experiences a pastoral longing for a perfect existence in nature unmarred by the realizations forced upon him by contemporary science.[20]

His is an '*incredulous* belief', full of the pastoral *desire* to believe; Synge's adult experience of nature is measured, detached, since his class allows him the privilege of observing nature without physical involvement or toil in the fields.[21] Synge moves in nature as an out-sider: he is a visitor to the small Wicklow and Kerry towns through which he walks, and is often recognized in Wicklow as one of a wealthy, estate-owning, landlord family. This distance between Synge and the world of nature would be, he seems to hope, eclipsed on Aran, where ubiquitous exposure to weather and wind was inevitable. In Aran, Synge hopes to find a way of bridging the gap between himself and the natural world as separately evolving entities, a way of denying historical time and events, a way of feeling connected to the people whom he has walked amongst and been separated from by class and religion, and a way of denying Darwin: a way, ultimately, of recovering pastoral.[22]

The loss of faith occasioned by Synge's reading of Darwin undoubtedly contributes to the strange presentation of time on Aran, which becomes a nostalgic representation not only of pre-colonial and pre-Christian but also pre-Darwinian modes of existence. Synge determinedly omits the processes of time whenever possible, even though this necessitates a silence on two remarkable features of Aran: the layers of rock immediately evident in the cliffs, and what Tim Robinson describes as 'the mighty stormbeach'.[23] Both formations, Robinson notes, 'insistently raise the question of geological origins, of the processes of time; it is as if [Synge] wanted to generalize his island into elemental simplicity and atemporality'.[24] Rather than address the temporal development of Aran as a geological formation, Synge opts to create an ancient Irish world that has been untouched by time except for the most immediate of natural cycles, resulting in the presentation of a world untouched by *evolutionary* time. The book, written over a period of several years, also ignores, but in one or two places, the cycles of time that dictate Synge's own life. Synge, then, makes a conscious choice to stress the atemporality of Aran. In its refusal to contextualize the writer's experience alongside contemporary events, the narrative procedure of *The Aran Islands* bears resemblance to Thoreau's compression of material into 'one year' of time at Walden, and also to Picturesque and Romantic travelogues, which frequently privilege 'timelessness' over historicism. And this timeless quality of Aran is symbolized, of course, by the islanders' lack of familiarity with, and seeming puzzlement at, Synge's clock: the island becomes literally timeless.

The timelessness of the space Synge presents is intimately tied to the use of the Irish language. 'I have decided', Synge writes after finding English too prevalent on the first of the islands, 'to move on to Inishmaan, where Gaelic is more generally used, and the life is perhaps the most primitive that is left in Europe.'[25] The people spoke 'with a delicate exotic intonation that was full of charm',[26] he found. The use of words like 'primitive', 'exotic' and 'charm' at the start of the book indicate the society that Synge is inclined to seek out: one removed from the 'civilized' world, and one that he sees from the standpoint of a man of urban, more worldly culture. This distance between Synge and the world in which he immerses himself, and the distance between his use of language and the islanders' use of language, was to prove valuable to Synge's art in the years to come. His characters, outside of those merely sketched in *The Aran Islands*, employ this exoticism constantly. But as an outsider and an observer, he does not see immediately that by emphasizing such things, he is participating in a colonialist move to identify the observed as an other who can only aspire to the knowledge of the observer.[27] Synge presents himself, in other words, as an early ethnographer, but one who is unaware of his own biases. Synge has been conditioned not only by his nostalgic – while studious – readings and considerations of Irish literature, but also, inevitably, by popular Picturesque conceptions of the west, of Aran, of the Irish language, and of the present state of Ireland under English rule. It is not until he has spent a substantial amount of time on the islands that Synge is awakened to his own role in this process of what is arguably another form of colonialism – in terms of the history of museums, an 'internal colonialism'[28] that objectifies the 'lost' aspects of one's own culture – and checks his nostalgia with a sharp realism. This process is evidenced in the text, which reads, curiously enough, as an evolution: rather than existing merely as a pseudo-anthropological record, the book also functions as a record of Synge's evolving attitudes towards the islands, and, by extension, to Irish culture and history.

Synge's early time on Aran is marked by the emphasis on atemporality, and the resulting emphasis on the primitivism of the islanders and their way of life. Synge wishes to see this way of life as timeless, and this desire aligns Synge's notions of the islanders with the attitudes identified by anthropologists in their assessments of the function of museums described at the start of this chapter. Because their way of life is pointedly at odds with modern Irish culture and actually quite settled, in Synge's mind, in the remote past, Synge must present the people of Aran as a museum display. In this sense, just as the Irish landscape became a 'live' museum that attested to the existence of Irish culture during the rise of the Picturesque and of Romanticism in the early and mid-nineteenth century, the Aran Islands become a living museum with interactive models that not only symbolize the past, but can trigger a sense of 'pastness' and participation in the past in the observer: the observer feels as if he has become part of the display. 'My sadness and delight', Synge writes, 'are older than the walls about me, and have lingered round these rocks since men were hairy and naked, for emotion is as inherent a property to this place as the colour or odour of the waves'.[29]

Despite having been so traumatized by his reading of Darwin, Synge observes as one who could only come after Darwin: not only is he conscious of the development of man as an animal, but also of the idea of antiquity, of ancientness, in everything he sees and experiences – he is fully aware, in other words, of evolution. Darwin's scientific reasoning allows Synge the space in which to imagine the distant past; but it is writing the likes of O'Grady's and Arnold's that influences his interpretation of that imagined past. Like Arnold and other Victorian writers on Ireland, Synge makes a connection between emotion and place, and implies that an immersion in the natural world somehow leads to an intense emotional life, as restless and unsettled and exuberant as the sea. Being a man of the post-Romantic, post-Darwin era, though, Synge cannot help but view this connection as primitive, and it is this aspect of the islands with which he is immediately enthralled. 'It gave me a moment of exquisite satisfaction to find myself moving away from civilization in this rude canvas canoe of a model that has served primitive races since men first went on the sea',[30] Synge writes of an early inter-island journey. Steeped in Irish literature, Synge cannot but make the connection between his journey and those journeys of early Irishmen like Bran, recorded in voyage tales from the seventh century onwards: and Synge, of course, had read Bran's voyage tale.[31] Synge's desire to make such links between the past and present leads to his feeling of 'exquisite satisfaction' at the use of 'rude' canoes that were the means of mobility for 'primitive' men. Such a response – to the primitive and its connection to the present – is standard in the early parts of the book. Synge manages to insert himself into the distant past by insisting upon its relevance and involvement in the present: 'I am in the north island again, looking out with a singular sensation to the cliffs across the sound. It is hard to believe that those hovels I can just see in the south are filled with people whose lives have the strange quality that is found in the oldest poetry and legend.'[32] The past is a constant presence for Synge as he exists on Aran, one that puts him in touch with a reality he has never known before. His language in such passages is, however, ironically prescient of his later thoughts on the island: it will indeed become 'hard to believe' in his imagined ideal of life on Aran.

Synge sees the past as present in almost every aspect of the islanders' lives. 'Every article on these islands has an almost personal character, which gives this simple life, where all art is unknown, something of the artistic beauty of medieval life.'[33] Editing his vision to focus on the benefits of the life he is observing, Synge initially ignores the very real poverty, isolation and hard work that accompany a 'simple', 'medieval' life. He also leaves out of sight the 'art' involved in the creation of his own book: just as medieval Irish monks wrote idealized pastoral versions of the possibilities of their future lives, Synge writes of an idealized, pastoral existence on Aran, a life in which everyone is in communion with each other and with the natural world. In this world there is 'the absence of any division of labour', and everybody 'can speak two langauges'.[34] Every man

> is a skilled fisherman, and can manage a curagh with extraordinary nerve and dexterity. He can farm simply, burn kelp, cut out pampooties, mend nets, build and thatch a house, and make a cradle or a coffin. His work changes with the seasons in a way that keeps him free from the dullness that comes to people who have always the same occupation. The danger of his life on the sea gives him the alertness of a primitive hunter, and the long nights he spends fishing in his curagh bring him some of the emotions that are thought peculiar to men who have lived with the arts.[35]

What Synge chooses to see, on Aran, is a life that resembles a communal Walden, where each individual is directly involved in almost every aspect of his own existence: from food and clothing production to the building of shelter, changing professions hour to hour as necessity deems. Having witnessed for himself the results of the inequities of life on the 'mainland' and, indeed, on Aran, when it came to land ownership and tenant rights, and unavoidably aware of the differences between his own and others' wealth, Synge views this 'absence of any division of labour' with favour. Ironically, though, his enthusiasm for what he sees as a form of natural communism is, of course, much more about his desire to overcome the distancing effect of his own social position – as a 'blow-in', an Anglo-Irishman, and as a tourist of sorts – than the reality of the islanders' working lives, which are, of course, limited to the work available to them and full of hardship. So enchanted is he with his own vision of this life that at certain moments he believes he would like to live permanently among the islanders:

> [T]hese men of Inishmaan seemed to be moved by strange archaic sympathies with the world. Their mood accorded itself with wonderful fineness to the suggestions of the day, and their ancient Gaelic seemed so full of divine sympathy that I would have liked to turn to the west and row with them for ever.

I told them I was going back to Paris in a few days to sell my books
and my bed, and that I was coming back to grow as strong and simple
as they were among the islands of the west.[36]

This, one of the few times that Synge allows his life beyond Aran to
insert itself into the text, is a clear representation of the pastoral
Synge is creating. He desires to live a 'simple' life on Aran, desiring to
abandon his own (by implication) complex life beyond the realm of
the islands. The result is almost startling: after being immersed in the
world that Synge sketches, the mention of Paris seems overwhelmingly worldly and foreign next to the simplicity he describes. In this
way Synge creates a text similar to traditional pastoral: a man of
urban education – if not a strictly urban upbringing – longs for the
simple life of nature as a remedy to the social and political complexities of his own world. Synge's nostalgia, which is explicit in such
a longing, is for a life that he has never lived, and one to which he is,
despite his recurring presence on Aran, an outsider. Synge's personal
nostalgia is extended, however, by his desire to make the life of the
islands available to an English language readership: his nostalgia
manifests itself in an act of cultural retrieval that posits the continued
existence of the 'ancient' Irish past through a process that glorifies the
islanders and their lives.

These glorifications result in the creation of a pastoral which
Declan Kiberd has claimed 'effects a revolutionary reversal',[37] but an
emphasis on Synge's pastoral form as 'revolutionary' ignores several
issues at work in the text of *The Aran Islands*. Synge does credit the
islanders with a great deal, but he is still conscious of a gap between
their experience and his own, and allows himself to edit – as he will
not in later texts – some of the experience in order to fit it in with his
ideal conception of the islanders' way of life. This editing process
results, I would argue, in a much more traditional *Irish* pastoral form
than has been recognized, and thus marks a return of sorts to an Irish
tradition with which Synge was, after all, so familiar. Synge's knowledge of medieval Irish sources would have meant a familiarity with
the representations of nature in the literature of the period: and he
would have thus been aware that those who experienced nature were
not only marginal figures, but also often aristocratic (as in the cases
of Sweeney and Finn) or significantly spiritual or visionary (as in the
cases of personae used in early medieval lyrics, and again in the cases
of Sweeney, Finn, and the *fían*). By making the peasants 'aristocratic',
Synge, far from employing the 'revolutionary reversal' that Kiberd

claims, is in fact transposing into the present an Irish tradition of the aristocrat pushed into the natural world and forced to come to terms with a natural existence. Synge himself, in his removal to the islands, is a 'noble in disguise', an upper-class Anglo-Irishman attempting to transcend class and rank, but he was aware from his study of Irish literature that many aristocrats pushed into the wilderness never recovered their assets and social position. The idea of the *islanders* as 'nobles in disguise', in effect, draws upon definite lines of Irish literature's characterizations: Sweeney, Caílte and countless bardic poets and their patrons all move in the natural world as a result of loss of status. The islanders' possible nobility would have been extraordinarily appealing to an Irish nationalist culture that was attempting to make claims for not merely the existence, but also the respectibility, of ancient Irish culture. This recovery of the peasants as aristocrats also, of course, conveniently fits in with Synge's own contemporary European sensibility, employing the familiar stereotype of the noble savage, and reflecting the European preoccupation with idealized notions of the primitive mind as pure and uncorrupted by civilization – ideas which, of course, themselves derive from colonialism and its legacies.

The transposition of such idealizations necessarily means that the text of *The Aran Islands* is edited; and Synge's editing processes result in a text that cannot be seen simply as an anthropological account. This editing does not apply only to matters of time, as Synge omits items that do not fall into line with his notion of what the Irish past should have been: in one encounter, Synge omits a story told to him by a local as 'a rude anecdote not worth recording'.[38] This is in itself an interesting commentary, a highlighted absence that suggests that Synge himself was beyond such 'rude' tales – whether rude is interpreted as 'primitive', 'unconstructed' or 'offensive' – and expected that his reader would be as well. In other cases, of course, the 'rude' – as in the 'rudeness' of the canoe above – is to be celebrated. Such linguistic tics indicate the form of pastoralism at work here: a certain amount of rudeness is cultivated as providing 'authentic' experience of the past, but when contemporary mores and ideas are offended or ideals let down, the rudeness is promptly omitted. As in Theocritus's pastoral poems, an amount of bawdiness provides a sense of rural 'reality' by presenting figures whose mode of speech corresponds to educated urban expectations of how an uneducated peasant might speak, but this might be pushed too far and offend the readership or might suggest that the figures are a- or immoral. To make this suggestion would be unconscionable, if one had nationalist beliefs as

Synge did: he was therefore put under the same burden as O'Grady and many others before him.

One of the most obvious areas in which Synge has edited to a purpose is in regard to religion. One islander with whom Synge converses 'wandered off into tedious matters of theology'.[39] Synge's turn away from religious faith partly explains why he fails to consider the islanders' religious attitudes within the context of his book, but to admit the presence of Catholic religiosity would also be to admit that Irish culture as it existed on the islands had absorbed what he perceived to be an 'outside' influence; as Nicholas Grene (among many other critics) concludes, 'he wanted to see [the islanders] not as the devout Catholics they no doubt were, but as people whose orthodox Catholicism barely covered primitive pagan attitudes'.[40] By editing out a significant element in the islanders' lives, Synge shapes his experience into what is a traditional pastoral, idealizing what corresponds with his expectations and hopes, and omitting what does not. His own nostalgia dictates, in a sense, what he can see in his early time on Aran. As a result, the text, while certainly allowing the reader access to parts of Aran culture, tells us just as much, if not more, about what the author perceives as lacking in present-day, modern Irish, and specifically Dublin – and perhaps more specifically Dublin upper-class Anglo-Irish – culture.

Synge's preoccupation with the primitive on the island suggests that modern life as he sees it has lost something significant in abandoning certain primitive ways: like all pastorals, Synge's offers a critique of the culture of which he is usually a part. When he has to return to the mainland on errands and business, he is unimpressed by what he finds. 'After my weeks spent among primitive men this glimpse of the newer types of humanity was not reassuring', he writes.[41] Again Synge's observations demonstrate the influence of Darwin: his consciousness that there are 'newer types of humanity' signals a recognition of the processes of evolution – and also, crucially, raises the question of where Synge sees himself as fitting in on this evolutionary scale. This recognition appears many times, as when he notes that 'The absence of the heavy boot of Europe has preserved to these people the agile walk of the wild animal.'[42] Synge acknowledges explicitly here the connection between animal and human that had so shaken the world when Darwin published *The Origin of Species* and *The Descent of Man*. Darwin deprived him of his faith, and Synge has absorbed his theories, repeatedly demonstrating observations that would not have been possible otherwise.

That he had absorbed Darwin, however, did not mean that Synge accepted his theories; as we have seen in his representation of the time of the islands as static and unchanging, Synge was capable of denying time or change altogether. And while Darwin's theories had negated the possibility of believing that nature cared particularly for man, the natural world of Aran, Synge insists, continually mirrors and reflects the lives and emotions of its inhabitants. Following a funeral, a thunderstorm mounts an attack on the sky, moving Synge to note the connection. 'In Inishmaan one is forced to believe in a sympathy between man and nature, and at this moment when the thunder sounded a death-peal of extraordinary grandeur above the voices of the women, I could see the faces near me stiff and drawn with emotion.'[43] Synge desires to believe in this sympathy above all things, wanting a connection between the physical, outside world, and the spiritual and emotional life of the interior mind. Having lost religious faith, Synge, like Yeats, turns to a faith in nature and place.

Nature on Aran has, however, as Tim Robinson puts it, a 'Darwinian ruthlessness' that is evidenced daily.[44] The danger to which islanders are exposed in their curaghs preoccupies Synge, whose fear out on the water is exhilerating: 'Even, I thought, if we were dropped into the blue chasm of the waves, this death, with the fresh sea saltness in one's teeth, would be better than most deaths one is likely to meet.'[45] Synge relishes the intimacy he can enjoy with the sea in Aran, but the threat of drowning is, for him as for the authors of early Irish voyage tales, pre-eminent. His exaggeration of the threat – clearly not every one of the men will be drowned, or the island's population would have died out – signals Synge's position as an outsider, as one who views the sea without personal knowledge of it. 'This continual danger, which can only be escaped by extraordinary personal dexterity, has considerable influence on the local character, as the waves have made it impossible for clumsy, foolhardy, or timid men to live on these islands.'[46] The natural world is unforgiving, and while Synge goes too far in believing that so many men will die by the waves each year, he insists on a symbiosis between man and nature on the island, and a popularized Darwinian influence of environment upon personal development and character. The struggle that he witnesses in Aran – with and against nature for a livelihood – impresses him as another example of the presence of the past in the islanders' lives.

All of these things – the 'timeless' simplicity of the islanders' occupations, their interaction with nature, and the thrill of danger that a natural existence adds to their lives – grant to the islanders' a certain beauty for Synge, but it is a beauty to which they are quite oblivious: their existence is not marked by the divide between culture and nature that preoccupies urban men, the creators of the pastoral ideal. A paradox exists, then: those closest to nature are not conscious of the intimacy. Too preoccupied with having to wrench a living from the land, the islanders surrounding Synge can afford neither to pause at length to consider natural beauty nor to go else-where and so gauge a comparison between their own and another landscape. Synge's privileges, which do not force him to work and which allow him mobility, contribute to his pastoral thinking, and to the analysis of the 'natural' from the position of the 'cultural'. In this sense, Synge seems to admit that he is himself not 'primitive', but one of the 'newer types of humanity'.

If the islanders do not distinguish between nature and culture, neither do they distinguish between the natural and supernatural, Synge believes. Because of the unreliability of the environment, super-stitions and folk beliefs abound on the island, and Synge is quick to fall under the spell of the possibility of himself believing in such supernaturalisms. While the practicalities and daily activities demanded by the natural world of Aran are necessarily a subject of constant conversation, they often give way to a different type of talk that relies upon folklore and myth. Among other things, Synge is told about fairies and their connection to the landscape. 'It is there the fairies do be playing ball in the night, and you can see the marks of their heels when you come in the morning', one man tells him.[47] The influence of such stories upon Synge is strong enough that he does end by believing in the possibility of the supernatural: 'Some dreams I have had in this cottage seem to give strength to the opinion that there is a psychic memory attached to certain neighbourhoods.'[48] Both of these incidents draw upon the traditional Irish practice of *dindshenchas* and the possibility of knowing the past through the present land-scape: but added to it is the kind of mysticism popular amongst Victorians of the upper-middle and upper-classes, the mysticisms of seances and secret orders like those in which Yeats was so involved, and of which Synge read. Synge, so aware of Irish literature, would have been conscious of *dindshenchas*, and so nurtured the tradition as well as its mystical possibilities as a way of replacing all that he has lost: faith in God, faith in man, faith in political action and Irish history. Like his contemporaries, Synge sought and found evidence for an intimate connection between nature and the Irish. Strongly influenced by both Darwin and by post-Romantic ideologies about the natural world, he seems to replace his lost faith with a belief in the connection between physical and spiritual worlds. 'These people', he concludes, 'make no distinction between the natural and supernatural.'[49] However, Synge was to come to a critique of such idealizations.

Synge's willingness to confront his own nostalgia sets him apart from other Revivalists: for Synge gradually checks himself with a hard realism, and in doing so aligns himself further with the medieval Irish literary tradition, pushing beyond surface similarities and coincidences between this tradition and contemporary ideals: moving, in other words, from traditional to Irish pastoral forms. This realism does not make itself felt in *The Aran Islands* immediately. The process by which Synge arrives at a more realistic view of the islands involves the passing of time, which, as we have seen, he initially resisted inserting into the narrative. An interesting example of the evolution of Synge's attitudes and pastoral representations lies in his view of the island women. At first, Synge finds that the red clothing of the women 'give a glow of almost Eastern richness'.[50] The emphasis on the exoticism of the women implies a foreignness with which Synge is utterly unfamiliar, emphasized by his choice of the word 'Eastern'. Synge later comes to see the women as exotic creatures of the sea, the element that dictates so much of the tenor of his visits to Aran, marking 'woman' out as 'nature': 'Their red bodices and white tapering legs make them as beautiful as tropical seabirds, as they stand in a frame of seaweeds against the brink of the Atlantic.'[51] As Joyce would do with his famous 'bird girl' scene in *A Portrait of the Artist as a Young Man*, Synge makes the observation of these women erotic, charged with a subtle sexual energy implied by his choice of words. By the second year of his visits, though, the girls on the beach 'looked strangely wild and seal-like with the salt caked upon their lips and wreaths of seaweed in their hair'.[52] Very subtly – almost imperceptibly – Synge's view of these women has moved away from the exotic, the erotic, towards a view of them as utterly foreign and animalistic. If they are at first the stereotype of feminine landscape, feminine nature made erotic, they become something more threatening, a form of Darwinian, sexualized nature, and utterly separate from Synge.

It is this separation from which Synge's classical pastoral form derives – the distance from the women is what allows them to be seen as exotic and natural – but it is also the cause of that form's demise in the text. 'In some ways', he writes, 'these men and women seem strangely far away from me. They have the same emotions that I have, and the animals have, yet I cannot talk to them when there is much to say, more than to the dog that whines beside me in a mountain fog.'[53] There is a mournfulness in such an admission; Synge longs to be able to communicate fully with the people he has come to so admire, but he recognizes a gap that, it seems, is overwhelming. In part this gap seems due to Synge's status as an outsider on the island, but he himself implies in such comments as the one above that the gap is more significant than that, arising out of the gap between 'civilization' and 'primitivism', and also, significantly, out of the sheer reality of nature. 'This year', Synge writes on a return, 'I see a darker side of life in the islands. The sun seldom shines, and day after day a cold south-western wind blows over the cliffs, bringing up showers of hail and dense masses of cloud.'[54] Gradually Synge is forced to look beyond the obvious beauties and advantages of a life on Aran towards the mercilessness of the weather and the poverty that affects everyone. Unlike others of the Revival, Synge 'worried constantly about the gap between a beautiful culture and the poverty that can underlie it', Declan Kiberd notes.[55] The realization of that gap comes on the islands, and impacts all of Synge's work to come. Towards the end of *The Aran Islands*, Synge writes that he became 'indescribably mournful, for I felt that this little corner on the face of the world, and the people who live in it, have a peace and dignity from which we are shut for ever'.[56] His longing to be a part of the community is overwhelmingly obvious, as is his awareness that he cannot transcend the casings of the very museum he has created for himself.

The gradual realizations of the life the men and women of Aran lead – forced to submit to the whim of weather and ocean, toiling without pause for mere survival – only increase Synge's admiration. Synge's Aran experience does not offer him simply a foray into the world of ancient Ireland and a space in which to indulge his nostalgia for that unknown time; ultimately the experience serves as an autobiographical voyage tale, in much the same way as Thoreau's *Walden* offers a personalized voyage of the mind. J.W. Foster has decribed *The Aran Islands* as

> a profound spiritual autobiography whose landscape, like that of the Medieval penitential voyages, is utterly essential but ultimately emblematic, a spiritual projection . . . Beneath the apparent symbolism of primal unity, the western island became for Synge the pared habitat of the self; his lasting vision was not that for which he travelled to the Aran and Blasket islands, nor was it like that of the Sons of O'Corra

who found God or Maelduin who found human companionship. Synge found his own solitariness, and so transposed the Medieval *Immram* into the 20th century.[57]

The voyage on which Synge set out was, in many ways, an uncertain one: he does not seem to have been sure of what he would find in Aran. And while the text of *The Aran Islands* is profitably viewed alongside the tradition of the early and medieval Irish *immram* or *echtrae*, it is also important to bear in mind the resemblances between it and *Walden* as a text that sets out to create a modern nation through the transcendental journey into the self *in nature*.

Synge's experiences on Aran also gave him a voice in which to write. In *The Aran Islands*, he had attempted a shift from oral to written tradition, just as his medieval forebears had, seeking to record what had not been recorded before in contemporary Ireland, and seeking to bring these oral tales to the attention of the public: Synge assigns himself the medieval role of scribe. Curiously, Stanley Cavell finds a similar shift taking place in Thoreau's work: Thoreau is searching, he argues, for a 'father tongue' – a matured language – and one that is necessarily written, not spoken. The fact that such different men on two different continents are involved in the same process suggests that a part of creating a modern national identity is this transformation from oral to written tradition. The oral tradition that Synge found in Aran was inspiration enough to alter his work irrevocably. What results is a language of '*created* authenticity', as Nicholas Grene has described it (my emphasis).[58]

This language, heavily reliant upon Irish syntax, is also, in many ways, pastoral, in its *created* naturalism, *created* rusticity. In this, Synge revives Theocritus's and Virgil's pastoral forms, which relied upon the creation by the poet of a rustic speaker who knew nothing of the artifice of poetics. Besides the invention and use of a rustic language, Synge revives other traditions of Theocritus's pastorals: the battles between old and young, love complaints and a natural, unaffected sexuality that would outrage many of his contemporaries. And, like Theocritus's pastorals, and like most classical pastorals, *The Aran Islands* and the plays that followed it were not written for a rural audience; Synge's works were constructed for Dublin theatre-goers and urban readers.

Perhaps more important than any of these elements, however, is the fact that Synge's *The Aran Islands* inaugurates, in a sense, the modern ideology of the Irish nation by melding classical and Irish pastoral models. As a celebration of 'traditional', 'authentic' and 'rural' Ireland in the days before the Free State's existence, *The Aran Islands* is arguably unequalled. If the Aran Islands are representative of the real Ireland, the lost Ireland, the rest of the country – rural or urban inhabitants, really – are sham Irish, 'plastic Paddies'. The result is that the 'real Ireland', as it has been so often called, was something to be not lived, but consumed, bought, experienced on internal holiday, attended like an exhibit, observed and visited.[59] Synge's text marks, in a sense, the inhabiting of another breed of colonial stereotype: that of the Picturesque countryside as outlined in nineteenth-century travelogues – this time, however, the observer was himself Irish, lending an 'authenticity' to the observations.

This sort of Irish pastoralism in which Synge engaged can be – and indeed has been – critiqued: for its employment of old stereotypes, for its encouragement of new ones, for its presentation of a peasantry that is overly simplistic and idealized. Seen, however, as part of a cultural process, *The Aran Islands* is much more than this. Certainly Synge's early reactions and attitudes are all that critiques have claimed; but the end of the text displays a canny understanding of his own idealizations, and offers a commanding critique of not only his own text, but of the Revival itself and its nostalgias. Synge has moved from a reflexive to a critical nostalgia, a nostalgia on to the wink and the nod, one that is aware and savvy. This, I would argue, is the movement from a colonial to a post-colonial nostalgia, one that is highly astute and political. Synge's text demonstrates an awareness of the need for nostalgia if a modern nation is to be created: the past must be recovered as a foundation, in effect. But foundations, once in place, become largely invisible: and Synge seems aware that he, like others, will need to move beyond such a nostalgia or become irrelevant. Hence the text employs a nostalgia and then moves deftly beyond it, into a realistic realm that would become Synge's hallmark.

In *The Aran Islands*, Synge removes himself to the physical and cultural margins of Irish society. In his sojourns on the islands, Synge thus creates for himself an existence that thematically resembles the medieval Sweeney's in a significant way: in situating himself in this natural world, he immerses himself in a nostalgia for another culture, of the past. There are, of course, major differences between the treatment and significance of nature in *Buile Suibhne* and *The Aran Islands*. For Sweeney nature is a place both of resignation and resigned love – for, inhospitable as the natural world may be at times, Sweeney emphatically declares his preference for it over the culture from which he has been displaced. In nature, then, as we have seen, Sweeney is subjected to a continual remembering of his now past life. Unlike Sweeney, Synge *subjects himself* to a world that he connects to nature, in the hopes of *recovering* memory. This fundamental difference suggests that the Irish cultural use of nostalgia itself has changed in the centuries between the two texts. Sweeney's nostalgia is indeed a form of the etymological homesickness; Synge's is far more complicated, in that he longs for a life he has never lived. This type of nostalgia is much more aligned with that present in traditional pastoral, which is most typically written by a privileged class of urban dwellers who express a nostalgia for the simple life of the poor country peasant, *a life with which they have only a literary familiarity*, and Synge, as we have seen, certainly fits into this class. Just as the *Eclogues* and the *Georgics* presuppose the existence of urban culture over the hills, *The Aran Islands* presumes the presence of Dublin and Paris as places hovering in the background of Synge's experience. And as the conception of nostalgia has changed, so too has the representation of nature in Irish literature. Nonetheless, Synge's work, like much medieval Irish literature, situates itself in the natural world and focuses its yearnings on lost culture.

Stanley Cavell remarks, after Emerson, that when we are attentive, watchful, our environment supplies us with 'the knowledge of what is needful'.[60] One could say that, like Thoreau's *Walden*, Synge's Aran writings attest to the truth of this idea, for the Revivalists' nostalgia needed a connection between past and present, and Synge, attentive and watchful as a gull perched on the craggy cliffs, finds that link; Synge found, we saw in an earlier passage, that 'those hovels I can just see in the south are filled with people whose lives have the strange quality that is found in the oldest poetry and legend'.[61] Situating himself in nature and forging a link between the present world and that world of 'the oldest poetry and legend', Synge writes in a nostalgic mode that constructs for himself – and for many of his generation – an intertwined idea of nature and nation, reflecting what he calls the 'psychic memory'[62] that haunts Ireland's landscape, and creating a culture, in the process, that relies on the natural world for continuity.

Synge's experience in writing *The Aran Islands* was to change his representation of nature and place and the Irish relationship to place drastically. The gradual move towards a critique of his own idealizations in that text is reflected in the work that followed. *The Playboy of the Western World* and *The Shadow of the Glen* both move away from the idealizations of *The Aran Islands* into realms that have been described as anti-pastoral but which are, in fact, reflections of the medieval Irish pastoral tradition. These reflections were, of course, to cause uproar when Synge's representation of the peasant was brought to the Abbey stage. This furore arose because of Synge's candour in relating tales of rural Ireland: while nationalism had already linked itself to rural Ireland, it had done so in a way that only idealized that rurality. Unlike many of his contemporaries, including Yeats in his early stages, Synge, after Aran, refused to present mere idealizations of rurality, choosing instead to present a reality instructed by his own study of Irish literature in the original, as well as rural Ireland in the original as he had witnessed it. In a letter to Stephen MacKenna, paraphrasing MacKenna's own description of contemporary Irish drama, Synge famously replied that 'no drama can grow out of anything other than the fundamental realities of life which are never fantastic, are neither modern nor unmodern and, as I see them, rarely spring-dayish, or breezy and Cuchulainoid'.[63] Despite his commitment to Irish literature and to the Irish past, Synge could not help but see that 'Cuchulainoid' drama was unrealistic, and avoided much of the experience of rural Ireland at the start of the twentieth century.

Synge's commitment to seeing – and not merely imagining – the realities of Irish life for the poor and the marginal developed in Aran, where, as we have seen, his vision sharpened, leading him away from a purely classical pastoral representation. Synge thus committed himself to exposing the 'reality' of Irish rural life, based not only on his reading of Irish literature, but also upon his experiences in the west as well as in Wicklow. The 'Playboy riots' signalled just how deep a resentment could be invoked by what was seen as a betrayal of pastoral Ireland. Synge's plays, while evoking 'traditional' Ireland through allusion to the old sagas and myths, ultimately refused to offer a simple idealization of that world. Rather than seeing the past as an idealized present, and the present as a declining version of the past, Synge saw instead the past as containing what we saw him refer to earlier as 'the fundamental realities of life'. Rather than idealizing those realities, he attempted to represent them, in his work following *The Aran Islands*, as truly as possible, relying on his reading of the past to inform the present. 'If Synge evoked the greatness of the saga life, the better to mock the littleness of the contemporary peasant, then the irony works both ways, mocking also the portentous bearing and blind violence of the ancient protagonists',[64] Declan Kiberd writes, identifying an irony that Synge's contemporaries, including Yeats, failed to recognize until later events forced it upon them. Synge seemed to recognize early on the danger of poets and writers glorifying a violent past without considering the implications for a soon-to-be nation that was fighting the bit and raring to be free.

The Shadow of the Glen, as a post-Aran drama, and in its evocation of medieval Irish literature and the Irish past, offers an example of the ways in which Synge's pastoral representations change. Synge exploits the theme of the tramp – a common figure in his essays on Wicklow – to full effect in the character of the chance visitor to Nora's cottage on the night of her husband's supposed death. The resulting drama pits the older husband against his younger wife, and the life of indoor comfort against that of wild nature. When Nora's husband awakens from his feigned death to denounce her behaviour, she is forced to choose to go with the tramp on his journeys around the countryside. The tramp in this play has evidently chosen his life on the road, living in the wilderness of the Wicklow mountains. Nora, however, does not choose a life in the wilderness at once; she is, by virtue of her situation, displaced, like Sweeney, into the natural world. Nora's situation invites comparison with those who turned to the *fían* for help or justice; just as the *fían* offered a form of protection to those living the life of nature, the tramp offers her protection and companionship in her future life. And, the play implies, she might well be better off in the wilderness, which at least affords freedom. The idealization of the tramp's description of the free life in nature is starkly contrasted with the wildness of the weather that, after all, forced him to seek shelter. Ideal and reality stand quietly side by side; Synge might prefer to believe in the ideal – to insist on the 'incredulous belief' in nature – but he cannot desist from providing that ideal's contrast.

As *Playboy* was inspired by Synge's experiences in the west of Ireland and the tales he was told, so *The Shadow of the Glen* was inspired by Synge's experiences in Wicklow. As in Aran, he was struck in Wicklow by the tremendous isolation of the people he met, and their separation from the 'modern' world. 'People like these', he remarked after a particular encounter, '. . . are a precious possession for any country. They console us, one moment at least, for the manifold and beautiful life we have all missed who have been born in modern Europe.'[65] In Wicklow, too, Synge sought out lives he believed held something that the modern world lacked, an indescribable something that he longed for and felt nostalgia for, despite having never experienced it. His descriptions in the essays, in their idealizations and mournful nostalgia, do not make it into the plays, however; after Aran, those idealizations are not allowed stand without challenge.

Compare, for example, the tension between ideal and reality in *The Shadow of the Glen* with Synge's writing of an evening in early autumn, when he feels a longing come over him, wishing that

> this twilight might be eternal and I pass these [cottage] doors in endless pilgrimage. Yet they make me and, I believe, many or most people who feel these things, more dejected than any sight of misery.
>
>   At such moments one regrets every hour that one has lived outside of Ireland and every night that one has passed in cities. Twilight and autumn are both full of the suggestion that we connect with death and the ending of earthly vigour, and perhaps in a country like Ireland this moment has an emphasis that is not known elsewhere.[66]

Synge's language is full of the influence of people like Matthew Arnold: he associates the moody sentimentalism he feels with the landscape, his longing with the sight of people he naively believes to be happier than himself and his urban contemporaries. Also, though, such a passage indicates the tragic element in Synge's philosophy. In Aran this made itself evident through Synge's preoccupation with the threat of drowning; in Wicklow, he saw the threat of the natural world being simply the impending threat of death. The liminality of twilight brings thoughts to Synge's minds much like those Thoreau experiences in winter at Walden when he witnesses the stripping of the ice from the pond. The natural world brings Synge to philosophical crisis, making him question the life he leads – in foreign lands and in cities – and forcing him to conclude that in nature is a purer, more satisfactory life: and, inevitably, that life is somehow separated from him. The natural world may be 'pure' and may offer a simpler existence than the one Synge is obliged by class and privilege (and ill-health) to live, but after writing *The Aran Islands* it is no longer so simple, as Synge's nostalgia is itself displaced.

The natural world serves, in Synge's works, as a site for reflection, a site of longing, and, in the case of his characters, of displacement. The power of nature, whether it is the power of the sea over the Aran islanders' lives or the power of the mountains over the Wicklow people's lives, is a dominating energy, one that Synge voluntarily submits himself to, again and again, in search of a more clearly defined reality. Within that search for reality, Synge focuses on marginal figures much as his medieval forbears did, whether the Aran Islanders, whose physical existence at the edge of Europe marks them as outsiders to much of Irish and European developments, or the rural peasants of Wicklow, Connemara and Kerry who are transformed into the characters of his plays. In transforming 'peasants' into 'players', Synge allies himself with much of the movement of the Revival, in a crucial way participating in the realm of Irish pastoral politics. However, through his determined realism after Aran, and in his commitment to Irish literature as it had been produced hundreds of years before and not in contemporary translation, Synge emerges as a writer who engages both Irish and classical pastoral forms while simultaneously demythologizing their power. That Synge's final, incomplete work, *Deirdre of the Sorrows*, continues this theme of demythologizing is telling, and indicates where his work might have gone.

Synge began his public literary career with an immersion in the Irish past, in his journey to the Aran Islands, and moved gradually towards the realization that the past could not offer a model for the present except by illuminating the constancy of human themes over time. In reaching this revelation, his work moved towards a realism that was paralleled in Yeats's development. Nature and landscape, while they are initially the sites for a reflexive nostalgia, gradually come to be much more complex in their signification, elements of an Irish past that contain both ideals and their opposites.

CHAPTER FIVE

Joyce and Beckett: Refuting Stereotypes

While Yeats and Synge came to critique their own brands of pastoral nostalgia, many other participants in the Revival did not, and the general atmosphere of the period leading up to and following Irish independence was thick with nostalgia: 'It is generally held', Luke Gibbons has written, 'that Irish society had to await the end of the de Valera era to awake from its nostalgic slumbers'.[1] Synge's realization about the useful limits of pastoral nostalgia came, by this measure, astonishingly early, considering that his death in 1909 prevented him from bearing witness to the violent formation of the Irish state that acted as one of several spurs to Yeats's own re-evaluation of nationalist idealizations. The new nation now possessed unequivocally[2] the land that only decades before had to be bought back from the colonizer in plots sometimes as small as two acres; the mood was jubilant with insights into Irish culture provided by nostalgia, with politicians glorifying an ancient pastoral existence that was perceived to have been ushered in and consolidated once again by independence. Pastoral politics were thus infamously used as the foundations of the nation, and would exert a vice grip on Irish culture: for even if key figures like Synge and Yeats had mounted an assault on the rural imaginary, that assault was kept in check by a popular desire that chose to see only the glorification of the rural, and ignored, protested against, or marginalized much else.

It would seem that once the Irish state was formed, nostalgia would have served its political purpose: having reminded an increasingly attentive public that Ireland had its own cultural past worth preserving, nostalgia had allowed for that past to be imaginatively retrieved. Nostalgia had effectively restored a sense of *national* culture to a colonized people, had bridged a long forgotten past and an unsatisfactory present, and had, in the process, made possible the imagination of a self-governed nation. But nostalgia continued to flourish as both an aesthetic and cultural form *after* independence. A difficulty lay in letting go of a sentiment that had long governed cultural nationalism and politics in Ireland: the land, so long a potent symbol for nostalgia, was now technically disengaged from that which had driven its meaning. An Irish government was in place and the land recovered, but the habit of attitude towards land was so deeply entrenched that it would not be shifted. Nostalgic attitudes towards land continued to deepen and were encouraged, in fact, by the events of the Civil War and by the fact of the North's now separate existence: land was still a potent indexical sign, in Pierce's terms, of fraught political issues.

There were many other Irish writers besides Synge and Yeats, of course, who chose to remove themselves from the grip of these 'nostalgic slumbers' – quite literally in the case of the voluntary exiles Joyce and Beckett. Neither Joyce nor Beckett is known for literary representations of nature and landscape, and so it appears initially that an Irish literary preoccupation with nature and landscape loses its force in the modern and post-modern periods as the urban becomes increasingly significant, and as the notion of 'place' itself is changed by exile and the experience of the Second World War. While earlier authors up to and including Yeats concerned themselves most obviously with an exterior landscape,[3] both Joyce and Beckett turn to the mapping of an interior landscape but one that, crucially, corresponds to, and/or correlates with, the external contemporary landscape represented in their works. The supremacy of place within the Irish tradition is thus challenged by the presence of mind, and by relationships between mind and place that move far beyond tropic interactions like the pathetic fallacy. Nostalgia would appear to be equally changed in representation. From their positions of self-imposed exile – stereotypically associated with nostalgic attitudes towards a homeland – Joyce and Beckett both challenge Irish cultural traditions: Joyce by explicitly questioning nostalgia's influence on and control of culture, and Beckett implicitly by defying his audience to remember, to feel at home. Both thus force a re-evaluation of the praxis of Irish culture by critiquing the ideology that relied so heavily upon a memory of the past to determine the value of the present. Both Joyce and Beckett, then, might be described as engaging in a process – to adapt Fred Davis's terminology once again – of Interpretive Nostalgia.

JOYCE AND THE REFIGURING OF *DINDSHENCHAS*

Joyce's writing is, quite obviously, urban: he repeatedly concerns himself with the Ireland that is to be found in the city of Dublin. In his emphasis on urban space, Joyce represents an obvious point of departure within the Irish literary tradition that wrote so over-whelmingly of the rural. Len Platt has argued that in opposition to the Revival's 'evocations of a timeless idyllic rurality are Joyce's exces-sively time-specific fictions'.[4] So dominant does the 'time-specific' urban environment seem within both Joyce's texts and in Joycean criticism that it might well appear an absurd exercise to attempt to discuss Joyce's work within the conceptual frame of this study. While a good deal might be said (and indeed to an extent has already been said) about 'Joyce and place', 'Joyce and nature' would seem to be a stretch even by the standards of Joyce criticism, which is, as Fritz Senn reminds us, given to stretching things 'too far' in response to Joyce's invitation to do just that.[5] What I would suggest, however, is that as critics we have not often looked beyond the template of the 'urban Joyce'; and this template disallows us from seeing, in *Ulysses*, a rather consistent engagement with pastoral images that do in fact point somewhere: towards, as we will see, Gibraltar, Palestine – and even the Dublin suburbs. While Joyce does not present his reader with an idealized rural Ireland on which to gaze nostalgically, he does present us with characters whose own imaginations not infrequently dwell on projected pastoral dreams, and pastoral dreams that are quite preoccupied with space not only beyond the Pale of Dublin, but beyond Ireland, too. Joyce's refusal to idealize rural Ireland does indeed pit him against 'tradition' and the tenets of much Revivalist literature: if one wants to imagine pastoral perfection, his texts sardonically suggest, one must look beyond Ireland. As will become clear, however, Joyce, like both Yeats and Synge, employs pastoral imagery to a purpose and with an equally politicized subtext.

If Joyce's pastoral representations are complicated by his urban textual world and his commitment to a 'scrupulous'[6] representation of reality that refuses idealizations of the rural, Joyce's relationship to nostalgia is equally complex. For most of his writing career Joyce was 'out of Ireland', removed from the space of which he so relentlessly wrote. As a self-proclaimed exile who frequently wrote 'home' seeking information about events, people and places 'at home' that were sneaking their way into his work, Joyce relied largely upon memory to provide him with the stuff of past reality to turn into fiction. Joyce's actions reveal a form of homesickness in that, like many immigrants or exiles, he surrounded himself with reminders of his homeland – whether in the guise of newspapers or visitors such as Beckett, who, like others, was initially welcomed in large part because he was from Dublin – and wrote almost exclusively of that home he had determinedly left behind. And yet, despite these facts, Joyce is rarely perceived as a nostalgic figure in the way that other writers are. Proust's reliance on 'involuntary' memory (in Beckett's terms[7]) to provide him with the details of a past lost to everyday remembrance has popularized him as the literary personification of nostalgic immersion in the past, so that to be 'Proustian' is possible without ever lifting a pen. Joyce is not, of course, connected with this type of sentiment – even though his attention to details of the past is arguably more obsessive than Proust's, which tends to be evocative rather than particular. Neither is Joyce associated with the type of nostalgia popularly perceived to hover over all of Yeats's work, even though Joyce's representations of Dublin are undoubtedly more thorough and exact than Yeats's representations of, say, Sligo, or Innisfree or Coole Park and its woods. Despite engaging in what might be deemed nostalgic actions and textual practices, Joyce is not 'nostalgic' in the modern Proustian or even Yeatsian sense of that word.

The manifestation of Joyce's nostalgia and 'homesickness' is, in fact, supremely rare. His absence from Ireland leads not to the idealization of Dublin or Ireland, but to a recognition of the *actual* sense of 'home' sickness that beset Ireland in what have been called the 'semicolonial' years[8] before independence, when so many felt a distinctly *colonial* longing for a sense of national home. It is his very attention to the detail of this reality that disallows the possibility of the memory of Dublin becoming nostalgic: Joyce's memory is too good to forget his sufferings at the hands of aspiring bourgeois Dublin society, or his acute observations of how others too were affected by petty corruptions, gross betrayals and lapidary morals in the almost independent nation. Joyce does not rely solely on his own voluntary memories, or on involuntary memory, however; he also devotes a formidable effort (or convinces others to 'volunteer' that effort) to fact checking. Joyce's commitment was to a literature whose basis was truth:[9] such a commitment forbade even a selective description of the past, and did not like to leave much to chance. Joyce's physical removal from Dublin after 1904 meant that the Dublin he recorded was one that was already gone, already in the past: his writing was itself an act of nostalgic preservation, but Joyce would go far in pursuit of a detail that meant that his preservation was accurate and not the invention or longing of memory. Distance from 'home' allowed him to create his epic tribute to the city of Dublin 'dirty and dear',[10] just as Spenser's removal from London and Yeats's from Sligo sparked them to their own literary tasks of spatial, cultural and personal remembrance. Joyce, however, would refuse to allow distance to affect his vision of Dublin.

The process by which Joyce disrupts Irish pastoral stereotypes and the conception of nostalgia begins with *Dubliners*, which immediately proclaims distance from countless other titles coming out of Ireland during the period: *The Untilled Field, The Aran Islands, Kathleen ni Houlihan,* and *In the Seven Woods* all affirm Ireland's traditional, rural nature. Not only does *Dubliners* operate in opposition to rural titles: it is, in a sense, a refutation of the tradition that focuses on place, since 'Dublin' is made subsidiary to the people that inhabit it; and this overtaking of place by people is, after all, the fact of urbanity. One would never describe 'Innisfree' or the Aran Islands as being dominated by population: as many critics have noted, both the Picturesque and the pastoral rely on a decided absence of people, since a landscape is simply not 'picturesque' if teeming with tourists. Dublin, however, is its people, and Joyce refuses to present an urban pastoral like Wordsworth's 'Lines Composed Upon Westminster Bridge', when the city is viewed before the stir of morning: the reader will not be protected from the swell of population so integral to the notion of the city.

The text of *Dubliners* denies the encroachment of even the suburbs; the city's inhabitants rarely venture beyond its borders. Mr Duffy of 'A Painful Case', who fancies himself a man living beyond the Pale, has actually been absorbed into it; Dublin Corporation absorbed several suburbs in 1900, Drumcondra among them,[11] so that he has been unwittingly drawn into the (colonial, bourgeois) urban space. In a select few narratives, memories of spaces beyond Dublin intrude: Howth, in 'Eveline'; Galway, in 'The Dead', for example. In other narratives, ideas of exotic and foreign spaces interrupt the otherwise banal present tenses of these characters' lives: the Orient, in 'Araby';[12] Buenos Aires, in 'Eveline';[13] Belgium, France, England and Germany, in 'After the Race';[14] London and Paris, in 'A Little Cloud'; the Aran Islands and 'the continent', in 'The Dead'. Curiously, the vast majority of non-Dublin space in *Dubliners* is foreign: not only not rural, but not Irish – with the Aran Islands a rare and pointed exception, reflective of the Revival's interest in them as well as Joyce's satirical glance at the movement. Dublin seems encroached upon far more by European cities than by its own suburban and rural border-lands. This is a pattern that Joyce will replicate in *Ulysses*, refusing rural Ireland a significant existence in his work just as the Revival seemed to deny urban Dublin life.

Of the few exceptions within *Dubliners* – when intrusions into Dublin are not other urban spaces – only the Hill family picnic on Howth Head might be said to embody a rural – or even pastoral – ideal within Eveline's bank of bleak memories. But even here there is something rather sinister in the image of Eveline's father dressed in her 'mother's bonnet'[15] like a fairy tale wolf, given what we are told about his 'violence'.[16] And while Gretta clearly harbours fond memories of the west of Ireland – fond enough that her attitude develops throughout 'The Dead' to become one of nostalgic reminis-cence[17] – when the memories are eventually unmoored towards the close of the story, they are not ideal or 'pastoral' in any simple way. Gretta's description of Michael Furey in the graveyard, with its exag-gerated weather and an equal emotional pitch, recalls Macphersonesque invocations of Irish landscape and character; the scene embodies stereotypical 'Irish' characteristics absorbed by Irish writing by the time of the Revival, as we have already seen – wild nature, and people whose sentimental existence is mirrored by dripping branches and rolling fogs.

Gretta is depicted as 'homesick' and full of nostalgia for her home and her lost past; Gabriel is, in contrast, 'sick of [his] own country'.[18] If Gabriel is indeed 'sick of [his] own country', remaining distant from the society of the annual dance and hidden behind his spectacles, Gretta's description of the graveyard scene is a certain way to emphasize it. The implication is that Gabriel, in his very inability to experience potent emotion as Michael Furey was, is not 'really' Irish. He has been accused twice of being a 'West Briton';[19] he is not inter-ested in Gretta's west or the Aran Islands; Irish is 'not [his] language';[20] he has 'never felt like that himself towards any woman'.[21] Gabriel does not experience the stereotypical characteristics of an Irishman: he does not display an attachment to land or Irish place, and remains outwardly dispassionate despite an emotionally tumultuous evening. Joyce thus exposes and challenges a (colonial) stereotype of Irish character. Far from experiencing the longing for home associated with the English word 'nostalgic', Gabriel is 'nostalgic' only in a Joycean play on the root meanings of words: he is sick of his own country, sick at home. It is not until Gabriel begins to consider the prospect of sexual intimacy in the hotel that he might be described as feeling nostalgia in the more usual sense, as he begins to think back over his life with Gretta to reassure himself in a disturbed present.

When Joyce penned 'The Dead', Ireland was submerged in the idealizations of the rural from an urban perspective. This trend is represented in the story by Miss Ivors, who arranges an 'excursion to the Aran Isles'[22] and speaks Irish as she exits.[23] Miss Ivors is, however, one in a cast of many; she might feel bound to rural, 'real' Ireland, but she is in a sense summarily and literally dismissed by Joyce half-way through the unfolding drama. Gabriel, among Joyce's first unlikely heroes, is urban and without connection to the rural – or, indeed, to the nationalist. In the story we witness Gabriel attempting to perform an act of delicate balance between the urban and continental mindset that he preens in himself and the rural nature of his wife's background and memories. The effectual result of this balancing act is an existence in the suburbs, which seems to satisfy neither party: Gabriel is unresponsive to Gretta's passionate desire to visit the west again, and Gretta is subject to her nostalgia for her country past within the space of the city. There is a sense that Gretta does not belong in the city, the idea and structure of which is a cultural import into Ireland and the sign of the presence of various colonizers. Gabriel and Gretta's home is towards the edge of the Pale, beyond the borders of Dublin City (Monkstown being a fashionable suburb within easy range of Dublin), which allows Gabriel to partake of the urban atmosphere of Dublin while allowing them both the opportunity to remain at what would appear to be a slight remove from the colonizer's grasp of governance that is Dublin. Ultimately, however, Gretta's memories reveal a colonization by nostalgic, romanticized pastoral notions of Ireland and its landscape, while Gabriel's mind has been colonized by a different set of Romantic views that lead him to idealize Gretta and feel a nostalgia 'for their secret life together',[24] and which lead him to disregard his 'own land'[25] in favour of continental attitudes. What is curious about viewing the story in this light is that it reveals an instability in *both* Gabriel and Gretta; so standard is it to read Gabriel as the character subject to a variety of illusions that Gretta's own inclinations to romanticize have been eclipsed. And Gretta's romanticizations are intimately connected to the pastoral stereotypes that had been proliferating in Ireland in the years before Joyce departed from Dublin. Gabriel might be under illusions, but he at least among the many we encounter in 'The Dead' seems to reach a level of recognition about his life, which is, ultimately, lived under the spell of a colonizing government.

If to be in the Ireland – and, perhaps, particularly Dublin – of 1904 was to be pummelled with the idea of rural Ireland being real Ireland, the seat of some essentialist Irish spirit connected to land and nature in an intimate way, Joyce's collection of stories, and the final story in particular, forcefully challenges that conceit. Nowhere in *Dubliners* do we receive an idealized picture of Irish rural society. Joyce presents figures who struggle with solitude and labyrinthine selves in an urban setting, passing through the community without necessarily feeling an integral part of it. The ideal of the rural community lectured on and written about in pre-independence Dublin is at odds, Joyce's text says, with the reality of stultified, colonial Dublin experience.

Joyce's characters are increasingly concerned with the attempt to define themselves in this space of the city of Dublin. In *A Portrait,* Stephen exemplifies this concern when he makes his memorable inscription in a school book identifying himself in local and then universal space. The insularity of Irish experience and culture is immediately challenged; Stephen positions himself in a wider and wider space, moving swiftly beyond the sense of the local that governed the *dindshenchas* tradition. This sense of abstract, linguistic exploration of the space around him is paralleled in Stephen's actual experience of the world as a child: as he walks around the city and to its borders, he learns streets and areas previously unknown to him, incorporates them into his knowledge, and remaps space again. While this same childish exploration would have occurred in rural areas as well, Stephen is part of a new generation reared in Dublin, the literary product of the late-nineteenth-century influx of rural inhabitants into the capital. Stephen is thus unfamiliar with the natural world, which seems strange and removed from his experience, and, as a result, while during the summer he enjoys the spectacle of cows and nature,

> when autumn came the cows were driven home from the grass: and the first sight of the filthy cowherd at Stradbrook with its foul green puddles and clots of liquid dung and steaming brantroughs sickened Stephen's heart. The cattle which had seemed so beautiful in the country on sunny days revolted him and he could not even look at the milk they yielded.[26]

Stephen distinguishes sharply between the ideal of 'the country on sunny days' and the 'sicken[ing]' reality usually removed from traditional pastoral and many Revival representations. Along with Synge's characters, Stephen represents the push of the *reality* of rural experience into modern Irish literature, marking a return to a medieval

Irish pastoral tradition. Rather than merely celebrating the countryside for its beauties, Joyce allows Stephen, the child of a city, to view
it in all its guises; and in this Joyce is substantially different from
many of his predecessors and peers.

   This lack of illusion about nature and landscape is related to
Joyce's own experience. Unlike Yeats and Synge, Joyce did not spend
any amount of time at rural retreats like Coole Park or on the Aran
Islands or even, like Beckett, in the hills around Dublin. Joyce's most
'rural' experience, one suspects, was his time at Clongowes, which
certainly replicated the experience of the demesne's 'big house'; but if
descriptions of Stephen's days at Clongowes are in any way reflective of
Joyce's own experience, the countryside held little interest for Joyce.
Besides Clongowes and brief periods of living beyond the city limits (in
Bray, for example), Joyce's experience of the world was profoundly
urban; and this urbanity has become his hallmark. The lack of the
country retreat in Joyce's imagination is, of course, reflective of class
issues that have been much addressed in recent criticism;[27] Joyce was
both Catholic and middle-class compared to the class position occupied
by Protestant Ascendancy Revival figures, even if they were, like Yeats,
frequently poor. Stephen's disgust with the realities of rurality is also
Joyce's disgust with a culture that idealizes rurality at the expense of
progress and realism, and with a class system by which he himself is
marginalized as a middle-class Catholic.

   The culture that Joyce seeks to represent is that of the new urban
sensibility. Still, Declan Kiberd argues, rurality inevitably lurks in the
background as a determining factor in characters' visions of the world:
'Dublin was in 1904 a classic example of a periphery-dominated-centre
. . . a conurbation dominated by the values and mores of the surrounding countryside.'[28] A growing and colonial metropolis whose population was never at far remove from the country (and indeed at the
turn-of-the-nineteenth-century Dublin was quite literally consuming
suburban and rural areas), Dublin is represented by Joyce as lacking
sophistication, still reliant on the old ideas and ways of rural Ireland
that do not apply to urban life and contribute to the paralysis of
inaction that determines *Dubliners*. Stephen's difficulty, in both
Portrait and *Ulysses*, is attempting to find his way as an urban man
through a labyrinth of the city (and thus the self) that has been
determined not only by colonial values, but by 'traditional', 'pastoral'
Irish ones. Joyce recognizes the influence of pastoralism on the era,
and it frequently becomes a target for his sarcasm and disdain. Part
of this disdain is undoubtedly wrapped up in the fact that, unlike

Yeats, Synge or Lady Gregory, he did not consider the rural to be a representation of the real Ireland. Not only would this have excluded himself and many others from an Irish 'reality'; it also celebrated the very backwardness and Catholic parochialism that Joyce could not abide, while ignoring the role played by the Anglo-Irish Ascendancy in the colonizer's continuing governance.

As a writer in progress, Stephen demonstrates Joyce's exposure to the Revivalist mythos as well as to a wide range of English and continental writers for whom nature and landscape were significant: Stephen is frequently preoccupied with images of the natural world that summon words to his mind. His experience of the natural world is always mediated through language and his experience of literature, however; he meditates on poetry and romanticism and then, afterwards, considers the world:

> He drew forth a phrase from his treasure and spoke it softly to himself:
> – A day of dappled seaborne clouds.
>   The phrase and the scene harmonised in a chord. Words. Was it their colours? He allowed them to glow and fade, hue after hue: sunrise gold, the russet and green of apple orchards, azure of waves, the greyfringed fleece of clouds. No it was not their colours: it was the poise and balance of the period itself. Did he then love the rhythmic rise and fall of words better than their associations of legend and colour? Or was it that, being as weak of sight as he was shy of mind, he drew less pleasure from the reflection of the glowing sensible world through the prism of language manycoloured and richly storied than from the contemplation of an inner world of individual emotions mirrored perfectly in a lucid supple periodic prose?
>   He passed from the trembling bridge on to firm land again. At that instant, it seemed to him, the air was chilled and looking askance towards the water he saw a flying squall darkening and crisping suddenly the tide. A faint click at his heart, a faint throb in his throat told him once more of how his flesh dreaded the cold inhuman odour of the sea . . . [29]

This is, of course, Stephen's tribute to (and Joyce's sarcastic take on) Romanticism and Yeats, and his attempt to be a similarly 'romantic' writer within the space of the city. By the time we meet him in *Ulysses*, Stephen is entangled in 'melancholy, sullen hatred, spiritual violence, a Manganesque despair of soul',[30] characteristics all tied to stereotypes of the nostalgic Irishman. Despite these romantic leanings, however, Stephen returns to the reality of the images the words for which spark his reveries: he cannot look at the milk of the cows, and dreads the sea. Thus the phrase 'day of dappled seaborne clouds' is initially connected to the scene ('The phrase and scene harmonised in a chord') but that connection is linguistically forced, and so tenuous, as represented by Stephen's passing over a 'trembling bridge'. The reality of the 'firm land' – he has had his head in the clouds, day-dreaming – changes his outlook, inevitably. Stephen's attempts to get lost in language, to lose the world of Dublin in his poetic dreams, always result in a stark realization of his 'fallen' state:

> Consciousness of place came ebbing back to him slowly over a vast tract of time unlit, unfelt, unlived. The squalid scene composed itself around him; the common accents, the burning gasjets in the shops, odours of fish and spirits and wet sawdust, moving men and women.[31]

The poetic dream of pastoral perfection is 'unlived', and Stephen cannot escape this fact; Joyce will not allow him to idealize, amidst the cityscape of Dublin, something that he does not know. Joyce thus makes it impossible for Stephen to experience a Revivalist nostalgia for the natural world, always checking the tendency with a strong realism; Joyce implies that nostalgia is the realm of the young writer, thus commenting upon the literary activities of the Revivalists as somehow immature and undeveloped. If Stephen experiments with the use of romantic language, that language rapidly gives way by the end of the novel, when his vow to 'fly by those nets' is implicitly accompanied by another to relinquish anything but a realistic language that accurately describes experience.

If Joyce does not allow Stephen to indulge too often in romanticisms and idealizations of the rural so common amongst his contemporaries, he does, nonetheless, engage other aspects of Irish literary traditions:[32] among many other things, *Ulysses* is an inheritance of the commitment of place to the page. This celebration of place takes the *dindshenchas* tradition of medieval Irish literature to its modern extreme, overlaid on the contemporary city instead of the general landscape of Ireland. This tradition had, as we have seen, been 'revived' in the literature of Yeats and Synge (amongst others), but rurality had been the focus for the majority of their celebrations of Irish place.[33] In memorializing 1904 Dublin, Joyce not only displaces the rurality of *dindshenchas* and the Revival's version of the tradition; he is also exercising a form of mental nostalgia, writing as he is from the space of exile and memory. Parallels to the Odyssey add to Joyce's concern with *nostos*, with homesickness, and the attempt to return home. Nostalgia makes its presence felt in the themes of the novel, as well, through Bloom. Bloom's preoccupation with the exotic Orient is also a concern with orientation, with his ability to locate himself in space, to make it familiar, and, in the process, to return to the known space of his home with Molly. Bloom's preoccupation with the world of Palestine, his unvisited 'homeland', signals a further nostalgia, this time for a life that he has never lived. Bloom's nostalgia for this unseen world, an Eden of the mind, and for his past life with Molly – also significantly connected with images of the natural world as a feminine space – allows him to continue to function in a present day that is dislocated and disturbing. In this, the intersection of nature and nostalgia in Bloom's mind functions as the preservative that it has been for many earlier Irish authors and characters.

The template of place established in *Dubliners* holds in *Ulysses*, but becomes much more complex. We begin towards the limits of the Pale and gradually move towards Dublin, where we then remain – with a few excursions back out of the city – for the duration of the novel. As in *Dubliners*, in *Ulysses* an Ireland beyond Dublin is referred to only infrequently. We do receive some sense of Dublin suburbs such as Sandycove (*U* 1.342);[34] Dundrum (*U* 1.366); Dalkey (*U* 1.576); Kingstown (Dun Laoghaire) (*U* 2.38); Ballsbridge (*U* 4.753); Finglas (*U* 6.862); Howth (*U* 8.900; 13.1178; 16.558; 18.371); and Sandymount (*U* 8.1045–6), for example, and of course we encounter several of these places not only by name, but with Bloom or Stephen during their day.

Of Irish place beyond Dublin and its suburbs, there is very little:[35] over half of the mention of placenames outside of Dublin seem to belong to the narrative of 'Cyclops', the episode which satirizes the Irish nationalist movement – and, very obviously, its celebration of rural Irish place. Despite occupying only just over six per cent of the total line count of the novel, 'Penelope' contains over ten per cent of *Ulysses*' references to Irish place beyond Dublin city centre. And Molly certainly considers Ireland more in the course of her comparatively brief monologue than Stephen or Bloom do. This might suggest several things: first, it consolidates the general (and often noted) sense of Molly's association with 'nature', land and fecundity. These associations have been read as confirmation of her role as stereotypical 'earth mother', the feminine landscape whose body bears fruit. The Irish (and, indeed, foreign) places of which Molly thinks, however, are resolutely non-rural: her mind skips over either places she has been, or places to which she and Blazes Boylan might bring a concert tour. Despite the fact of her foreign birth, Molly's relative preoccupation with Irish place also suggests that she is somehow 'more Irish' than Bloom or Stephen – both of whom lack a particular place in the society, and both of whom thus fittingly think little of Irish place. Only places of immediate personal importance enter Bloom's mind; there are, in fact, particular places which reference important people: Ennis his father; Mullingar, Milly; Howth, Molly. Stephen thinks only of Irish places through which he passes, in general preoccupied with more distant lands like Paris.

As in *Dubliners*, Joyce in *Ulysses* thus presents an urban space that is – except in the mind of the Citizen – almost islandized, unconnected to the rural or the provincial. What results is not 'a miniature cameo of the world we live in' (*U* 16.1225), but a distinctive representation of the way that the *mind* perceives geography. Joyce represents place as it exists in the imagination, the unknown looming small unless personally, emotionally connected to us. Place in mind and place in actual, cartographic or spatial geography are out of all proportion. Mullingar is of particular significance to Bloom because Milly is there; Paris looms large for Stephen because it had seemed his means of escape. But both Mullingar and Paris – despite their own very obvious differences in size, international cultural significance, et cetera – are of lesser importance than Dublin, which is largest in both Stephen and Bloom's mental 'maps', simply because of their presence in it.

We might not make much of the lack of Irish placenames in *Ulysses*: the novel is, after all, set in Dublin city centre, and does not aim to take the reader on a tour of all Ireland. Extraordinarily, though, places *beyond* Ireland's borders are present to a large degree in the text. So much so, in fact, that a reader altogether ignorant of geography might be excused for thinking Dublin very near indeed to Gibraltar, Egypt, Palestine and Paris, the four of which figure most prominently of all places beyond Dublin in the novel,[36] which is worthwhile considering more closely.

As a presence in the novel, Paris represents Stephen's desires to flee Ireland for a permanent continental (and more enlightened and non-colonial) existence as an artist; Paris thus comes to signify a type of freedom not to be found in 1904 British-controlled Dublin. If Paris would seem to be the obvious sign of cultural, artistic sophistication, freedom and even ribaldry, Gibraltar, Egypt and Palestine are not so easily deciphered. All three places certainly index a Joycean concern – traceable to *Dubliners* – with orientalism and exoticism that has been well documented. They also represent, of course, a concern with origins: Molly's birth in Gibraltar, and Bloom's Jewish ancestry in Palestine and Egypt. Beyond these factors, however, is a curious commonality. In 1904, Gibraltar was, like Ireland, a British colony; having been captured in the early-eighteenth century, it formally became part of the British Empire in 1830 (and remains a protectorate today). Egypt had been under British rule since 1882, the year of Joyce's birth, and would not become independent until after the Irish Civil War, by which time the 'Egypt for the Egyptians' movement had succeeded in forcing Britain's hand. Palestine was not yet under British control in 1904 when *Ulysses* takes place, but by then the first Zionist Congress had been held, and the programme to create a Jewish national homeland had begun; and by the time Joyce was working on his novel and reading about the programme,[37] Britain's involvement in Palestinian affairs had become clear. Indeed, by 1920, three years after the Balfour Declaration, Palestine's governance came under a British mandate. A strange cycle of colonialism is thus set up in the novel, with Stephen, the future artist, the only one to think beyond the geographical boundaries of British colonialism.

The British colony of Gibraltar is the site of Molly's birth to an Irishman who serves in the British Army and so is a colonial servant; her subsequent 'return' to Ireland, another British colony, ties her to both the role of governor (which she seems to adopt in the Eccles Street household) and that of the colonized. Susan Bazargan notes that

> besides being an imperial crossroads, Gibraltar, occupied by the British, in population African, Spanish, Jewish, Moroccan, Maltese, and Genoese, presents the modern-day colonial situation in which the categories of colonizer and the colonized are splintered to reveal multiple layers of subcolonization, conflicting interests among oppositional groups of various nationalities, which are separated not only by class and economic distinctions but also by race and religion.[38]

With inseparable Spanish, Jewish and Irish connections, Molly herself comes to represent these 'layers'. Her attitude towards Gibraltar is similarly layered; she vacillates between an indulgent nostalgia (in her remembrances of Mulvey and the Moorish Wall), a recollection of her irritation with British militarism in Gibraltar,[39] and a sense of Gibraltar as a space of the eclipsed past (evident, for example, in the sparing detail about her mother and in her forgetting of Spanish[40]). Gibraltar thus comes to have a much broader signification in the text than places in texts from the Revival: not simply idealized or demonized, it reflects historical and cultural developments within the

British Empire, and the processes through which memory itself is colonized. Since Molly's monologue is defined by her ability to remember and so her ability to integrate memories of different places, it is unsurprising that, at the novel's close, she attempts a 'fusion of presence and absence, of Gibraltar and Dublin, of the Moorish Wall and Howth Hill'.[41] The hybrid identity forced upon Molly is one that her mind re-enforces through a melding process.

Bloom does not reconcile his identity as easily. The grandson of an immigrant (presumably fleeing persecution), Bloom now lives in a British colony where he is persecuted for his Jewishness; in response he dreams of a 'return' to a 'homeland' – not the birth land of his grandfather but a homeland in the process of being created: and by Bloom's own definition Jewish settlement in Palestine at the turn of the twentieth century constituted a nation. He begins his consideration of Palestine by reading the ad[42] for a 'model farm' that could 'become ideal winter sanitorium' (*U* 4.154–6); he then considers the 'dead sea in a dead land, grey and old' (*U* 4.223). This shows Bloom's savviness: as an ad man himself, he is not susceptible to all that he reads. 'Nothing doing' (*U* 4.200), he thinks; and then, the ad man's mind stirred, 'Still, an idea behind it' (*U* 4.200). Bloom's idealizations of Palestine are thoughts of a promised land, and Molly is implicated in this procession of thoughts: she too is a sort of promised land to which Bloom might return. Ireland was often represented by Joyce's contemporaries as 'woman', and Joyce plays with this representation here, making Molly into a figure of both Ireland and Israel.[43] Throughout the day, Bloom returns to images of pastoral perfection in the guise of Palestine, but, while allowing himself this indulgence, also questions the reality of such images:

> Lovely spot it must be: the garden of the world, big lazy leaves to float about on, cactuses, flowery meads, snaky lianas they call them. Wonder is it like that. Those Cinghalese lobbing about in the sun in *dolce far niente*, not doing a hand's turn all day. Sleep six months out of twelve. Too hot to quarrel. Influence of the climate. Lethargy. Flowers of idleness. (*U* 5.29–34)

Martha follows up his thoughts by sending him a little piece of a pastoral in the guise of a 'yellow flower with flattened petals' (*U* 5.239). Bloom's next significant return to thoughts of the Palestinian plantations comes in 'Lestrygonians' when, worried that a nearby Boylan will see him, occupies himself with the ad: 'took out, unfolded Agendath Netaim' (*U* 8.1183–4). This being Joyce, it is surely no accident that Bloom's hand finds the advertisement for an escapist pastoral dream when he is confronted with the sight of his wife's lover who is so blatantly challenging his personal sense of place. Despite the ad's appearance at such a key moment, when in 'Circe' Bloom is shown slides of the plantations, we are informed that 'The *image* of the lake of Kinnereth with *blurred* cattle cropping in *silver haze* is *projected* on the wall' (*U* 15.986–7, my emphasis). Joyce and Bloom display a keen awareness here of the act of 'projecting' pastoral ideals. At day's end, Bloom burns the ad he has kept carefully, and which has drifted in and out of his consciousness for some sixteen hours. He

> produced from his waistcoat a folded page of prospectus (illustrated) entitled Agendath Netaim, unfolded the same, examined it super-ficially, rolled it into a thin cylinder, ignited it in the candleflame, applied it when ignited to the apex of the cone till the latter reached the stage of rutilance, placed the cylinder in the basin of the candlestick disposing it unconsumed part in such a manner as to facilitate total combustion. (*U* 17.1324–9)

Bloom's idealizations of and nostalgia for Palestine have quite literally burned themselves out.

Bloom's sense of marginalization in Ireland, and his subjection to anti-Semitic ideas aimed at him by a people themselves subjected and colonized, contributed to his early in the day thoughts of an idealized pastoral life in Palestine. The prose that Joyce penned to suit these idealizations is classically pastoral: Palestine, Israel and the holy land are beautiful and also bountiful, prosperous, fertile. The pastoral language is consistently undermined, however; Bloom realizes that the settlement might become something productive and lush, but that in the present it is a wasteland.[44] Despite his almost sentimental musings about Palestine and its lush, Edenic climate that might produce melons and exotic fruit, Bloom does not seriously consider the possibility of moving or even investing in the plantation scheme; the sentimental dream of pastoral perfection is a private one that remains in the realm of Bloom's mind and is not acted out in the present as it was for Yeats's characters or for Synge. Bloom himself recognizes that his consideration of the plantation scheme has been 'superficial'; he abandons and 'disposes' of the idea with no display of sentimental loss.

What Bloom would really like, we learn in 'Ithaca', is not a 'return' to pastoral Palestine, but a *suburban* existence: 'a thatched bungalow-shaped 2 storey dwellinghouse of southerly aspect' (*U* 17.1504–5), 'not less than 1 statute mile from the periphery, of the metropolis, within a time limit of not more than 15 minutes from tram or train line' (*U* 17.1514–16), and outfitted with all manner of modern conveniences. The consideration of the perfect suburban existence at 'Bloom Cottage. Saint Leopold's. Flowerville' (*U* 17.1580) seems to be recurring; the narrative supplies such details of the property, its furnishings and gadgets that this is clearly not Bloom's first time to dream it up; this fantasy is of far greater significance to him than the thought of buying land in Palestine. The dream of his 'country residence' (*U* 17.1657) remains, of course, a dream; it is a far off and imagined prospect only. The explanation for this suburban dream that fuses pastoral and urban existences is provided by Bloom himself: we are told that he 'meditate[s] on schemes so difficult of realisation' (*U* 17.1754) because:

> It was one of his axioms that similar meditations or the automatic relation to himself of a narrative concerning himself or tranquil recollection of the past when practised habitually before retiring for the night alleviated fatigue and produced as a result sound repose and renovated vitality. (*U* 17.1755–8)

Bloom, in other words, allows himself dreams and projections since they help him to sleep well and peacefully: he submerges in a Romantic nostalgia – 'tranquil recollection of the past' – because it is comforting, and 'renovate[s] vitality'. Bloom's awareness of the benefits of nostalgia, immersion in 'tranquil recollection' or in dreaming of his ideal existence '*Rus in Urbe*' (*U* 17.1503) is, in one sense, quite startling, since it is marked by an equal awareness of the limits of these benefits. Bloom might spend some of his pre-sleep time concocting fantasies of a future life, but during the day he does not allow such dreams to interfere with his realistic vision of the world. Bloom is thus a savvy employer of nostalgia or comforting memory for his own purposes, but is not subject to these things as, it would seem, so many of his real life contemporaries were. Indeed, even Bloom's suburban dreams seem eminently practical, preoccupied as they are with the price of such an estate and its associated costs. Estates like the one that Bloom imagines himself owning were, of course, in 1904, largely part of an Ascendancy lifestyle. Andrew Gibson notes that

> It is only such a lifestyle, after all – the lifestyle of a gentry with English connections . . . – that could ever provide one with a 'botanical conservatory' or a glass summerhouse 'equipped in the best botanical

manner' (i.e. from the colonies . . .), or the luxury and freedom for proper 'contemplation of the celestial constellations'.[45]

Bloom thus moves away from the pastoral fantasy of life in a Palestinian settlement; the far more 'practical' fantasy is the one that he would have witnessed for himself in 1904 Dublin. Rather than focusing on the relentlessly rural idyll, Joyce turns our attention to that which was so often elided from Revival fantasy: the Anglo-Irish demesne house such as Coole Park. Even after Yeats's purchase of the tower at Ballylee, he did not turn down offers for a stay in the 'big house', preferring its marvels of comfort to the often flooded tower. Bloom, in other words, wants what Yeats, Lady Gregory and Synge have, but pointedly do not write of, and he wants it as near to the metropolis as possible. Bloom thus becomes an early spokesperson for the benefits of suburban living as offering the best of both worlds.

Through his employment and subsequent deconstruction of pastoral ideals, Joyce comments upon the inheritance of Irish literature, and particularly upon the movement of the Revival that saw such emphasis placed upon rural Ireland, its peasantry and the exoticism associated with 'primitive' cultures believed to be close to nature. Far from engaging nostalgia for lost culture as many of his near contemporaries were doing, Joyce offered instead a critique of that nostalgia by turning away from the country towards the city, which, he saw, had determined the romanticism with which the countryside was viewed. In creating his urban Irish world, Joyce offered what was the closest Irish literature had come to a map of contemporary Ireland: the geography of mind that Joyce invented is also a geography of space,[46] and particularly of Dublin. Within this cityscape, Joyce also offered his take on the pastoral ideal, slimming it down to a modern size – a specific plot of gated and walled land to replace endlessly rolling hills – and planting it near enough to the city to be accessed by public transportation. Instead of the idyll of Innisfree or the Aran Islands, Joyce settles on an idyll left out of other Irish accounts of pastoralism, that of the suburb.

BECKETT

Despite his internationalism and his life on the continent, Joyce has been easily claimed by critics as a quintessentially Irish author due to his settings and subject matter. To make the same claim for Beckett has proven more difficult, as the mature Beckett's work rarely offers

anything so obvious as a solid geography, Irish or otherwise, oper-
ating in defiance of the Irish tradition that grants nature and place a
significant role. Beckett's work does not offer the reader or theatre-
goer the deceptively simple beauty of medieval Irish nature poetry,
none of the magnificent artifice of Spenser, no Syngian celebrations of
wild Connemara winds, not even a Joycean dream language to
ascribe a surreal, seductive voice to the land and sea. Beckett seems
to exist beyond the bounds of Irish literary tradition.

However, while Beckett clearly operates outside of the stereotypical
traditions of Irish and English nature writing, he does engage with the
Irish tradition in which nature is the site of nostalgia. Vladimir and
Estragon exist symbiotically in *Waiting for Godot*; so nature and the
intersection of memory and time function symbiotically in Beckett's
major plays. In the present tense of the plays there is rarely a sense of
any external, physical world; memories of nature and place frequently
come to signify a past existence better than the present. The natural
world evoked by Beckett frequently functions as a bank of memories of
an imagined time before the plays begin. Read this way, Beckett's plays
are an interesting depiction of an Irish pastoral mode: there is a tendency
to think of the past in idealized terms, and yet the present tense of the
characters' existence undercuts not only the reality of these fleeting
memories of a better life, but the reality of the present as well.

Beckett's simultaneous engagement with and undercutting of a
pastoral mode should not come as a surprise, in one sense: he consistently engages with dialectical tensions – between hope and despair,
ceasing and going on, birth and death. The tensions between
philosophical extremes drive much of Beckett's dramatic and fictional
material. While there has been a decided tendency within Beckett
studies to treat his texts as philosophical treatises independent of
material, cultural and historical developments, this tendency is
gradually being challenged. What I would suggest is that Beckett's
engagement with the theme of nostalgia as connected to nature reflects
not only his well known experiences during the Second World War; it
also reflects a personal attachment to place that dictated much of his
own childhood existence. More importantly, however, it indicates
another major shift for Irish literature, in that Beckett's work, in its
near denial of place, nature and memory, speaks volumes of the new
Irish state and its rural, Catholic and essentially nostalgic propaganda.
Beckett is decidedly removed from the new state and its ideology, in
part because of his class and religious background, but also because
of his – like Joyce's – determined devotion to an international

literature. While Beckett displayed a personal affection and even nostalgia for his childhood haunts in the Wicklow and Dublin mountains, his world view forbade idealization; all around him was a world so far from ideal that it would be sheer folly to insist on the illusion of a pastoral existence, Irish or otherwise. Beckett thus offers a commentary on the past and present states of Ireland; in his very removal, and in Ireland's relative absence from his work, Beckett critiques threatening atmospheres of colonialism and its dictatorships, and also the insular, self-reflective, self-specific and censored literature encouraged by the young Irish state.

Rather than an idealization of the natural world and man's place in that world, Beckett's plays offer a nightmarish vision of a world in which nature is all but absent. A dated but nonetheless interesting book on pastoral drama describes the pastoral's aspiration to

> a fundamental idealism which led men to envelop [man and nature] in a certain opalescent, unreal atmosphere. A large part of mankind is usually engaged in longing not so much for a better life but for an easier life, in which 'nothing to do' makes the dream more golden.[47]

One could very well substitute 'pessimism' for 'idealism', 'nightmare' for 'dream', and have an apt description of the world of Beckett's plays. Besides the extreme lack of activity, there is a nostalgia for the past, for some idyll that haunts the characters by its absence. When anything of the natural world is present in the plays – a tree, the memory of a lake or mountains – the characters are reminded of their despair, lamenting not only the loss of that world but their memory of it.

One of Beckett's signatures is the ability to draw out the time of a play's performance into what is a torturous experience of an eternally lived present. In an eternal present, the past – whether immediate or distant – is questionable, memory is questionable, and consequently reality itself an uncertainty. *Godot's* tree is the focal point of this theme, setting in motion the question of reality and the possibility of knowing reality. By tracing the revolution of the play about the tree, a 'sign of life', it is possible to trace the links between nature and nostalgia in Beckett.

At various times, Beckett referred friends and critics to the German Romantic painter Caspar David Friedrich's 'Mann und Frau den Mond betrachtend' and 'Zwei Männer betrachten den Mond' as the inspiration for *Godot*. The paintings, of silhouetted figures near a solitary tree gazing at the moon are, as James Knowlson notes, mimicked at the close of both acts.[48] Symbolic landscape thus serves as a starting point from which to approach the play. Among other possible inspirations for the play are Synge's wanderers. If the set and the two tramps have roots in Friedrich and Synge – both very obviously concerned with landscape and its effect on dramatic atmosphere – it is clear that the play's mood was born of the Second World War. While Beckett's work has long had the reputation for being anti-autobiographical, *Godot* draws fundamentally upon his experience of the Second World War, as do later plays. So thoroughly imbued with events of the war is Beckett's dramatic corpus, in fact, that Hugh Kenner identifies a 'Gestapo theme' that leads from one play to the next.[49] Work in the French Resistance and bearing witness to the arrest of friends (while barely avoiding arrest himself) influenced Beckett deeply: horror of war and at people's fates inform this play from the first.

The play begins with a description of landscape: 'A country road. A tree. Evening'. As the spot where Godot is supposed to appear, this tree – bare in the first act – is vital to the play:

> Estragon: [Despairingly.] Ah! [Pause.] You're sure it was here?
> Vladimir: What?
> Estragon: That we were to wait.
> Vladimir: He said by the tree. [They look at the tree.] Do you see any others?
> Estragon: What is it?
> Vladimir: I don't know. A willow.
> Estragon: Where are the leaves?
> Vladimir: It must be dead.
> Estragon: No more weeping.
> Vladimir. Or perhaps it's not the season.
> Estragon: Looks to me more like a bush.
> Vladimir: A shrub.
> Estragon: A bush.
> Vladimir: A – . What are you insinuating? That we've come to the wrong place?[50]

Their recognition of the tree is tentative. Vladimir wants Estragon to confirm that they are there at the tree and that they will later on remember this fact; 'he must', as one critic has put it, 'confirm this present tense by reference to an anticipated retrospect'.[51] Vladimir will repeatedly re-enact this role, attempting to move beyond the present to a moment in which he can know the past and predict or plan for the future: an impossibility within the world of the play. In this uncertainty, both characters' anxiety over the long-awaited meeting surfaces. What if it is the wrong tree? What if it isn't a tree at all? There is no certainty, no assurance that the natural world and humankind exist, because there is no possibility, without memory, for the certainty that comes with retrospect. The tree, then, becomes the sign of the longing for memory. In this, Beckett employs a trope – the tree of life – to signal not a nostalgic or pastoral longing for the past, but instead the futility of that longing. The characters inevitably return to the tree as a topic of conversation – discussing in turn its significance as the potential meeting place, the possibility of hanging themselves from its branches, or hiding behind its too thin trunk – but the possibility of creating an idealization out of its presence is gone. Landscape has been whittled away to a state of meaninglessness, and the tree remains to haunt the characters as a symbol of the hope for the very possibility of memory.

Following this first encounter with the tree, Didi and Gogo's anxiety extends from doubting the tree to doubting that they have gotten the date for their appointment right. Vladimir's anxiety is expressed in the stage directions when he looks 'wildly about him, as though the date was inscribed in the landscape'.[52] The irony here is that the date and time are inscribed in the landscape, which reflects the war – and, indeed, the post-war – era, hopelessly barren, hopelessly uncertain. The two realize that they must attempt to forget this uncertainty and thus attempt to make conversation to ward off the silence. In the search for something to do they focus on the tree, no longer significant because it is the site of the future meeting but because it suggests the idea of suicide. The tree of life, in its lifelessness, suggests death. This idea is even more appealing because they have heard that hanging men experience arousal; thus the idea of death rouses the life in them. Having realized, however, that the tree's branch will not support the dead weight of desperate men, the tree is useless to them. The fear of remaining alone in a world that offers only one tree as hope and the meanest of vegetables as sustenance is horrifying for both men. 'Don't let's do anything', Estragon concludes, 'It's safer.'[53]

Towards the end of Act I, after Lucky and Pozzo's departure, Gogo forgets the earlier conclusion that the bough would break and leave one of them to fend for himself: looking at the tree, he remarks, 'Pity we haven't got a bit of rope . . . Remind me to bring a bit of rope tomorrow.'[54] In his despair, Gogo forgets, hopes; this function of memory abounds in the play. It is necessary to forget in order to survive; otherwise one is in danger of realizing the hopelessness of

eternal waiting. Didi, however, does not forget as easily as does Gogo.
In Act II the differences in their memories become further apparent
when they examine the tree for what we presume is the second day in
a row.

> Vladimir: Look at the tree.
> Estragon: It's never the same pus from one second to the next.
> Vladimir: The tree, look at the tree.
> [Estragon looks at the tree.]
> Estragon: Was it not there yesterday?
> Vladimir: Yes, of course it was there. Do you not remember? We
> nearly hanged ourselves from it. But you wouldn't. Do you
> not remember?[55]

Memory, of the kind that would allow Estragon to recall recent
events, does not exist. Vladimir, with his seeming ability to remember
the day before, is tortured by doubt as to whether his memories are
real or not. He pushes Estragon to remember, for an admission that
he does indeed recognize the place.

> Estragon: [Suddenly furious.] Recognize! What is there to recognize?
> All my lousy life I've crawled about in the mud! And you
> talk to me about scenery! [Looking wildly about him.] Look
> at this muckheap! I've never stirred from it!
> Vladimir: Calm yourself, calm yourself.
> Estragon: You and your landscapes! Tell me about the worms!
> Vladimir: All the same, you can't tell me that this [Gesture] bears any
> resemblance to . . . [He hesitates] . . . to the Macon country,
> for example. You can't deny there's a big difference.
> Estragon: The Macon country! Who's talking to you about the Macon
> country?
> Vladimir: But you were there yourself, in the Macon country.
> Estragon: No, I was never in the Macon country. I've puked my puke
> of a life away here, I tell you! Here! In the Cackon country!
> Vladimir: But we were there together, I could swear it! Picking grapes for
> a man called . . . [He snaps his fingers] . . . can't think of the
> name of the man, at a place called . . . [Snaps his fingers] . . .
> can't think of the name of the place, do you not remember?[56]

Vladimir struggles to remember vague events: picking grapes, the
landscape of a different life, his clothes drying in the sun. In his
forgetting, Estragon seems happier than Vladimir, who goes through
contortions to prove to himself that his memories of humanity are

indeed real and, by extension, that he exists. Where the medieval Irish tradition recorded the history of placenames to ward off the oblivion of generational forgetting, Vladimir is unable to remember even places where he himself has been. Without any validation – even self-validation – the past simply fades, so that there is no sense of the collectivity of an activity like *dindshenchas*, since even personal experience goes unremembered. The erasure or impairment of individual memory through traumas like war, imprisonment or life under a brutal regime has, of course, massive implications for cultural memory. All five of the characters of *Godot*, even the small boy whose answer so infuriates Didi at the end of the play, display degrees of memory loss. If the characters are taken as a microcosm of culture, the signs are clear: cultural memory is disappearing, being erased through trauma. For one witness to the wars in Europe in the 1940s, and who had seen in his lifetime the violent formation of his home nation, such cultural disappearances, such cultural silences, would have been easy to recognize. To forget, to allow one's self the seeming liberty of oblivion, was to allow oneself to carry on. This is the other extreme of the pastoral, political nostalgia that Beckett witnessed in Ireland (and, indeed, in pre-war Germany): instead of a reverence for the past that elides the possibility of that which is not 'traditional', the world of *Godot* offers the opposite phenomenon, when cultural memory is so overwhelmed by trauma as to itself become elided.

No matter how irritated Didi and Gogo become with one another, however, they are in fact 'incapable of keeping silent'.[57] In silence are 'all the dead voices'[58] that taunt them with memories of a time and place when life was not so barren or hopeless.

> Vladimir: They make a noise like wings.
> Estragon: Like leaves.
> Vladimir: Like sand.
> Estragon: Like leaves.
> [Silence.]
> Vladimir: They all speak together.
> Estragon: Each one to itself.
> [Silence.][59]

The music of this language is emphasized by the silences, the pauses before the return to the recitative. The dead voices, which are memory, speak through nature, and are like nature. Sand slipping through a sieve of fingers and leaves scattering on a wind are both metaphors for time, and the dead voices that are so vigilantly avoided speak of time's passage, a passage that neither can quite fathom any longer. Didi and Gogo battle to slay silence in order to avoid hearing the voices of time past, but they battle silence with an invocation of the voices themselves. When they lose themselves in this process and forget what it was that sparked the conversation, they return to the tree, the staged symbol of time and nature.

> Vladimir: Wait . . . we embraced . . . we were happy . . . happy . . . what
>   do we do now that we're happy . . . go on waiting . . . waiting
>   . . . let me think . . . it's coming . . . go on waiting . . . now that
>   we're happy . . . let me see . . . ah! The tree!
> Estragon: The tree?
> Vladimir: Do you not remember?
> Estragon: I'm tired.
> Vladimir: Look at it.
>   [They look at the tree.]
> Estragon: I see nothing.
> Vladimir: But yesterday evening it was all black and bare. And now it's
>   covered with leaves.
> Estragon: Leaves?
> Vladimir: In a single night.
> Estragon: It must be spring.
> Vladimir: But in a single night!
> Estragon: I tell you we weren't here yesterday. Another of your night-
>   mares.[60]

The dynamic of memory here is poignant: Vladimir, struggling to validate some reality – that they were indeed here yesterday, and the day before, and an eternal number of days before that – bows to Estragon's forgetfulness that allows them both to live. Vladimir gives up an attempt to convince his companion that they were in the same place on the previous day, and lapses into wonder at the state of the tree, and, undoubtedly, at the state of his own memory. The tree haunts the play as the dead voices haunt Didi and Gogo's memories.

Vladimir, while realizing the tree is a sign of some sort of life in the barren landscape, does not allow it to have any meaning. When they grow frightened at the approach of Pozzo and Lucky in the second act, Estragon tries to hide behind the tree and realizes he is unhidden. 'Decidedly this tree will not have been of the slightest use to us', Vladimir remarks.[61] Nonetheless it is the tree that brings the play to a close.

> Vladimir: . . . Everything's dead but the tree.
> Estragon: [Looking at the tree.] What is it?

Vladimir: It's the tree.
Estragon: Yes, but what kind?
Vladimir: I don't know. A willow.
[Estragon draws Vladimir towards the tree. They stand motionless before it.]
Estragon: Why don't we hang ourselves?
Vladimir: With what?
Estragon: You haven't got a bit of rope?
Vladimir: No.
Estragon: Then we can't.
[Silence.]
Vladimir: Let's go.
Estragon: Wait, there's my belt.
Vladimir: It's too short.
Estragon: You could hang on to my legs.
Vladimir: And who'd hang on to mine?
Estragon: True.[62]

Estragon has forgotten all of their encounters with the tree; Vladimir seems to remember, although his language suggests that he is masking this remembrance, just as he did at the start of the play: 'I don't know. A willow.' His memory does not serve him with answers useful in any way, and so the tree is not, at the end, of the slightest use to them – practically. As a symbol, however, the tree plays an obvious role: despite everything, despite the nothingness of their existence, it has life, and heralds a spring of its own, persevering. Didi and Gogo, in their own meaningless perseverance, resemble the tree. Ultimately Beckett moves the tree beyond trope; this is not a tree symbolic of hope and a new era. The tree, changing and growing in the most unyielding of earth, somehow survives, despite its circumstance, but for no good reason at all, just as St Augustine's thieves are saved or damned for no reason. Just as Didi and Gogo cannot think of any good reason to give up their wait for the eternally tardy Godot, and so continue their banter in order to pass the time, so the tree continues to live, to shed and grow leaves, and, undoubtedly, to weep.

If nature has been shattered and has lost its place of privilege in the world of *Godot*, in *Endgame* it has all but disappeared. As in *Godot*, the presence of any natural elements is linked to time and memory: memories of a world before the unnamed and unknown event that has levelled the world into 'zero'[63] consistently invoke natural landscapes, which serve as a constant reminder of time's dictatorship, even more forcefully present than in *Godot*. In *Godot*, with its open set and stark, bare landscape, it is clear that there is more than 'world enough', as Andrew Marvell put it, as far as the characters are concerned. The opposite is true of *Endgame*, whose (in)action confines itself to a claustrophobic room with two small windows, sparking some early interpretations of the play as taking place within a skull, a drama of the interior mind. But the time that weighs so heavily on Didi and Gogo's hands weighs even more heavily in *Endgame*; the characters have far more time than they would ever wish to have. This overabundance of time has replaced the natural world, which has been reduced to greyness.

A picture remains hanging on the wall but is reversed so that the painting itself is invisible, and is eventually replaced with the alarm clock; the onslaught of time has replaced the possibility of viewing landscapes so that 'nature' becomes 'time'. Blind Hamm relies on Clov to interpret the visual world for him; his memories of the natural world differ sharply from the reports that Clov offers of the greyness of earth and sea. A good deal of the conversation between Hamm and Clov involves such fleeting images of what the stage directions refer to as the 'without'. Trapped inside what seems to be a fallout shelter, Clov informs Hamm of what he sees through the windows, and Hamm, a teller of broken tales, weaves narratives that centre on the loss of the natural world:

> Hamm: Nature has forgotten us.
> Clov: There's no more nature.
> Hamm: No more nature! You exaggerate.
> Clov: In the vicinity.
> Hamm: But we breathe, we change! We lose our hair, our teeth! Our bloom! Our ideals!
> Clov: Then she hasn't forgotten us.[64]

As in *Godot*, the decline of the characters, both physically and psychically, is equated with and, in this case, has replaced, the natural world. Nature functions as death, as absence; there is 'no more nature', just as there are no more painkillers, no more pap, no more sugarplums, tides, coffins. 'Something', Hamm repeats, 'is taking its course.' The 'something' is a decline that extends to the limits of the world. Hamm and Clov, while resigned to the fact of inexorable decline, seem to retain a certain hapless hope at moments, forgetting for instants the futility of such hope.

> Hamm: Did your seeds come up?
> Clov: No.

Hamm: Did you scratch round them to see if they had sprouted?
Clov: They haven't sprouted.
Hamm: Perhaps it's still too early.
Clov: If they were going to sprout they would have sprouted.
[Violently.] They'll never sprout.[65]

Clov does not hope that time will bring any change here; at later points in the drama Hamm will take on this role of ultimate pessimist. As is the case with Didi and Gogo, Hamm and Clov need each other desperately, and although both long for the release of death, they persevere, Schopenhauer-like, beyond their own desires.

With their limited physical abilities, Hamm, Nell and Nagg all travel to distant, almost forgotten landscapes in memories and dreams. At one point Hamm says, 'If I could sleep I might make love. I'd go into the woods. My eyes would see . . . the sky, the earth. I'd run, run, they wouldn't catch me. [Pause.] Nature! [Pause.] There's something dripping in my head. [Pause.] A heart, a heart in my head.'[66] In sleep he might be able to reach back to a world that was far more expansive than the single room containing, he assumes, all of the life left in the world. Nell and Nagg's memories are similarly related to landscapes: the Ardennes, the road to Sedan, Lake Como. These visions of forests and lakes are juxtaposed against their present living conditions: legless, unable to touch, unable even to satisfy an itch 'in the hollow', they now inhabit separate, shrunken deserts in the form of ashcans filled out with sand. Vague memories provide the only oasis.

Clov, the only one able to view 'the without' for himself with the telescope, offers no such memories, as if the vision of the actual world has banished all possibility for an alternative. 'I say to myself that the world is extinguished, though I never saw it lit.'[67] As the only viewer of the scene beyond the high windows, he interprets not only for Hamm, but for the audience. His view of the world reveals that there is simply nothing about. Hamm comes to rely on this changelessness as an indication that at some point the 'something' that is taking its course will indeed lead to the final moves in this bizarre game that 'me – [he yawns] – to play'.[68] What we witness is enough to reveal the stagnation of the days that has taught them to hear differences between the beginning, middle and end of the clock's alarm. Hamm's reliance on such stagnation is vehement; when Clov announces that on this day he has found not only a rat but a flea, Hamm urges him to kill the flea. 'But humanity might start from there all over again! Catch him, for the love of God!'[69] This is not merely pessimism; it also expresses the hope that nihilism itself will be validated and become certain. Despite this, Hamm maintains what can be described only as a Beckettian hope, forgetting occasionally, as Didi and Gogo do, the plight of the world. He speculates that beyond their immediate environs, 'perhaps it's still green. Eh? [Pause.] Flora! Pomona! [Ecstatically.] Ceres! [Pause.]'[70] In his fragmentary tales, Hamm reveals himself as one who was not always so accepting of pessimism. He tells Clov of a friend, a painter in an asylum (possibly the artist of the painting turned to the wall): 'I'd take him by the hand and drag him to the window. Look! There! All that rising corn! And there! Look! The sails of the herring fleet! All that loveliness! [Pause.] He'd snatch away his hand and go back into his corner. Appalled. All he had seen was ashes.'[71] Now Hamm has only the memory of 'all that loveliness', and the unimaginable ashen grayness of the world he cannot see, and yet cannot avoid seeing. 'Use your head, can't you, use your head, you're on earth, there's no cure for that! . . . But what in God's name do you imagine? That the earth will awake in spring? That the rivers and seas will run with fish again? That there's manna in heaven still for imbeciles like you?'[72] Hamm, speaking aloud, addresses himself as much as the original audience to this remark; he no longer hopes. He cannot believe in any pastoral dream, any Eden. He goes through the motions of praying to God, insisting that the others join in, and then bursts out, 'The bastard! He doesn't exist!'[73]

The elimination of nature and of the natural world has eliminated the possibility for a normal existence in *Endgame*; the possibility of regeneration is gone, and is in fact dreaded by both Hamm and Clov at different moments. The absence of nature thus comes to signify the lack of human possibility, of any change or movement. Times when nature and landscape were present, then, become significant memories to the characters. This theme is also present in *Godot*, when the absence of nature signals the absence of the possibility of memory. Beckett's work employs nature in a way that thus seems to recognize the link between nature and memory. This recognition is made most clear in *Krapp's Last Tape*, a short piece written in English in 1957, in which all of the character's significant memories are connected to the natural world in some way, and indicate an intense and overwhelmingly nostalgic longing for a lost and unlived past.

Instead of taking place in a surreal landscape or within the confines of a bunker-like room cut off from the world, *Krapp's Last Tape* is set by Beckett in a den, on 'a late evening in the future'.[74] This alone is striking; we are in a world much more recognizable. With his taped and 'live' monologues, Krapp bridges a gap between Beckett's early drama and the late drama, which moves towards the monologue and frequently involves one (usually male) character. While Didi and Gogo indirectly quote themselves in their repetitions and Hamm and Clov swirl through a repetitive, speculative banter about the world beyond their room, Krapp's tape recorder 'makes possible the absolute retrieval of spoken words'.[75] In this way, Beckett again stretches the time of the drama so that the audience is aware of the stagnation and sameness of Krapp's life over a period of approximately forty-five years. Sitting down at his desk to record what we are told is the final tape in a series, in a 'scriptless'[76] state, Krapp resembles Didi and Gogo, who constantly talk about what to talk about; Krapp is relieved of this difficulty by having something to listen to. Hamm's broken narratives become Krapp's taped narratives, but they are still marred by silences and Krapp's impatience with the stop and rewind and fast forward buttons. With these buttons he is thus able to accomplish what the characters in the two earlier plays were not: he can fast forward and rewind time at will, although in the end the audience realizes, if he does not, that this capability ultimately makes no difference and is an illusion.

The memory that interests Krapp the most on his sixty-ninth birthday is not the death of his mother or the scant publication history of a work he apparently wrote, but the 'farewell to love'. With great impatience he rewinds a tape until he reaches the section that interests him:

> – upper lake, with the punt, bathed off the bank, then pushed out into the stream and drifted. She lay stretched out on the floorboards with her hands under her head and her eyes closed. Sun blazing down, bit of a breeze, water nice and lively. I noticed a scratch on her thigh and asked her how she came by it. Picking gooseberries, she said. I said again I thought it was hopeless and no good going on and she agreed, without opening her eyes. [Pause.] I asked her to look at me and after a few moments – [Pause.] – after a few moments she did, but the eyes just slits, because of the glare. I bent over her to get them in the shadow and they opened. [Pause. Low.] Let me in. [Pause.] We drifted in among the flags and stuck. The way they went down, sighing, before the stem! [Pause.] I lay down across her with my face in her breasts and my hand on her. We lay there without moving. But under us all moved, and moved us, gently, up and down, and from side to side.
> [Pause.]
> Past midnight. Never knew such silence. The earth might be uninhabited.[77]

What is curious about Krapp's lost love is that, like the characters in *Godot* and *Endgame*, he associates memory with the natural world. Again there is a recognizable landscape, of a lake, the sun, and the flags that catch the boat, a landscape that has no place in Krapp's present-day world of his study, surrounded by darkness and his boxes of tapes. Each year, the audience presumes, Krapp goes through the ritual of not only recording a new tape, but remembering the girl in the boat and convincing himself that he 'wouldn't want [the years] back. Not with the fire in me now.'[78] As with other Beckett characters, he is unable to move beyond his present situation, and unwilling to admit to the illusion of his final claim. 'Everything there, everything on this old muckball, all the light and dark and famine and feasting of . . . [hesitates] . . . the ages! . . . Let that go!'[79] Krapp has attempted, over the years, to resign himself to the 'muckball', trying to forget that once the earth 'moved, and moved us'. He denies his regret to the end, despite having 'scalded the eyes out of me reading *Effie* again, a page a day, with tears again. Effie . . . [Pause.] Could have been happy with her, up there on the Baltic, and the pines, and the dunes.'[80]

Krapp, and all of Beckett's characters, attempt to rid themselves of desire; the philosophers whom Beckett read espoused such an attempt. Like most in the Beckettian universe, though, these attempts are futile. Vladimir and Estragon will persist in hoping that Godot will come; Clov will hold out a belief that one day he might leave Hamm and perhaps go in search of the small boy; and Krapp, despite forty-odd attempts, will continue to deny regret at the loss of the girl in the boat and will tell himself that it is just as well. All of them, in their stagnation, are haunted by memories of nature, which continues only in memory, obliterated. Nature, and the absence of the natural, reflects the characters' states of mind; place, and landscape, are inextricably bound to mind. The natural world, in these three plays, functions as a reminder of all that has been lost, and the enormity of the time that has engulfed and thus replaced it. It is possible, in fact, to conclude that the absence of landscape and nature in Beckett's drama is as significant as their presence might be in Synge's. The impossibility of attaching oneself to an unrecognizable landscape impacts on characters' abilities to remember, and it is that *impossibility* of memory – and the equal (and ironic) impossibility of forgetting that impossibility – that haunts Beckett's works. Even though Beckett's drama is certainly not consciously engaged with an Irish literary tradition in the way that even Joyce was, his works none-theless offer a commentary on that tradition by moving away from it.

While Beckett's dramas frequently represent landscapes decon-
textualized and barren of obvious historical geography, his fiction is
occasionally much more concrete in its representations of landscape.
The ghosted presence of Irish landscapes that hovers in the trilogy has
allowed the publication of texts such as *Beckett Country*,[81] but this
attempt to claim Beckett for the Irish tradition and connection to
place often seems a forced one. Beckett's works, so profoundly void
of the hope of any sort of pastoral retrieve, suggest that in the post-
Second World War era the question of a national literature is eclipsed
by far more pressing questions about the nature of humanity and
man's place – or placelessness – in the world. In many ways, Beckett's
social position and the time he lived in allowed him and, indeed,
forced this concern with broader questions about the nature of the
world. Irish independence became a reality while he was still quite
young, and the urgency of political activity subsequently dimmed in
Ireland. The urgency of the political situation in Europe did, of
course, compel Beckett to involve himself, and on the side of the
oppressed; he would not flirt, as others did, with fascism. Witnessing
the systematic displacement that occurred during the war must, I
would suggest, have disrupted his sense of place: attachment to landscape and 'home' might have been something that Beckett himself
experienced and even celebrated on occasion in his writing, but that
same attachment to landscape and the desire to own and rule over
land was what drove much of the destruction to which he was a
witness during the late 1930s and 1940s – and which would continue to
provoke his dismay in the years that followed. Placelessness, and
displacement, subsequently become much more significant in his work.
Murphy's realistic, recognizable sketches of Dublin and London give
way, after the war, to the shattered places of *Godot* or *Endgame*. What
has been lost in between is not only a sense of place, but the power of
memory to retrieve, to heal, to build bridges. 'Remembrance', Terry
Eagleton has written, 'is a way of possessing the past, but even this
feeble degree of agency is a luxury in Beckett's world.'[82] That Beckett's
first published writing focused on Proust, the author most associated
with memory in modern literature, is curiously and fittingly ironic. The
'luxury' of memory in Beckett's oeuvre disallows for the kind of
Proustian memories that Beckett described in his essay; by the time
Beckett comes to write his major dramatic works, memory, along with
place and nature, seems to have evaporated. Only when remembrance
assaults does the possibility of even an imaginative possession of place
and nature emerge, only to be eclipsed once again by forgetfulness.

CHAPTER SIX

Contemporary Versions of Irish Pastoral: Heaney and Boland

The Irish pastoral mode used by Yeats and Synge first idealizes and then critiques idealizations of rurality, marking a return in Irish literature to both the classical pastoral forms of early medieval literature and to the nostalgic mode of the later medieval period. Joyce, inheriting this mode, employs it to celebrate only ironically, savagely undercutting idealizations of the rural as outmoded and suggesting an alternative model of 'real Ireland' as urban or, eventually, suburban. By the time we reach Beckett's writing, a challenge is posed to the very notions of idealization and memory which form the basis of pastoral literature in general; and in their nostalgia for memory itself, the characters of Beckett's major plays deconstruct the tradition of Irish pastoral so that the possibility of retrieving a lost past in an eternal present becomes absurd. Despite Beckett's challenge to the Irish pastoral tradition and to the very idea of place, however, Irish writing has continued to explore pastoral modes as a way of critiquing culture or highlighting crisis. As shapers of Irish pastoral in the twentieth century, Yeats, Synge, Joyce and Beckett all serve as possible influences on the continuing representation of nature and place in writers as different as Patrick Kavanagh and John McGahern, Seamus Heaney and Nuala Ní Dhomhnaill, Medbh McGuckian and Eavan Boland, Peter Fallon and Michael O'Siadhail. What Seamus Heaney refers to as 'the sense of place' in Ireland has been preserved, in many ways, through what I have argued is an Irish pastoral tradition.

The *actual* place of Ireland has changed dramatically since the mid-twentieth century, however. Ireland's population has become increasingly urban, and the landscape of the nation has become increasingly industrialized. Nostalgia for landscape and natural beauty has consequently become focused, more often than not, on the *lost possibility* of the rural ideal. In part because of the removal of the population from rural conditions, 'nature, like culture itself, is more and more being tacitly understood as *the representation of itself*, and "itself" is often understood as *its former self*'.[1] As the possibility of believing in a mythos of rural Ireland as real Ireland has diminished, nature has been increasingly turned to as a representation of 'its former self'. Thus 'natural' sites such as the vales of Glendalough or the lakes of Killarney have been turned into 'cultural centres' where categories of 'nature' and 'culture' are blurred and blended and produce a form of (national) nostalgia: one is present in a natural world, but one that is deemed to be part of the past; visiting such 'natural' sites thus becomes like a trip to a museum that plays upon the received notion of rural Ireland as somehow more genuine than urban Ireland, triggering a self-reflexive nostalgia. This sort of nostalgia is not limited to the visual images of 'interpretive centres' or even postcards, however; the prevalence of rural images and narratives even in contemporary Irish television and cinema shows that these themes have not disappeared in contemporary Irish culture.

The idea of Irish rurality thus persists, and seems to contribute to the nation's ability to absorb change. This is particularly evident if one considers that Ireland's rapid social and economic transformation since becoming a member of the European Community has taken place amid a proliferation of rural imagery that proclaims social stasis. The pace of change in modern-day Ireland seems to have forced a continued reliance on the idea of the rural nation, with the result that, as Fintan O'Toole has described it,

> an increasingly urban and industrialised reality [is] made palatable, both to ourselves and to those whom we wish to attract, by being wrapped up in harmless rural folksy images. For the last hundred years, Irish culture and in particular Irish writing has been marked by this dominance of the rural over the urban, a dominance based on a false opposition of the country to the city which has been vital to the maintenance of a conservative political culture in the country.[2]

Images such as those used in Industrial Development Authority advertisements – attempting to entice foreign business into Ireland – picture, as Luke Gibbons has noted, serene landscapes more often than they do factories and industrial estates.[3] Irish Tourist Board commercials, particularly those aimed at North American audiences, tend unfailingly to show rural scenes, with little sign of Temple Bar or the chaos of Dublin traffic, while even recent advertisements in the English press name Ireland 'the land of memories', which, when combined with the images of the Cliffs of Moher, the Aran Islands and other rural sites, suggests that a visit to Ireland will submerge the tourist in the past. Nostalgia continues to makes its presence felt within Irish society, then, as a marketing and advertising strategy, and, pointedly, as a political strategy as well. The divide between country and city, if imaginatively maintained, pits the 'simple' country life against the 'corrupt' values of the city, and so, as O'Toole notes above, maintains current conservative political strains in Ireland.

Despite efforts by advertisers and politicians to maintain an image of rural Ireland, though, the increasing urbanity of Irish life has led to the production of a new literature: writers as different as Roddy Doyle and Frank McCourt indicate the attention now granted to urban realities previously underrepresented by the national literature. Even the Abbey Theatre, which from its foundation granted a forum to an overwhelmingly rural representation of Ireland, has resolutely turned to the production of plays by a generation of dramatists like Frank McGuinness and Marina Carr, whose work does not focus exclusively on the concerns of rural Ireland. Prose writers such as John Banville, Dermot Bolger, Anthony Glavin, Desmond Hogan, Neil Jordan, Claire Keegan, Colum McCann and Colm Tóibín have lent to the writing coming out of Ireland a determinedly international setting and appeal, and continue to challenge an insular notion of just what it means to be Irish, or where.

However, the most critically acclaimed and exported writer of recent decades is much more obviously aligned with the Irish pastoral tradition that has been under discussion here. Seamus Heaney's international appeal and marketability suggests not only the strength of his poetic, but also the coincidence between his work and defined ideals of Ireland as a rural space. In his attention to the rural spaces of Ireland, Heaney is not alone amongst contemporary writers, of course. A study of recent Irish poetry notes that much Northern poetry has focused on 'more traditional and often pastoral subjects, and derives its origin, energy, command and strength from them . . . Only among poets from the South, poets physically removed from the duress of the situation in the North, is there emerging a poetry which reflects modern city life'.[4] In his study of Irish literature 'after Yeats and Joyce', Neil Corcoran also notes an emphasis on land and landscape in Northern poetics, after describing the ways in which mid-twentieth-century Irish poetry

> made it clear how inseparable from matters of Irish history ideological representations of rural Ireland are: whether because the Famine is

inscribed so deeply into the Irish landscape and psyche . . . or because of the de Valeran valorization of an impossible ideal, or because, in a colonial and post-colonial country, matters of the land's ownership are inevitably more fraught . . . In many other post-Yeatsian poets of Irish rural life, *particularly those from the North*, these recognitions are also made, even in the great act of establishing Irish topographies with great imaginative definition and richness.[5] (my emphasis)

While there are inevitably exceptions to such generalizations – Paul Muldoon, for example, escapes easy categorization – it is nonetheless an interesting delineation of Irish poetic development, suggesting that an engagement with land, landscape and place in literature continues to remain a significant way of expressing cultural, social and political upheaval. If the issues of land ownership and territorial rights seemed to subside for both Joyce and Beckett, with Heaney they revive forcefully. With his consciousness of both rural and urban life, and life in Northern Ireland and in the Republic, Heaney engages a vast number of themes, but none of them, perhaps, as enduring as that of the 'imaginative definition' of rural place. Like other Northern poets of the period,[6] and like many of his Irish predecessors who had written through tumultuous times, Heaney was led into an intense relationship with land, landscape and place in his writing; place and nature could suggest stability and continuity of identity during a time when stability was lacking and both personal and national identity were under severe pressure.

That Heaney came to international prominence during a period of violence and chaos is significant: bearing witness to territorial and sectarian battles of 1960s and 1970s Northern Ireland led Heaney to conclude – as many others had before him – that the Irish people maintained an intensity of emotion for place.

> We are dwellers, we are namers, we are lovers, we make homes and search for our histories. And when we look for the history of our sensibilities I am convinced . . . that it is to . . . the stable element, the land itself, that we must look for continuity.[7]

Heaney's early metaphors – 'digging' and the 'bog' in particular – signify the attempt to establish 'continuity', to 'search for our histories' and attempt to recover memory eclipsed; identity can be established or stabilized through a sense of *spatial* continuity. Through the bog's physical preservation of past lives and objects, or through the psychological preservation of attitude towards natural space

evidenced by placenames, for example, Heaney attempts to find a
way of uniting infinite strands of identity from past and present.

Many of these strands and much of the complexity in Heaney's
poetry would seem to arise out of the relationship between Ireland
and England, a relationship which, he has claimed, determined his
poetic language: 'I think of the personal and Irish pieties as vowels,
and the literary awareness nourished on English as consonants. My
hope is that the poems will be vocables adequate to my whole experience.'[8] Aware of the necessity for both vowels and consonants,
Heaney's 'whole experience' encompasses the Irish and the English,
and the awareness of the tension and relationship between them.
Much of the past relationship between Ireland and England had been
determined by strife over territorial rights and land ownership; the
Northern Ireland of the 1960s and 1970s that Heaney witnessed was
marked by public and often violent debate over similar issues of
rights and territory, alongside the strains of a civil rights movement
and general sectarian unrest. It is unsurprising, then, that Heaney's
poetry often makes place, nature and landscape central in delineating
the political and social climates of his time. Just as the essential interaction between vowels and consonants can metaphorically point to a
simultaneous Irish–English divide/relationship, so too place and nature
begin to function as signifiers of the historical events that created and
continue to create that divide/relationship. So far does this signification
develop in Heaney's poetry that, one critic concludes, 'the rural life
becomes synonymous with Irish life, and the resulting tension involves
more than an opposition of the rural and the urban; it involves an
opposition of Irish and British. Pastoral tensions in Heaney's verse often
represent national ones'[9] indicative of an ongoing battle to establish
continuity of identity within a hybrid – and still contested – space. For
Heaney, as it was for Yeats, place is a reliable aid in this battle.

In a 1977 lecture, Heaney credits the Revival with having renewed
'The Sense of Place' in Irish culture that generations of English rule
had dulled. Yeats, Heaney writes, had a double purpose: 'to restore a
body of old legends and folk beliefs that would bind the people of the
Irish place to the body of their world' and 'to supplement this
restored sense of historical place with a new set of associations that
would accrue when a modern Irish literature, rooted in its own region
and using its own speech, would enter the imagination of his country-
men'.[10] 'The sense of place' becomes a potential unifying factor in
Irish culture of particular relevance to Heaney's own historical
moment:

> Irrespective of our creed or politics, irrespective of what culture or subculture may have coloured our individual sensibilities, our imaginations assent to the stimulus of the names, our sense of place is enhanced, our sense of ourselves as inhabitants of not just a geographical country but of a country of the mind is cemented. It is this feeling, assenting, equable marriage between the geographical country and the country of the mind . . . that constitutes the sense of place in its richest possible manifestation.[11]

If such public expressions are taken as political acts, Heaney's reaction to the situation in the North is diplomatic in its stress on similarities 'irrespective' of differences. In a culture charged with change – whether from invasion, colonization, religious conversion, poverty, famine, civil war or political and sectarian violence – nature and landscape serve as a steady realm both beyond the clutches of change and a testimony to it; the sense of place can unify these disparate histories of Ireland and of the Irish people in their relationship with England. Where Yeats was interested in antinomian tensions – between Irish and English, nature and culture, spirit and material, past and future – Heaney attempts to focus on similarity and continuity, on 'equable marriage' between Irish and English, past and present, country and city, woman and man, or self and other. Nonetheless, his work exhibits an awareness that, while the natural world is underwritten with the histories of many cultures and times and so signifies the simple persistence of humanity and culture, it cannot serve as a salve for instability; it is not possible to establish similarity and continuity on all fronts. Heaney's work thus becomes – as Yeats's was – aware of its own nostalgic idealizations of nature, place and landscape.

While many critics have noted the poet's engagement with place and nature, there has been surprisingly little considered analysis of Heaney's pastoral forms. There is a general sense that Heaney operates outside of 'tradition': Sean Lysaght, for example, has argued that 'The luxuriant vocabulary of the pastoral genre, implying a fruitful, accommodating environment, is quite out of place in Heaney's sparse, rather comfortless landscape.'[12] The most exacting work on Heaney's engagement with nature is Sidney Burris's impressive study, which examines Heaney's 'pastorals' within the framework of the *English* pastoral tradition, and which I would like to consider in some detail. Heaney's work, Burris argues, bears relation to the work of George Crabbe, often credited with introducing a shock of reality into the English tradition (although, as we have seen, Spenser did this as well,

and earlier), offering 'the same climate of particularized description
that distinguishes much antipastoral poetry'.[13] If Heaney seems to
function on the edge of the English pastoral tradition, in the space of
the 'antipastoral', Burris strengthens this claim by demonstrating
particularly strong thematic links between Heaney and John Clare.
Clare, a distinctly liminal poet,[14] is unusual within the English tradition
of nature writing not least because he was not a part of the upper
classes and dwelt in nature; Heaney and Clare share 'their firsthand
knowledge of farm life, their sense of a community under siege, and
their awareness of the pastoral's ability to glance at other matters'.[15]
Both Clare and Heaney employ 'aggressive rural imagery' that 'revises
the conventional posture of the carefree shepherd' in order 'to represent the silent communities that have remained outside of pastoral
writing'.[16] The consideration of Heaney's poetry alongside English
pastoral models is revealing, particularly since Burris's study seems to
situate Heaney on the edge of the English pastoral tradition: Crabbe
and Clare both write as a corrective to other pastoral models.

Having established Heaney's connections to English pastoral traditions, Burris demonstrates Heaney's engagement with classical
pastoral models:

> Heaney, who sees a dim present clouded by a dimmer future, resorts to
> myths and histories that would explain his predicament and so comfort
> the sufferer, and these myths and histories represent an ironic reversal
> of the traditional – Virgilian – pastoral perspective. But the imaginative
> direction, the strategies that govern the rural imagery, and the con-
> solations derived from their nurturing nostalgias are remarkably
> similar to Virgil's pastoral both in technique and, most important of
> all, in their generic orientation.[17]

While Virgilian pastorals represent a nostalgic view of a now lost
paradise, Heaney's poems frequently engage historical pasts far from
paradisial to represent a negative continuity between past and present
in the form of violence, inhumanity and static cultural rituals. If
Heaney's work seems to thus reverse Virgilian and classical tradition,
it nonetheless evokes the classical pastoral's tension between oppo-
sitional states, the most traditional of which is that between country
and city; Heaney focuses instead primarily on the historical, cultural
and political tensions between England and Ireland. Heaney's use of
the pastoral, a 'genre susceptible to social and political commentary',[18] allows him to subtly critique his society, Burris argues, and to
explore these tensions.

However enlightening this is, we are receiving only part of the story: the consonants, but not the vowels, in Heaney's terms. The failure to consider Heaney's simultaneous relationship to the Irish tradition is also a failure to recognize the layering of identities that necessarily occurs in colonial and post-colonial societies. Just as Yeats's was, Heaney's pastoral is, ultimately, a hybrid mode that contains elements of Irish, English and classical pastoral traditions. The failure to recognize the tradition of *Irish* pastoral, and the consideration of Heaney's poetry only in the context of classical and English pastoral models is indicative, in fact, of a type of colonial thinking that considers English and continental tradition to be the 'standard' or 'norm'. It is worth recalling, in this context, Edward Said and Seamus Deane's arguments about the imaginative reclamation of space in post-colonial cultures; Heaney, whose work functions as an embodiment of much of the academic debate over ideologies of colonialism and independence, seeks to restore space itself as an historical context. David Lloyd has argued that Heaney, like Yeats, engages in a 'reterritorialisation' that 'symbolically restores the interrupted continuity of identity and ground'.[19] While engaging in a process that consciously reclaims place, Heaney is also aware of the impossibility of a complete restoration, as the landscape bears witness to many cultures in a sometimes literal layering, as in the bog. What results out of this consciousness is a sense of shifting identities and shifting loyalties within the reclaimed space, and this sense is often bound together with nostalgia and longing and an acute presence of an illusive past that is often as violent as the present. Heaney's pastorals are, in other words, particularly Irish, and particularly post-colonial, in their combination of literary models.

Heaney's first collection, *Death of a Naturalist*, marks a first attempt to sort through strands of these themes. The book graphically charts the process that gives the work its title and one of its central poems (which, one critic notes, 'could have been more accurately entitled 'Death of a Pastoralist', since it is the notion of a pastoral, childhood Eden that actually dies'[20]): the poet moves from childhood to adulthood and from the ideal that was the classical pastoral into the realm of rural realities. Like Yeats and Synge and other Irish writers before him, Heaney moves away from traditional and English modes of pastoral towards a more clear representation of his experience. The resulting mode digs deeper and deeper into the idealizations of landscape and nature in order to reveal the violence and hardship of the reality of such a life: nature itself can issue 'obscene threats' ('Death of a Naturalist', l.30).[21] The violence in the collection 'reminds us that Heaney has never been a pastoral poet oblivious to the awkward realities of political (and therefore in Ireland, paramilitary) power';[22] the result of Heaney's awareness of violence is a 'militarized pastoral'.[23] The threat of the natural world had been present in medieval Irish writing on nature; Heaney updates the Irish pastoral tradition by writing of the threatening violence of life in the Northern Ireland of the day. Heaney will delve beneath surfaces and find realities largely unrepresented by traditional and English pastoral poetics in a seductively material language that seems to defy classical pastoral tradition and that is reminiscent of Patrick Kavanagh's; Heaney has directly acknowledged a debt to Kavanagh, as we will see. What is important to note at this juncture, however, is that Heaney is consciously drawing upon a tradition of 'nature writing' that is not a mere imitation of English or classical pastoral tradition. Through Yeats and Kavanagh, as well as anonymous medieval authors, Heaney is exposed to a tradition of Irish pastoral forms that becomes increasingly significant in his work.

Heaney's essays reveal awareness of the development of an Irish tradition of nature writing distinct from classical or English pastoral tradition: he recognizes, in effect, the changes in Irish literature's representation of nature described in Chapter Two. Citing a poem ascribed to Oisín on Ben Bulben, Heaney writes that

> Scholars might classify this as an elegiac poem as much as a poem of place and it does indeed have a backward look which gives it a more modern tone, a more alienated stance: but in the first flush of the hermit poetry six or seven centuries before this poem was written, it is not to the tears of things but the joy, the lifting of eye and heart, that we respond.[24]

Heaney's work has itself been described as marked by a 'constant self-evaluative backward look';[25] what is interesting is that Heaney cites the backward-looking nature of the poem as 'modern', noting that something changed after the time of 'hermit poetry' to create a 'more alienated stance' in Irish literature:

> It almost seems that since the Norman Conquest, the temperature of the English language has been subtly raised by a warm front coming up from the Mediterranean. But the Irish language did not undergo the same Romance influences and indeed early Irish nature poetry registers certain sensations and makes a springwater music out of certain feelings in a way unmatched in any other European language.[26]

Like many critics and scholars of early Irish literature, Heaney argues for something unique in the earliest Irish representation of nature. Early *and* later medieval Irish poetry, he argues, is 'sustained by a deep unconscious affiliation to the old mysteries of the grove, even while ardently proclaiming its fidelity to the new religion'.[27] In the context of such arguments Heaney's poetry can be seen as attempting to represent that 'deep unconscious affiliation' with the natural world; in this Heaney bears resemblance to earlier theorists like Arnold, seeming here to believe in an almost ethnically or racially determined attachment to place.

While idealizing such a connection to land and nature, however, Heaney's poetry addresses the unavoidable realities of that world in both past and present – and in this, he goes beyond Arnold's cultural stereotypes and steps into the imaginative space occupied by Yeats in his later poetry. Aware of the trend in Irish literature that turned towards nostalgia and the backward look, and aware too of more recent developments like that of Yeats and later Kavanagh's ruthless assessment of the de Valeran dream, Heaney attempts, by looking backwards himself, to return to 'the joy, the lifting of heart and eye' of early Irish poetry, but to learn from cycles of history as well, thus integrating the past into the present. One critic notes that Heaney's poetry 'is not about the pastness of that past but its presence. This is in accord with the living in a critical space of Ireland' which is a 'paradigmatic postmodern condition'.[28] It is certainly true that the Ireland that has informed Heaney's poetics is a 'critical space' contested and inscribed with various histories that, particularly in 1960s and 1970s Northern Ireland, were actively resistant to inter-involvement. To claim that this is a postmodern condition, however, ignores the realities of Irish life over many centuries and the realities of colonial and post-colonial experience: the past has, as we have seen, been a strong presence for authors as far back as the thirteenth century. Heaney, by addressing this space and by attempting to write from and through it, aligns himself with much of the Irish tradition.

Following *Death of a Naturalist*, Heaney further develops his thematic engagement with this tradition. *Wintering Out* relies more heavily on the type of Irish pastoral with which Heaney seems to most identify, that of Kavanagh, whose 'The Great Hunger' Heaney describes as 'a kind of elegy in a country farmyard, informed not by heraldic notions of seasonal decline and mortal dust but by an intimacy with actual clay and a desperate sense that life in the secluded spot is no book of pastoral hours but an enervating round of labour and lethargy'.[29] While Yeats offered a model or paradigm for a poet's movement through modes of pastoral, he did not offer the same experience of farm and rural life that Kavanagh did, and which Heaney shared. The combination of the elegiac and the realistic that Heaney learned from Kavanagh's poetry – and which recalls medieval Irish literature's simultaneous celebration and deflation of nature – is a felt presence in *Wintering Out*, as is the direct influence of medieval Irish literature through texts like *Buile Suibhne*. In poems such as 'Bog Oak', 'The Backward Look' and 'Traditions', Heaney continues digging – as Kavanagh did – removing himself to the outdoors – as Sweeney did – in order to assess again the strands of thought and theme that inform life in Ireland and Northern Ireland.

Following his much remarked upon move to the Republic,[30] Heaney's writing takes a new approach to Irish pastoralism, when he more fully adopts the figure of Sweeney as a metaphor of the con- dition of being an 'inner émigré' ('Exposure' from 'Singing School', l. 31).[31] Like the poet, 'Heaney's Sweeney' struggles to balance culture and nature, living both within and without, struggling to repossess a composure of selfhood while consigned to a wilderness: like Sweeney, Heaney engages in 'the poetic quarrel with the self rather than the political quarrel with others'.[32] Besides struggling against a public expectation to take sides and to be a visible exponent for various political positions in Ireland, Heaney's struggle is also against pastoral models which he recognizes to be a part of the colonizing tradition in Ireland: Spenser, for example, makes an increasing appearance in his poetry through allusion and by name, and lurks even in essays like the one cited above on Kavanagh, with its emphasis on the unreality of a 'book of pastoral hours'. Like Empson, Heaney believes in 'versions' of the pastoral, which allows him to differentiate between a writer like Spenser and Irish authors like Synge and Kavanagh, whom he iden- tifies as working on what he tentatively calls 'frontier pastoral',[33] a phrase which bears witness to the influence of American writing on his thinking, but also indicates an awareness that Irish pastoral forms are somehow on the border of other pastoral traditions.

Heaney's brand of pastoralism is particularly evidenced in his representation of nature as Ireland/female/other, or as colonized subject revealed to a male/English/colonizing gaze, and poems like the bog series and like 'Act of Union' have resulted in controversy for those who see the representation as reductive or dissembling. 'Act of Union'[34] describes the colonizing relationship as a sexual act in which aggression is almost veiled ('conquest is a lie' (I l. 11), we are told) and in which responsibility is thus almost removed; within the body of the woman/the colonized/Ireland, 'my legacy now culminates inexorably' (I l. 14). While the layering of allegorical meanings in the poem has offered critics much fodder and has fuelled debate over the adequacy of Heaney's response to fraught political issues, I would argue that it is the poem's form that provides Heaney's most significant response. As a pair of Shakespearean (and pointedly not Spenserian) sonnets, 'Act of Union' 'unites' an English literary form (itself shaped by the 'foreign' influence of the sonnet's Italian Petrarchan origins) with Heaney's own particular take on that form: slant and half rhymes, unpredictable metrical patterns, and slight shifts in rhyme schemes and tone from one part to the second. 'Act of Union' thus becomes a commentary on poetic form and tradition under colonial circumstances, offering an 'Irish' take on an 'English' form, thus suggesting the inseparability of cultural strands. The sonnet – traditionally a 'little song' about love – is united with the 'hatreds and behindbacks' ('North' l. 25)[35] of historical invasion and colonialism as a literal breeding ground for bitter and bloody revolution that leaves the population 'raw, like opened ground, again' (II l. 14). Heaney's version of Irish pastoral – with its reliance on place as English or Irish, male or female – here forcefully invades an English sonnet tradition. Accompanying this invasion is an implicit, pastoral lament in the poem's final lines, with the realization that 'No treaty / I foresee will salve completely your tracked / and stretchmarked body' (II ll. 11–13): the poet concedes the impossibility of a union that will heal scars; the poem's two parts remain distinct and separate, the sonnet form itself 'stretchmarked' by Heaney's original usage. That the two sonnets are gathered under one title, however, indicates Heaney's insistence on the attempt at unification.

'Rather than harp on differences', one critic notes, 'between metropolitan artist and rural craftsman, between sophisticated poet and illiterate potato farmer, [Heaney] emphasizes the similarities between them.'[36] This focus on similarity and the attempt at union are ultimately an emphasis on continuity which, given the political situations in which Heaney found himself embroiled in 1960s and 1970s Ireland, would seem not only understandable, but historically predictable: Synge and Yeats both attempted to link past and present in their own earlier, literary bids at continuity. Heaney's sense of personal, generational rupture – his father and grandfather were farmers, but he is a poet – he attempts to bridge with metaphor, with language: son, father and grandfather are all engaged in the act of digging, of rooting out. Metaphorical resemblances become a way of recognizing a continued, if not literal, pastoralism, a way of asserting a longing and nostalgia for the world from which he has broken – 'They seem hundreds of years away', he begins 'The Seed Cutters'[37] – while also representing with the clearsightedness of distance the cold realities of the longed-for life. In this way nature is almost always a site of nostalgia in Heaney's work, but it is nostalgia of tremendous complexity, one that recognizes the impossibility of recovery in the face of contemporary social and political life. Place and the natural world become a site of longing – for the past of childhood, for the past of Ireland – but one that is imagined and permanently out of reach, 'a frieze' like the Breughel images evoked in 'The Seed Cutters' (l. 13). The pastoral past remains, to cite an essay of Heaney's out of context, an 'imagined realm . . . a placeless heaven rather than a heavenly place'.[38]

Heaney's poetry remains pastoral in its engagement with Irish tradition – whether in its representation of Ireland or of landscape as feminine, yielding and other, or in its employment of literary figures like Sweeney and Spenser. Despite a non-rural adult existence, Heaney, like many Irish authors before him, continues to represent what is now non-lived experience and cultural memory. In a wonderfully ironic way, it has been left to Ireland's pre-eminent female poets to most forcefully challenge the Irish pastoral tradition and to record 'other' experience.

The Irish pastoral mode that has been under discussion here has been largely a male preserve, as, arguably, is the pastoral tradition in general. From the preceding analysis of Yeats, Synge, Joyce and Beckett, it would appear that the tradition of Irish pastoral writing that stretches back to the middle ages has not been merely maintained, but has in fact reasserted itself, through Heaney's work. While it would, of course, be most useful to examine the ways in which Irish women's writing has engaged with this theme over the centuries, such an analysis is out of the range of the present study; but it is significant that in contemporary Ireland the voices challenging and rewriting the tradition belong to Ireland's most prominent female poets. Nature in Irish literature is often feminine and the landscape of Ireland often personified as a woman (or Shan van Vocht, or Kathleen ní Houlihan), which inevitably means that to confront the Irish pastoral tradition as a woman is problematic. Among Irish women writers, Eavan Boland offers an exemplary way of addressing this problematic. Boland's work disrupts and in many ways dismantles the gendered nature of Irish pastoral, challenging the direction of the tradition and offering a final window through which to view Irish attitudes towards land, landscape, place and nature and their relationship to nostalgia.

As an Irish poet, Eavan Boland has developed an international reputation rivalled only by Heaney's and, more recently, Paul Muldoon's. Cited in President Mary Robinson's first official speech, and as prolific an essayist and critic as Heaney has been,[39] Boland has become the counterpoint voice to Heaney's, the south to his north, the female to his male – but, pointedly, not the city to his country. In a 1970 *Irish Times* article 'The Future of Poetry', Boland wrote about Joyce's city and Kavanagh's countryside, and posed a question: 'What new realities are there in Ireland to match these two equally rich realities pushing each other aside?'[40] Securing her work a unique place in Irish literature, Boland herself answered this question by forcefully introducing into an equation delineated by two prominent Irish male authors a third space: the suburbs.

Boland's mapping of the suburbs is a particularly interesting poetic phenomenon in the context of the Irish tradition that saw nature as the site of exclusion from culture, a sign of marginal existence. Both cultural exclusion and marginalizaton have been part and parcel of women's experience in general, and Irish women's experience in particular. Twice colonized – by both the invaders of the landscape and by the men that were their husbands, fathers, brothers and sons – Irish women suffered the double burden of being twice refuted, twice silenced. In this sense, women *were* nature in their signification of exclusion and the margins of culture. The representation in seventeenth- and eighteenth-century *aisling* literature of Ireland as a woman raped, plundered or displaced reinforced this marginalization by making woman the defeated, the colonized: and it is her defeat, in fact, that marks the colonization. This displacement of historicity onto an at once mythical and erotic image of land as female is extraordinarily problematic, since it decontextualizes Ireland's political disenfranchisement, demasculanizes the Irish male population, and so introduces a way by which the forming nation will further enforce colonial-type mentalities in its own population by deeming women weaker/other/colonized even in the event of 'independence'. The assertion of a kind of machismo becomes increasingly important in colonial and newly post-colonial cultures, as Joyce, for example, is only too happy to demonstrate with his drawing of the Citizen in 'Cyclops'.

Boland came to poetry aware of this inheritance, and aware that her relation to literary and, specifically, Irish literary tradition was problematized by gender and sexuality. Boland's career runs parallel to Heaney's, with publication in the 1960s and 1970s of several collections of poetry that attempted to come to terms not simply with the politics of Northern Ireland, from which she was physically removed, but with larger cycles of history that had dictated the removal of women from literary traditions. Her earliest poetry, noted for its remarkable formal coherence, gradually loosened to incorporate more personal rhythms. Boland has described the poem that she initially 'intersected' with in Ireland in the 1960s and 1970s as not her own but 'an inherited mixture of the British Movement poem – overtones of Larkin, with postures of irony – and the Irish lyric, with postures of mood and melancholy'.[41] This poetic she perceived was, interestingly, an intertwined, palimpsestic, hybrid, colonial form, both English and Irish, ironic and sentimental. Despite the fact that as a young poet Boland unreservedly admired Yeats – undoubtedly the contributor of 'sentiment' to the poetic equation she outlines above – she gradually came to see his influence as a 'poisoned chalice he had handed on to the poets who came after him'.[42] 'Postures of mood and melancholy' were inevitably part of the poison, but were not merely Yeatsian, of course, but part of an Irish tradition from which Boland felt herself removed by virtue of gender.

The 1970s and 1980s in Ireland reinforced 'the perception of the poem as political'[43] for Boland. But the notion of the poem as a political unit or as a political act was pointedly limited to the realm of the hero, to 'politics' as male domain (made more concrete, perhaps, by her own childhood as the daughter of an Irish diplomat). To this dilemma Boland responded with an assault on the binary either/or of Irish pastoral tradition, and began her disruption of the urban/rural divide. In 'Suburban Woman', Boland describes the birth of the suburbs in terms of a rape, which recalls Heaney's 'Act of Union' as well as the mythological rapes to which both poems are indebted; but Boland's poem goes further than a delineation of Irish and English relations.

> Town and country at each other's throat –
> between a space of truce until one night
>
> walls began to multiply, to spawn
> like lewd whispers of the goings-on,
>
> the romperings, the rape on either side.
> The smiling killing. That you were better dead

than let them get you. But they came, armed
with blades and ladders, with slimed

knives, day after day, week by week –
a proxy violation. She woke

one morning to the usual story. Withdrawing
neither side had gained, but there, dying,

caught in cross-fire, her past lay. Like a pride
of lions toiled for booty, tribal acres died

and her world with them. She saw their power to sever
with a scar. She is the sole survivor. (Ill. 1–16)[44]

Suburbia becomes a feminine space, and the space in which the silent past of the contemporary woman lies. There is, Boland writes in 'Ode to Suburbia', 'No magic here' (l. 25);[45] the mythology that is the pastoral existence, that is feminine nature, is reduced to 'the claustrophobia / Of . . . back gardens' (ll. 3–4).[46] The suburbs become the marginalized realm of the marginal within independent Ireland, housewives and mothers beyond the boundaries of the city, out of the reach of the countryside that governed so much of Irish ideology. The almost literal no man's land of the suburbs is made central in such poems, retrieved from the margins by metaphoric force. So successful, in fact, has Boland's act of retrieval been that it is possible to see her as having redrawn the parameters of Irish literature. It is important, she has said,

> that critics realize that they are not dealing with a marginal project
> when they talk or write about women's poetry. They are not discussing
> a detour or a digression. They are talking about poetry itself, all that
> leads into it in the past, and everywhere it is going in the future. When
> the history of poetry in our time is written – I have no doubt about this
> – women poets will be seen to have re-written not just the poem, not
> just the image. They won't just have re-balanced elements within the
> poem. They will have altered the cartography of the poem. The map
> will look different.[47]

Within the context of Irish writing, Boland has been one of few responsible for making it possible to perceive women's poetry as not a merely 'marginal project'. Besides publishing poetry that itself challenged the position of women in Irish culture, history and literature, Boland was also among those responsible for forcing recognition of the lack of inclusion of women's writing in the *Field Day Anthology of Irish Writing*, and so, one might argue, responsible in part for the recent publication of the *Field Day Anthology of Irish Women's Writing*. Her public outspokenness on such political issues is thus also a counterpoint to Heaney's relatively veiled statements.

The 'map' that is Boland's poetry certainly does look different to what has gone before. Unlike the male authors examined in earlier chapters, Boland brings the reality of suburban existence into Irish poetry instead of retreating imaginatively into rurality. Many critics have remarked upon the fact that '. . . after *Night Feed*, it was clear that the suburb was as legitimate a landscape for Irish poetry as the canals of Dublin, the towns of the Gaeltacht or the shipyards of Belfast'.[48] While earlier Irish poetry had focused relentlessly on the countryside as the bastion of the real Ireland, and while fiction like Joyce's had turned with equal fervour to the site of the city to counteract that relentless ruralism, little writing had attended to the spaces that were springing up between these extremes, possibly because these spaces were so much the arena of women. (Leopold Bloom, who entertains the fantasy of a suburban home, is pointedly described as the 'new womanly man') (*U* 15.1798–9).[49] The space that fell between the cracks of Irish literary vision was part of the 'hidden Ireland', and that space contained Irish women's experience, which had also remained largely hidden from view and unexpressed.

Boland has described these acts of retrieval of Irish women's experience as 'subversive'. Curiously, she compares her own 'subversion' to that of what she calls 'nature poets':

> Good nature poets are always subversive. Someone like Frost, or the best of John Clare for example. Their lexicon is the overlooked and disregarded. They are revelatory poets. They single out the devalued and make a deep, metaphorical relation between it and some devalued parts of perception . . . What happens is that the poet becomes the agent in the poem for a different way of seeing. And not just for seeing that particular thing. The project in the nature poem is a revised way of seeing, rather than the thing that's seen. After a while, I came to think of myself as an indoor nature poet. And my lexicon was the kettle and the steam, and the machine in the corner and the kitchen, and the baby's bottle . . . They assumed importances . . . I felt about them, after a day spent in the house or with little children, exactly the way the nature poet feels after taking the same walk for several days and seeing the same tree or the same bird. So I had something of the agenda of the nature poet in all that.[50]

Boland's notion of nature poetry as a subversive way of visualizing, seeing and presenting the world suggests that while she represents a new space in Irish literature, she does so by delineating that space from within the linguistic territory of the pastoral and its sub-genres, which provide the opportunity for critique. Her revision of both classical and Irish pastoral forms results in what one of her poems calls 'The New Pastoral' which, as Patricia Boyle Haberstroh puts it, 'reflect[s] a woman's life' and 'imagines a new muse, one who speaks a mother tongue'.[51] 'The New Pastoral' rejects the bind to place that classical, English and Irish pastoral insist upon – 'I am a lost, last inhabitant – / displaced person / in a pastoral chaos' (ll. 4–6) – as unavailable to real women: 'I'm', the voice tells us, 'no shepherdess' (l. 10).[52] The weight of the pastoral tradition, which in Ireland is intrinsically tied to the idealization of women as land and nature, is spelled out: 'I could be happy here' (l. 15), we are told, except for the whisperings that tell her

> there was a past,
> there was a pastoral,
> and these chance sights
>
> what are they all
> but amnesias of a rite
> I danced once on a frieze. (ll. 20–5)[53]

The poem suggests that 'pastoral' is itself 'past', and the present-day, real-life woman is haunted by 'amnesias of a rite' and the notion of woman frozen in time and space 'on a frieze'. The 'pastoral' and the 'rite' are both implicitly deconstructed by forcing remembrance, and by including what has been silenced or elided from Irish literature. In writing out Irish women's experience, Boland has created a new form in her poetry that is at once realistic – in its insistence upon the inclusion of women's daily experience – and imaginary – in its retrieval of experience outside of her own lifetime. Her project is thus on the one hand at odds with Irish tradition, and on the other very much aligned with it; she rejects, Anne Fogarty writes, 'attempts by postcolonial studies to make the past malleable and amenable to restatement',[54] and at the same time forces the recognition that that same past must be revisited, if not restated, in order to be accurate and to include women's experiences.

Boland's pastoral tendencies do not focus on nature as woman or as Ireland; she is, in fact, concerned to overturn such stereotypes and tropes. 'I won't go back to it', 'Mise Eire'[55] begins, in a declamatory tone and a refusal of the specific that recalls the opening of Yeats's 'Sailing to Byzantium': just as we might ask, 'what country?' after reading Yeats's opening line, here we are forced to enquire 'go back to what?' Among other things, the 'it' is the reduction of woman and self into 'scalded memory' (l. 9), into 'A palsy of regrets' (l. 15), and into herself as 'Eire'.[56] Boland's poetic imagination stretches in such a poem, again like Yeats's, over many times and places, compressing, in a visionary way, the experience of many into one. The 'I' becomes an all-encompassing female voice able to embody and expose the lost voices of the past. Boland will repeatedly concern herself with these acts of retrieval, speaking for those who are silent, and speaking against the imaginary projections of woman, Ireland and nature.

Boland's attention is often turned to natural cycles of life, particularly those associated with motherhood and birth. Natural images thus play a role in her work, but do not come freighted with the nostalgia that so marks Heaney's poetry: Boland swerves out of reach of an Irish tradition that is at times cloyingly sentimental for the past. But since this past is one that excludes her and other women's experience – they are *Outside History*, as she puts it – Boland is forced to create a present moment that is ghosted with the presence of the unwritten and unrecorded past. Augustine Martin's assessment summarizes Boland's turn away from her Irish forebears:

> She maps out a territory . . . This is of course a region of the imagination, as much a fictional construct as [Austin] Clarke's Celtic-Romanesque or Kavanagh's childhood country of Ballyrush and Gortin – though less haunted with history as the one, or without topography as the other, and quite without the savage nostalgias that alternately energise and disable their sense of experience.[57]

While it begins as an actual place, Boland's suburbia does become, of course, like Yeats's Innisfree, a projection, and an imaginary space. Her recognition of the status of such space is immediately evident in the title of her most recent collection of poetry, *The Lost Land*. While Boland's work is not marked by 'savage nostalgias', nostalgia does function as a type of protest against oblivion; in this, Boland's work engages with the tradition of Irish pastoral while pushing it beyond its known boundaries. *The Lost Land* becomes that space eclipsed by the maintenance of a silence about women's role in multiple histories; the actual land of Ireland left behind by emigrants; the territory lost under colonization; the space that is a 'lost' language; and it also becomes the loss of the imaginary Ireland, the loss of 'Mother Ireland'. In the collection's two sequences, 'Colony' and 'The Lost Land', Boland moves between the concepts of overt colonization and the colonizations that are internal and of the mind, and ends the second series with a reiteration of her disrupting notion of suburbia:

> *Beautiful land* the patriot said
> and rinsed it with his blood. And the sun rose.
> And the river burned. The earth leaned
> towards him: Shadows grew long. Ran red.
>
> *Beautiful land* I whispered. But the roads
> stayed put. Stars froze over the suburb.
> Shadows iced up. Nothing moved.
> Except my hand across the page. And these words. ('Whose?')[58]

This poem subtly ties together many of Boland's themes. While 'the patriot said' his piece, the poetic persona's is 'whispered': the contrast between the very register of their voices reveals the lack of place given to the woman within Irish and Irish nationalist culture. The patriot declaims his love of the land and the land replies with change: the male is linked to the land by the force of the pathetic fallacy. When the poet's persona speaks the same words, what results in the physical world is a Beckettian stasis: 'Nothing moved'. While the trope of the male patriot provides equally trope-like consequences of violent change, the admiration of the land by the female subject (and, crucially, not object) does not fit in to received notions of patriotism or of the relationship between 'man' and nature. The final line of the poem further disrupts all that has gone before. There is a strength of movement that is writing, that is voice: even if whispered, the voice that is on the page, that is put there by the hand of the woman poet, will go on, and will have effect. The patriot, whose actions are swallowed up by the land and by his love of it, does not live to see change; the poet, penning 'these words', operates within a different set of conventions, removed from both city and countryside, in a middle ground that allows for a kind of revolutionary act of liberation that is new language. Most crucial, however, is the discovery of 'lost land' that is suburbia; and the challenge it poses to the Irish tradition, creating, in Boland's own words, a 'new pastoral'.

Pastoral Speculations

'Nostalgia', the sociologist Fred Davis notes, 'thrives on transition, on the subjective discontinuities that engender our yearning for continuity'.[1] As a sociological phenomenon, as well as a literary, aesthetic one, nostalgia serves as a preservative, stablizing the sense of the present. Infusing the present, nostalgia charges it with the knowable, predictable past so that the present no longer seems as unsettled, since a continuous identity is posited. In the face of changing or threatened social structures such as Ireland experienced – during, for example, the consolidation of Christianity's presence at the end of the twelfth century, during English colonization and the resulting loss of the Irish language, and in the tumultuous period leading up to Irish independence – place and nature could be conceived of as a steady and unaltered realm beyond the reaches of the fluctuating culture. For this reason, Irish literature seems frequently to use the natural world as a site for heightened nostalgia that stretches other pastoral representations, with the result that nature becomes a site from which to express the longing or mourning for lost or threatened culture.

This study has attempted to demonstrate the existence of a tradition of Irish pastoral writing that both draws upon and deviates from other pastoral models. The Irish pastoral mode reflects not only the pastoral's tendency to offer veiled critiques, but also the historical circumstances that have shaped the mode over time. Yeats and Synge set out to consciously recover, remember and commemorate Irish cultural forms of the past, and their texts initially reflect conscientious attempts to experience that which they had not lived personally. The realization that such attempts did not allow for any absolute retrieval led to a reshaping of their nostalgia: at once deflating it – making it more critical – and intensifying it, since the longing for a lost past was now genuine. Joyce, learning from the lessons of the Revival, leaps

directly to this phase of reflexive, critical nostalgia, engaging idealizations ironically, but nonetheless preserving an intensely specific
Irish past. By the time we reach Beckett, the Irish pastoral's concern
with preservation of the past has become impossible; the mode seems
to have reached its useful limitations. We have moved from one end
of a spectrum to another, between what Terry Eagleton refers to as
the 'terrible twins' of '[a]mnesia and nostalgia, the inability to remember
and the incapacity to do anything else'.[2]

When cultures are under threat from any number of sources –
particularly, I would suggest, the enormous threat to culture that is
colonialism and imperialism – the value placed on cultural memory
seems to increase immensely: the fear of elision or erasure often
sparks an intense movement of activity to preserve and remember,
with the urgent sense that this must be done before it is 'too late'.
While this type of attitude can be taken to extremes and used as a
defensive manoeuvre to thwart necessary change and progression, it
can also serve to do, simply, what it aims: prevent cultural artefacts
from being forgotten. While the Irish Revival's nostalgic aesthetic
certainly contributed to a problematic of identity in de Valera's
Ireland, when the defined notion of what it meant to be Irish was
rigidly inscribed into the constitution, this aesthetic also allowed for
a continuity of Irish literary and cultural identity to be reasserted.
Nostalgia, far from being an indulgent, sentimentalizing exercise,
provided a political impetus that allowed, in many ways, for the
movement from 'homesickness' to 'home rule'.

Because cultural upheaval has continued, the need for the pastoral
mode has also continued; Beckett's dismissal of the notion of the
graspable, palpable past of a particular place in favour of an examination of the larger question of man/woman's very place in the world
was not a permanent one. The circumstances in Northern Ireland
from the 1960s through to the present have almost demanded an
attention to the notion of the land and the question of past and future
ownership. Seamus Heaney's attempts to focus on the landscape of
Ireland as a site of stability and so one of reverence have imaginatively retrieved the medieval Irish pastoral tradition as well as the
Revival's version of the mode. The Irish pastoral mode continues, in
other words, to function as a way of expressing cultural upheaval and
the longing for lost or threatened culture. The mode has seen a
significant reinterpretation in recent decades, however, through the
poetry of Eavan Boland and many other gifted writers. Moving
beyond the divide of country and city, Boland inserts a third space

into the see-saw equation that is pastoral, and forces a recognition of the fact of women's exclusion from many aspects of Irish cultural history, including the Irish pastoral mode.

I would like to return to a quotation of Harold Toliver's cited at the beginning of this study: 'Whether or not the texts examined here need all be considered "pastorals" is not as important finally as our discovering something in them through this lens that would be less noticeable through another.'[3] While outside of the context of this study it might seem difficult to classify Beckett, for example, as a pastoral writer, my hope is that this study has indeed managed to allow for the 'discovery' of something. It has not been my aim to force the authors and texts examined here to be deemed 'pastoral' in an overdetermined, exacting way. Instead, what I have attempted to show is that the examination of these authors under the umbrella that is pastoral can reveal cultural traditions otherwise left sheltering and frequently unnoticed. And while it would seem true that Irish authors have almost continually looked to landscape as a site of stability and continuous identity, it is worth speculating that other cultures, particularly those that have found themselves under the yokes of colonialism and imperialism, have also turned to nature as a stabilizing, constant realm that is the site of their own lost or elided culture. In examining 'pastoral' representations of nature and landscape in literature and their coincidence with nostalgia, the underlying cultural and social histories can be illuminated in a new way, and can cast light on the resistance and adaptation to social change.

Notes

1 'Landscape' is used throughout this work to represent the natural, physical world in all its guises; in defining the word in this way, I am following the second offering of the Oxford English Dictionary: 'A view or prospect of natural inland scenery, such as can be taken in at a glace from one point of view: a piece of country scenery.' As J. Barrell notes in *The Idea of Landscape and the Sense of Place 1730–1840: An Approach to the Poetry of John Clare* (Cambridge: Cambridge University Press, 1972), 'There is no word in English which denotes a tract of land, of whatever extent, which is apprehended *visually* but not, necessarily, *pictorially*. The nearest is probably "terrain", but in practice the uses to which this word can be put are very limited . . . The word we do use, of course, is "landscape"' (p. 1). Barrell notes that 'landscape' in this sense came into use in the mid-eighteenth century, after having been introduced from the Dutch in the sixteenth century (p. 2).

2 S. Schama, *Landscape and Memory* (New York: Vintage Books, 1996), p. 61.

3 *Dindshenchas* or the lore of place was a widely practised branch of traditional Irish poetics; E. Gwynn's *The Metrical Dindshenchas Volumes I–V* (Dublin: The Royal Irish Academy Todd Lecture Series, Volume IX, 1903) collects a wide range of the poetic material, but tales and poems of place are inserted into almost every medieval Irish manuscript collection.

4 Johannes Hofer coined the word in his 'Medical Dissertation on Nostalgia'. See F. Davis, *Yearning for Yesterday: A Sociology of Nostalgia* (New York: The Free Press, 1979), Chapter One.

5 In the contemporary use of the word 'nostalgic', there is also often a link with 'sentimentality', a link which seems to go back to the nineteenth century, as will be seen in Chapter Two.

6 The idea of the 'lost past' applies if time is conceived of as linear and so forward moving, as M. Shaw and C. Chase point out is the case in the western cultures. Chase and Shaw add two other factors – a sense of lack in the present and an access to the past through physical and visual objects – as determining the extent to which nostalgia can permeate a culture's consciousness ('The Dimensions of Nostalgia', in M. Chase and C. Shaw (eds), *The Imagined Past: History and Nostalgia* [Manchester: Manchester University Press, 1989], p. 4).

7 In *Modern Ireland and the Erotics of Memory* (Cambridge: Cambridge University Press, 2002), N.A. Miller writes that 'Knowing the past . . . amounts to a kind of transmigration of the subject beyond the prison-house of presence that defines it, an entry into a historical space other than that which is the subject's own' (p. 30). Nostalgia, I argue, is key to this process of accessing the past.

8 G. Bachelard, *The Poetics of Space*, trans. Maria Jolas (Boston, MA: Beacon Press, 1994 [1964]), p. 9.

9 See W.J. Ong, *Orality and Literacy: The Technologizing of the Word* (New York: Methuen & Co. Ltd., 1982), pp. 43–5; 57–67; 96–100.

10 In *Postmodernism, or the Cultural Logic of Late Capitalism* (London: Verso, 1991), F. Jameson has used 'nostalgia' to discuss American cinematic culture of the 1970s as a form of 'aesthetic colonization' of earlier time periods,

particularly the 1950s (p. 19). Jameson's argument, however, focuses upon the notion of the post-modern as raiding the past and its voices for contemporary authenticity; my own argument is that nostalgia as an aesthetic is in place long before the post-modern period. I would, however, agree with his assessment that a nostalgic aesthetic 'lay[s] siege either to our own present and immediate past or to a more distant history that escapes individual memory' (p. 19).

11 Frank O'Connor's assessment in *The Backward Look* (London: Macmillan, 1967) is typical: 'I am not sure that any country can afford to discard what I have called "the backward look", but we in Ireland can afford it less than any other because without it we have nothing and are nothing, and we must not cease to remember Yeats' final words:

> Cast your mind on other days
> That we in coming times may be
> Still the indomitable Irishry.' (p. 230)

12 L. Gibbons, citing the historian Oliver MacDonagh, notes that the

> tendency to collapse the past into an ever-receding present, is one of the distinguishing features of Irish political culture . . . As nationhood belonged to the cultural as much as to the political domain, what Frank O'Connor referred to as 'the backward look' also fixated literature and the arts within its controlling vision. While T.S. Eliot was trying earnestly to renew contact with a literary heritage in his famous essay 'Tradition and the Individual Talent', Irish writers such as James Joyce and Sean Ó Faoláin were attempting to escape the nightmare of history'. (*Transformations in Irish Culture* [Cork: Cork University Press, 1996], p. 82)

13 T. Eagleton, *Crazy John and the Bishop and Other Essays on Irish Culture* (Cork: Cork University Press, 1998), p. 68.

14 This mode has been identified by the sociologist Fred Davis in his study of nostalgia:

> So frequently and uniformly does nostalgic sentiment seem to infuse our aesthetic experience that we can rightly begin to suspect that nostalgia is not only a feeling or a mood that is somehow magically evoked by the art object but also a distinctive aesthetic modality in its own right, a kind of code or patterning of symbolic elements, which by some obscure mimetic isomorphism comes, much as in language itself, to serve as a substitute for the feeling or mood it aims to arouse. (*Yearning for Yesterday*, p. 73)

15 H. Toliver, *Pastoral Forms and Attitudes* (Berkeley, CA: University of California Press, 1984), p. vii.

CHAPTER ONE

1 Hagiographical and other religious material has been excluded from the present study; its inclusion would change this project's scope and, indeed, necessitates a study of its own.

2 See, for example, J. Kenney, *The Sources for the Early History of Ireland: An Introduction and Guide. Volume I: Ecclesiastical* (New York: Columbia University Press, 1929), pp. 190–1; 286–7; and also G. Murphy, 'Vergilian Influence Upon

the Vernacular Literature of Medieval Ireland', *Studi Medievali*, 5 (1932), pp. 372–81.

3   While this term's Romantic associations are troublesome, my usage follows K. Jackson's in *Studies in Early Celtic Nature Poetry* (Cambridge: Cambridge University Press, 1935; reprinted Felinfach, Wales: Llanerch Publishers, 1995), the only study of nature in Irish literature of any period.

4   Besides K. Jackson, see, for example, R. Flower, *The Irish Tradition* (Dublin: The Lilliput Press, 1994 [Oxford: Oxford University Press, 1947]).

5   While hagiographical texts describe the lone monk abandoning society for a sojourn in the wilderness, such journeys were in practice rare and discouraged as disruptive to monastic communities: see L. Bitel, *Isle of the Saints: Monastic Settlement and Christian Community in Early Ireland* (Cork: Cork University Press, 1990), pp. 229–30; and D. Dumville's introduction to *Ireland's Desert Fathers* (forthcoming). Of actual lone hermits (such as Baitanus and Cormac in Adomnán's *Life of Columba* (A. Anderson and M. Anderson, eds. and trans., *Adomnán's Life of Columba* (Oxford: Clarendon Press, 1991)), many went on to found monasteries or become heads of churches: the pursuit of the ideal of hermit life leads to their elevation within the Church.

6   Jackson, *Studies in Early Celtic Nature Poetry*, p. 108.

7   M. Tymoczko, 'A Poetry of Masks: The Poet's Persona in Early Celtic Poetry', in K.A. Klar *et al.* (eds), *A Celtic Florilegium: Studies in Memory of Brendan O Hehir* (Laurence, MA: Celtic Studies Publications, 1996), p. 187.

8   See, for example, 'Manchán's Wish' (ninth or tenth century), where the 'mask' of Saint Manchán of Líath, who died in 665 (G. Murphy [ed. and trans] *Early Irish Lyrics: Eighth to Twelfth Century* [Oxford: Oxford University Press, 1956], p. 29), allows for a projected, as yet unrealized life with 'A beautiful wood close by . . . for the nurture of many-voiced birds' (Murphy, p. 31 st. 3). Because the focus of this study is primarily Irish literature in English, the decision has been made to provide only translations of early Irish material; translation sources provide the Irish originals as well, with the exception of the *Acallam na Senórach*. It should be noted as well that titles of old and middle Irish poems and tales in this chapter are conventions imposed by modern editors.

9   Monastaries functioned as Ireland's earliest 'cities' in an essentially rural society; they 'may have carried out some of the functions of urban communities' (N. Edwards, *The Archeology of Early Medieval Ireland* [London: B.T. Batsford, Ltd, 1990], p. 6). Monastic 'cities' were created by a Church which had itself imported organizational structures from the Roman empire; thus urban centres were cultural imports into medieval Ireland. Seán Ó Tuama also makes this point: 'Cities and towns – particularly on the east coast – have historically been the creations and preserves of invading colonists' ('Stability and Ambivalence: Aspects of the Sense of Place and Religion in Irish Literature', in J. Lee [ed.] *Ireland: Towards a Sense of Place* [Cork: Cork University Press, 1985], p. 22). Authors of these poems, then, wrote about nature from the distance that traditionally defined the pastoral.

10   In Murphy, *Early Irish Lyrics*, pp. 10–19.

11   D. Ó Corráin, 'Early Irish Hermit Poetry?', in D. Ó Corráin *et al.* (eds), *Sages, Saints and Storytellers: Celtic Studies in Honour of Professor James Carney* (Maynooth: Maynooth Monographs 2, 1989), p. 258.

12   Manuscript instances of *fían* literature increase throughout the medieval period: see K. Meyer, *Fianaigecht* (Dublin: Royal Irish Academy, Todd Lecture Series Volume XVI, 1910), pp. xv–xxxi. From the twelfth century onwards, *fían* lore was considered a significant part of Irish literature, possibly because of its association with almost every part of Ireland. Unlike Cuchulain, who is

predominantly associated with, and placed in, Ulster, Finn and *fían* lore cover a much wider territory, and so could appeal to a wider audience.

13 While the *Táin* contains many references to place (and is one of the most significant pieces of Irish literature) it has been omitted here because it follows a pattern similar to the Finn tales: place rapidly gives way to battle and adventure tales. Nature is also insignificant within the *Táin* tales: the characters are, like their Finn-cycle counterparts, aristocratic and unconcerned with a life in nature. And while even the title of the collected tales tells us that animal farming was a particularly important aspect of medieval Irish life, the tales themselves avoid the detail that might allow us to claim significance for a literary pastoral attitude towards nature; the 'cattle raid' seems to allow only for a frame in the manner that the hunt does for early Finn tales.

14 Nagy draws on the work of E. MacNeill (ed. and trans., *Duanaire Finn*. 2 vols. [Dublin: Irish Texts Society, 1908], who noted that the *fían* exists outside of the landowning community and perform rites of passage (pp. xvii–xlii). The *fénnid*, as an outlaw, or literally 'outlandish' figure, joins the *fían* 'as an extraordinary means of reacquiring what one is legally entitled to within society' (J. Nagy, *The Wisdom of the Outlaw: The Boyhood Deeds of Finn in Gaelic Narrative Tradition* [Berkeley, CA: University of California Press, 1985], p. 48). In ensuring property rights, the *fían* is concerned with the perpetuation of a class system in which the aristocracy owned land. The *fían*'s service thus acts as both 'a cause and effect of social change' (Nagy, p. 49), but also forces the continuation of societal practices like the passing on of land to rightful heirs.

15 Meyer, *Fianaigecht*, pp. 22–7.

16 Ibid., p. 25.

17 See also 'Reicne Fothaid Canainne' (K. Meyer, *Fianaigecht*, pp. 10–21); 'The Fight of the Ford'; and 'How Finn Obtained Knowledge, and the Slaying of Cul Dub' (both in K. Meyer, 'Two Tales About Finn', *Revue Celtique*, XIV [1899], pp. 241–9).

18 Gwynn, *Metrical Dindshenchas*, p. 72.

19 See also W. Stokes (ed. and trans.), 'Finn and the Phantoms', *Revue Celtique*, VII (1896), pp. 289–305.

20 Murphy, *Early Irish Lyrics*, p. 161.

21 J.G. O'Keeffe (ed. and trans.), *Buile Suibhne* (Irish Texts Society Vol. XI. 2nd edn, London: Irish Texts Society 1996), p. 15.

22 Ibid., p. 115.

23 Gwynn's *Metrical Dindshenchas* collects a wide range of placelore, some of which is present in the *Acallam*.

24 On place in the *Táin*, see G.C. Haley's 'The Topography of the Táin Bó Cúailnge' (unpublished Ph.D. dissertation, Harvard University, Cambridge, MA, 1973).

25 *Finnegans Wake* is similarly circular, and makes the landscape of Ireland a central character.

26 A. Dooley and H. Roe (eds and trans.), *Tales of the Elders of Ireland* (Oxford: Oxford University Press, 1999), p. 39.

27 P. MacCana, 'Placenames and Mythology in Irish Tradition: Places, Pilgrimages and Things', in G.W. Maclennan (ed.), *Proceedings of the First North American Congress of Celtic Studies* (Ottawa: Chair of Celtic Studies, University of Ottawa, 1988), p. 335.

28 Dooley and Roe, *Tales*, p. 49.

29 J. Leerssen, *Mere Irish and Fíor-Ghael* (Cork: Cork University Press, 1996), p. 153.

30 The Marquis of Clanricade's 1722 account of a bardic school tells us that 'The Qualifications first requir'd were reading well, writing the Mother-tongue, and

a strong Memory' (in O. Bergin [ed. and trans.], *Irish Bardic Poetry* [Dublin: Dublin Institute for Advanced Studies, 1970], p. 6). The significance granted to memory confirms that bards – as the aristocratic and educated in a culture in which literacy was far from universal – preserved Irish history as it had occurred and as it continued to unfold.

31 On 'pseudohistory' in other Irish literature, see J. Carey, *A New Introduction to Lebor Gabála Érenn* (Dublin: Irish Texts Society, 1993), p. 1 and note 1.

32 M. Caball notes that the gradual acceptance of the Normans 'typifies bardic capacity for conceptual innovation in the midst of structural dissolution' (*Poets and Politics: Reaction and Continuity in Irish Poetry, 1558–1625* [Cork: Cork University Press, 1998], p. 102).

33 Following the Norman invasion and changes to the Irish Church, 'Irish rulers had to turn elsewhere to find a theoretical justification for their authority – to the secular learned classes of bards, brehons, and historians, and to the immemorial tradition expressed in the secular inauguration-rites' (K. Simms, *From Kings to Warlords: The Changing Political Structure of Gaelic Ireland in the Later Middle Ages* [London: The Boydell Press, 1987], p. 16).

34 N.J.A. Williams (ed. and trans.), *The Poems of Giolla Brighde Mac Con Midhe* (Dublin: Irish Texts Society, 1980), p. 275.

35 Ibid., p. 57 st. 13.

36 Ibid., p. 63 st. 29.

37 Bergin, *Irish Bardic Poetry*, p. 101 st. 2; p. 102 st. 8; st. 11; st. 12.

38 Ibid., p. 249 st. 2; st. 7; st. 11.

39 W. Gillies, 'The Classical Irish Poetic Tradition', in D.E. Evans *et al.* (eds), *Proceedings of the Seventh International Congress of Celtic Studies* (Oxford: Oxford University Press, 1986), p. 111.

40 See M. Dowd, 'Gaelic Economy and Society', in C. Brady and R. Gillespie (eds), *Natives and Newcomers* (Dublin: Irish Academic Press, 1986), p. 125.

41 In 'Native Culture and Political Change in Ireland, 1580–1640', B. Cunningham writes that 'Sixteenth century Irish writers had not distinguished between conflict with the English on the one hand and the ongoing disputes among the Gaelic lords themselves on the other . . .' (in Brady and Gillespie, *Natives and Newcomers*, p. 155). On British aims of confiscating and controlling land, see N. Canny, *The Elizabethan Conquest of Ireland* (Sussex: The Harvester Press, 1976), pp. 114–15; 118–19.

42 Bergin, *Irish Bardic Poetry*, p. 232 st. 2.

43 Ibid., p. 233 st. 9.

44 Ibid., p. 268 st. 1.

45 Ibid., st. 2–3.

46 Ibid., st. 5.

47 J. Carney, *The Irish Bardic Poet* (Dublin: Dublin Institute for Advanced Studies, 1958), p. 11.

48 Bergin, *Irish Bardic Poetry*, p. 269 st. 8.

49 Kinsale was the largest rebellion in Ireland up to that time; led by the O'Neill family, the rebels were joined by troops from Munster as well as Ulster. The Spanish had also been fighting the English before the battle itself. For an account of the events leading up to the battle, and the subsequent flight to the continent, see *Beatha Aoda Ruaidh Uí Dhomhnaill* (*The Life of Aodh Ruadh O Domhnaill*) 2 Vols., ed. and trans. by P. Walsh (Dublin: Irish Texts Society 1948–49). It offers a fascinating prose account of the defeat at Kinsale: 'Sad indeed that 'twas not side by side these heroes launched the attack on their enemies and directed their energies towards their foes, and that they were not on good terms, for their success was unbroken while they remained so, and they were victorious in the

neighbouring territories they entered, and they would not have been banished from their native land by a foreign race, as happened afterwards' (I, p. 273).

50 Fear Flatha Ó Gnímh's work also demonstrates the increasing concern during the late fifteenth and early sixteenth centuries with the demise of the bardic order, and his 'The Death of Ireland' offers another look at the state of Irish culture following Kinsale; see Bergin, *Irish Bardic Poetry*, p. 264.

51 Ibid., p. 222 st. 2.

52 Ibid., st. 4.

53 Ibid., p. 223 st. 13–14.

54 Ibid., p. 226 st. 2; st. 11.

55 Ibid., p. 227 st. 20; st. 23.

56 Ibid., p. 226 st. 14; st. 15.

57 In the 1580s and 1590s, the Munster plantation had a population of about 400 English (M.M. Morrogh, 'The English Presence in Early Seventeenth Century Munster', in Brady and Gillespie, *Natives and Newcomers*, p. 171). Only three decades later, according to N. Canny, the adult British population in Ulster, for example, was approximately 12,000. Movement from England to Ireland compares to that from Spain to the Americas, 'which averaged 2,583 a year during its sixteeenth-century phase . . .'; Britain's population was, however, 'less than half that of the Iberian peninsula' (*Making Ireland British 1580–1650* [Oxford: Oxford University Press, 2001], p. 211).

58 See, for example, R. Gillespie, 'The End of an Era: Ulster and the Outbreak of the 1641 Rising', in Brady and Gillespie, *Natives and Newcomers*, p. 195.

59 Canny, *Making Ireland British*, p. 327.

60 J.E.C. Williams, *The Court Poet in Medieval Ireland* (Oxford: Oxford University Press, 1972), p. 19.

61 The first maps deemed reliable by those who knew the landscape were prepared by John Speed for the Irish section of the 1612 *Theatre of the Empire of Great Britaine* (J.H. Andrews, 'Paper Landscapes: Mapping Ireland's Physical Geography', in J.W. Foster [ed.], *Nature in Ireland* [Dublin: The Lilliput Press, 1997], p. 202).

62 Renaissance cartography and cosmography had advanced so quickly that, from 1475–1575, according to one historian of mapmaking, 'European perception of the world land and water relationships changed more than it did in any comparable period' (N.J.W. Thrower, *Maps and Man: An Examination of Cartography in Relation to Culture and Civilization* [Englewood Cliffs, NJ: Prentice-Hall, Inc., 1972], p. 48). By Spenser's era, there was communication between geographers and the Elizabethan court, resulting in 'the parallel development of models of the globe and of the state', which was 'fundamental to the creation of that consciousness of an outward-looking empire which became so important in the centuries to come' (L.B. Cormack, 'The Fashioning of an Empire: Geography and the State in Elizabethan England', in A. Godlewska and N. Smith [eds], *Geography and Empire* [Oxford: Blackwell Publishers, 1994], p. 16). For contemporary Irish critics, this mapping is the beginning of the colonial venture. 'These maps and documents are triumphant symbols of the power of the colonial government to penetrate and appropriate every corner, every placename and every person in the land' (W.J. Smyth, 'Explorations of Place', in J. Lee [ed.], *Ireland: Towards a Sense of Place* [Cork: Cork University Press, 1985], p. 3).

63 F. Lestringant, *Mapping the Renaissance World*, trans. D. Faussett (Berkeley, CA: University of California Press, 1994), p. 5.

64 While '*mappa mundi*' was used to describe earlier maps, those drawn during the Renaissance were the first to represent the actual globe as we know it, as opposed to what was known of the globe in earlier eras.

65 Giraldus Cambrensis, *The History and Topography of Ireland*, trans. J.J. O'Meara (New York: Penguin Books, 1982), p. 238.
66 Ibid., p. 239.
67 Céitinn, in his 1634 treatise, *Foras Feasa Ar Éirinn* (4 vols., D. Comyn and P.S. Dinneen ed. and trans. [London: Irish Texts Society, 1902–14]), attacks Cambrensis, but also Stanihurst, Spenser and others for writing falsely about Ireland: 'inasmuch as it is almost according to the fashion of the beetle they act, when writing concerning the Irish'; a beetle 'keeps bustling about until it meets with dung of horse or cow, and proceeds to roll itself therein' (Vol. I, p. 5).
68 Part of the problem was Ireland's Catholicism. The Elizabethan era witnesses a change, however, as the Irish are seen as 'pagan'. Canny notes that 'To admit that the native Irish were Christian would . . . acknowledge them as civilized also. By declaring the Irish to be pagan, however, the English were decreeing that the Irish were culpable, since their heathenism was due not to a lack of opportunity but rather because their system of government was antithetical to Christianity. Once it was established that the Irish were pagans the first logical step had been taken towards declaring them barbarian' (*Elizabethan Conquest*, p. 125). C. Carroll traces the change in the idea of barbarity to John Derricke's *Image of Ireland* (1581): his 'notion of the Irish as inherently and innately evil and so fit for extermination marks a real departure from the medieval discourse of barbarism, in which the Irish are evil not by nature but by custom, and so capable of improvement' (*Circe's Cup: Cultural Transformations in Early Modern Ireland* [Cork: Cork University Press, 2001], p. 18). It should be remarked, as well, that the title of Derricke's tract, like Spenser's, aims to be a visual aid – a map – of Ireland.
69 The Irish economy was not entirely pastoral, however; this was in part an English fiction. See Dowd, 'Gaelic Economy and Society', in Brady and Gillespie, *Natives and Newcomers*.
70   . . . for though the Irishry . . . *possessed a land abounding with all the things necessary for the civil life of man*, yet, which is strange to be related, they did never build any houses of brick or stone, some few poor religious houses excepted, before the reign of King Henry the Second . . . Neither did any of them in all this time *plant any gardens or orchards, enclose or improve their lands,* live together in settled villages or towns, nor make any provision for posterity, which, being against all commonsense and reason, must needs be imputed to those unreasonable customs which made their estates so uncertain and transitory in their possession. (J. Davies, *A Discovery of the True Causes Why Ireland was Never Entirely Subdued Nor Brought Under Obedience of the Crown of England Until the Beginning of His Majesty's Happy Reign*, in Henry Morley [ed.], *Ireland Under Elizabeth and James the First* [London: Routledge, 1890 (1612)], pp. 291–2 my emphasis)
71 For evidence that wherever possible the land was, in fact, under cultivation, see Canny, *Elizabethan Conquest of Ireland*, p. 14.
72 R. Beacon, 'Solon His Follie', in V. Carey and C. Carroll (eds), (Binghamton, NY: *Medieval and Renaissance Texts and Studies*, Vol. 154, 1996 [1594]), p. 75.
73 Ibid., pp. XIII–XLIII.
74 'For the husbandman must first break the land before it be made capable of good seed; and when it is thoroughly broken and manured, if he do not forthwith cast good seed into it, it will grow wild again and bear nothing but weeds' (Davies, *A Discovery*, pp. 218–19). Davies is, however, unusual in attempting to justify conquest through law, and in his willingness to point out the repeated errors of earlier Englishmen in Ireland.

75 A significant element of English 'civility' was language; the Irish language was almost entirely ignored in these prose 'maps'. As P. Palmer puts it, 'There is an outflow of *Views, Discoveries, Descriptions, Images, Platts, Anatomies*, but, as the relentlessly visual register of these titles insists, Irish-speakers are looked at rather than heard. Their story is told almost without quotation marks' (*Language and Conquest in Early Modern Ireland* [Cambridge: Cambridge University Press, 2001), p. 40).

76 P. Coughlan, '"Some secret scourge which shall by her come to England": Ireland and Incivility in Spenser', in P. Coughlan (ed.), *Spenser and Ireland* (Cork: Cork University Press, 1989), p. 52.

77 E. Spenser, *A View of the Present State of Ireland*, A. Hadfield and W. Maley (eds) (Oxford: Blackwell Publishers, 1997 [1633]), p. 156.

78 Ibid., p. 27.

79 Recent scholarship attempts to address this gap in Spenser studies. Carroll argues that Irenius's outline of invasions in *A View* corresponds to that in *Leabhar Gabhála*, suggesting that Spenser did have direct knowledge of some Irish literature (*Circe's Cup*, p. 65).

80 'Colin Clouts Come Home Againe', in *The Works of Edmund Spenser: A Variorum Edition* Vol. 7: *The Minor Poems* (Oxford: Oxford University Press, 1966 [4th edn]), p. 157; p. 155. The theme of exile and its nostalgic elements is also, of course, Ovidian, and Ovid's well-documented influence on Spenser is thus also at work here.

81 Ibid., p. 165.

82 There was famine in late-sixteenth and early seventeenth-century Ireland as well, of course.

83 Citations for *The Faerie Queene* are taken from the Penguin edition (London, 1978; reprinted 1987); line numbers are provided to facilitate the use of other editions. For the dedication, see p. 37.

84 Some of Yeats's early poems, as well as Joyce's *Ulysses*, are written from a similar space.

85 W. Maley writes about Spenser's archaic English in relation to English as it was spoken in Ireland: 'Spenser's Irish English: Language and Identity in Early Modern Ireland', *Studies in Philology*, 91 (1994), pp. 417–31.

86 S. Stewart, *On Longing: Narratives of the Miniature, the Gigantic, the Souvenir, the Collection* (Durham, NC, and London: Duke University Press, 1993), p. 142.

87 This argument was presented in a series of lectures given at the Graduate School and University Center, the City University of New York, autumn 1997.

88 These cantos share with Finn literature the theme of the hunt; while we assume that Spenser had Ovidian sources for Faunus, it is plausible that he knew tales of the Finn cycle, which were widely collected in manuscripts after the twelfth century.

89 This question echoes another: 'Who knows not Colin Clouts?' (VI.16). The connection between the phraseology, and the obvious identification between Colin and Spenser, has led critics to argue that the voice in the *Mutabilitie Cantos* is, like that of Colin Clouts, personalized. J.R. Lupton argues 'that it is precisely the mythopoetic demarcation of the poet's home-away-from-home which permits the appearance of a more concretised narrative persona' ('Mapping Mutability: or, Spenser's Irish Plot', in B. Bradshaw *et al.* [eds], *Representing Ireland: Literature and the Origins of Conflict, 1534–1660* [Cambridge: Cambridge University Press, 1993], p. 105). This argument is particularly interesting due to the element of nostalgia that Spenser evidently experiences as an exile.

90 The reader of *The Faerie Queene* thus also becomes a participant in the charting of empire.

CHAPTER TWO

1 G.W. Stocking, Jr, 'Essays on Museums and Material Culture', in G.W. Stocking, Jr (ed.), *Objects and Others: Essays on Museums and Material Culture* (Madison, WI: University of Wisconsin Press, 1985), p. 6.

2 Collecting, as J. Clifford describes it in 'Objects and Selves – an Afterword', in Stocking, Jr (ed.), *Objects and Others*, 'has long been a strategy for the deployment of a possessive self, culture, and authenticity' (p. 238); Stocking, Jr points out that 'the very materiality of the objects of material culture entangled them in Western economic processes of the acquisition and exchange of wealth' (*Objects and Others*, p. 5), and that collection itself resulted from historial processes that have to do with 'on the one hand forces of economic development and nationalism that transformed Europe in the nineteenth century, and on the other with those of imperial domination' (pp. 4–5). S. Stewart demonstrates how objects in museums are forced, by their decontextualization, to 'represent' or become the signifier for an entire culture (*On Longing*).

3 On the museums and societies of nineteenth-century Ireland, see J.W. Foster, *Recoveries* (Dublin: University College of Dublin Press, 2002) and T. Eagleton, *Scholars & Rebels in Nineteenth-Century Ireland* (Oxford: Blackwell Publishers Ltd, 1999).

4 Stocking, Jr, *Objects and Others*, p. 5.

5 Antiquarianism was, as T. Eagleton describes it, a 'dissident' occupation, since in Ireland 'remembering the past has been, unlike in England, largely a radical pursuit' (*Scholars & Rebels*, p. 10). M. Tymoczko notes that that translation of early Irish texts that took place within the antiquarian movement focused on 'the reclamation of Irish culture' (*Translation in a Postcolonial Context* [Manchester: St Jerome Publishing, 1999], p. 20); as a result, 'Translation in the Irish context . . . is not simply a locus of imperialism, but a site of resistance and nation building as well. The apparently neutral, academic, and recondite translation of medieval Irish texts has been an arena of intense ideological and even political activity' (p. 21).

6 M. Andrews (ed. and introduction), *The Picturesque: Literary Sources and Documents*, 3 Vols (The Banks, East Sussex: Helm Information Ltd, 1994), Vol. I, p. 33.

7 M. Andrews has described the Picturesque as a 'squirearchy' (ibid) that functions by 'coming up with a set of aesthetic criteria which makes scenes of poverty and dilapidation attractive', thus enabling the viewer to 'suppress any moral sympathies which might find it hard to tolerate the misery of rural poverty . . . The Picturesque thus supports a deeply conservative ideology at the same time as, for the privileged beneficiaries, it eases the spectacle of the painful transition to a new order' (ibid., Vol. I, p. 22).

8 On the rise in tourism, see S. Thompson, 'The Postcolonial Tourist: Irish Tourism and Decolonization Since 1850' (unpublished Ph.D. dissertation, Notre Dame University, 2000), p. 32, n. 14, in which Thompson charts the numbers of guides to Ireland produced for tourist consumption. In 'Samuel Ferguson: A Tourist in Antrim', in G. Dawe and J.W. Foster (eds), *The Poet's Place: Ulster Literature and Society* (Belfast: Institute of Irish Studies, Queen's University Belfast, 1991), E. Patten notes that the Napoleonic Wars forced English tourists to turn away from the Grand Tour to the 'domestic circuit' (p. 98).

9 Among them were Percy Bysshe Shelley (who famously delivered a speech at Trinity College Dublin, only to be answered with thrown tomatoes), William Wordsworth (who came to visit the scientist William Rowan Hamilton in 1829 and who described Ireland as 'a romantic itinerary, a sucession of picturesque

scenes with priority given to ruined monastaries' (in Patten, 'Samuel Ferguson', in *The Poet's Place*, p. 100), and William Thackeray (whose 1843 trip was recorded in a travelogue).

10 The penchant for 'wildness' is highlighted by William Gilpin's *A Dialogue Upon the Gardens at Stowe* (1748), which argues that 'Regularity' – the very land-scape of post-enclosure England – was unappealing to the imagination: 'Thus a regular Building perhaps gives us very little pleasure; yet a fine Rock, beau-tifully set off in Claro-obscuro [sic], and garnished with flourishing Bushes, Ivy, and dead Branches, may afford us a great deal; and a ragged Ruin, with venerable old Oaks, and Pines nodding over it, may perhaps please the fancy yet more than either of the other two Objects' (in Andrews, *The Picturesque*, Vol. I, p. 73). Gilpin's enthusiastic capitalization lends additional force to his argument.

11 The Claude-glass is one of the most fascinating objects of this period. Named after the landscape painter Claude Lorrain, the Claude-glass was a piece of convex glass backed with foil (which could be coloured, like contemporary film filters, to create visual effects like those of sunlight, sunset, etc.) through which the landscape could be 'framed' and viewed. That the viewer was required to turn away from the landscape in question, and that the glass distorted the image (due to its convexity) makes it a wonderfully apt metaphor for the distancing involved in picturesque and pastoral ideologies.

12 'Francophobia played its part in defining the character of the English Picturesque, not just in the familiar comparison of free, open English landscapes with the oppressive artifice of Versailles: after the French Revolution, the whole issue of landscape management became peculiarly politicised and xenophobic' (Andrews, *The Picturesque*, Vol. I, p. 12).

13 Macpherson came quickly to the spotlight with the publication of *Fragments of Ancient Poetry* (1760). The appeal that this brief pamphlet had led to a period of research in Scotland that produced *Fingal: An Ancient Epic Poem in Six Books. Together with several Other Poems composed by Ossian the Son of Fingal*, and *Temora: An Ancient Epic Poem in Eight Books. Together with several Other Poems composed by Ossian the Son of Fingal*, in 1765.

14 J. Macpherson, *The Poems of Ossian and Related Works*, ed. Howard Gaskill, Introduction by Fiona Stafford (Edinburgh: Edinburgh University Press, 1996), Fragment VII, p. 16; Fragment X, p. 21.

15 Ibid., *The Poems of Ossian*, p. 35.

16 M.H. Nicholson's seminal work, *Mountain Gloom, Mountain Glory* (Washington, DC: University of Washington Press, 1997), provides an indispensable social history of how nature in Europe came to be revered.

17 Cited in S. Deane (ed.), *The Field Day Anthology of Irish Writing*, 3 Vols, (Derry: Field Day Publications, 1991), Vol. I, p. 980. M. Tymoczko argues that while Brooke 'follows Macpherson in creating a translation that is self-standing within the English literary stystem', she also 'shows pains to avoid the criticism levelled at Macpherson by providing scholarly commentary in footnotes, by carefully specifying her sources, and by including . . . the originals of almost all the texts she translates' (*Translation in a Postcolonial Context*, p. 132).

18 J. Walker, *Historical Memoirs*, p. 125.

19 T. Eagleton notes that 'Sentimentalism and sensibility are, so to speak, the eighteenth century's phenomenological turn, rehearsing in the realm of the passions and affections a ritual of subjecthood which is already well-established in the fields of economic and political life' (*Crazy John*, p. 77).

20 J. Hardiman, *Irish Minstrelsy*, Vol. I, p. ii.

21 Ibid., Vol. I, p. xxxvii.

22 Ibid., Vol. I, p. ii. James Clarence Mangan, of course, also played the game of 'discovering' and 'translating' texts. L. Platt has described Yeats's and Joyce's very different reactions to Mangan: Yeats 'the landless landowner regarded the one Catholic poet of any significance from this period as a rootless, self-destructive figure outside the mainstream of Gaelic culture. The churchless Catholic [Joyce], on the other hand, presented Mangan as summing up Catholic dispossession, the last and most passionate representative of a dead culture' (*Joyce and the Anglo-Irish: A Study of Joyce and the Literary Revival* [Amsterdam: Rodopi, 1998], p. 29).

23 Hardiman, *Irish Minstrelsy*, Vol. I, pp. 201–2; Vol. II, p. 178.

24 While Romanticism was more widespread in England, even there Romantic attitudes towards landscape 'were the property of a very few social groups' who were mobile: 'This mobility is an essential condition . . . : it meant that the aristocracy and gentry were not, unlike the majority of the rural population, irrevocably involved, so to speak, bound up in, any particular locality which they had no time, no money, and no reason ever to leave. It meant also that they had experience of more landscapes than one, in more geographical regions than one; and even if they did not travel much, they were accustomed, by their culture, to the *notion* of mobility, and could easily imagine other landscapes' (Barrell, *The Idea of Landscape*, p. 63). If mobility and so the defining attitude towards landscape that governed Romanticism was an impossibility for much of English society, it was even more of an impossibility for the Irish at this time.

25 John Clare, an exception within the English nature poetry tradition, is one of the few writers for whom the distance between subject and object did not exist.

26 T. Eagleton, *Heathcliff and The Great Hunger: Studies in Irish Culture* (London: Verso, 1995), pp. 7–8.

27 'Given the "romance" of colonization, it is not surprising to find a resistance to the cult of the wilderness, and the idealization of solitude and nature, in Irish culture . . . Where the colonizer saw nature, the colonized saw culture. Accordingly, landscape in Irish romanticism answered not so much to the call of the wild as to the return of the native, its ruins, antiquities and associations with myths and legends testifying to the existence of disparate national narratives which asserted a tenacious hold on popular memory' (Gibbons, *Transformations*, p. 14).

28 'Nature and Nation in the Nineteenth Century', in J.W. Foster (ed.), *Nature in Ireland* (Dublin: The Lilliput Press, 1997), p. 413.

29 W.E. Montgomery, *The History of Land Tenure in Ireland* (Cambridge: Cambridge University Press, 1889), p. 85.

30 See J.H. Andrews, *A Paper Landscape* (Oxford: Oxford University Press, 1975), and Brien Friel's *Translations* (London: Faber & Faber, 1981).

31 T. Eagleton remarks that the Ordnance Survey served an ironic purpose: 'Since some of this scholarship was to inspire later nationalist writers, it could be claimed that the Irish Revival was funded in part by the British state' (*Scholars & Rebels*, p. 130).

32 Thompson, 'The Postcolonial Tourist', p. 34. Thompson notes that Thomas Cook of travel guide fame completed one of his most successful tours to Ireland in 1847, one of the bleakest years of the Famine.

33 This is also in sharp contrast to the English situation, according to Eagleton:

> [W]hereas in the British context history becomes Nature, in Ireland Nature becomes history. And this both in the sense that, in a largely pre-industrial society, the land is the prime determinant of human life, and in the sense that in the Famine history appears with all the brute, aleatory power of seismic upheaval, thus writing large the course of much Irish history. The

British have naturalized their own social relations as providential; and the effects of Nature in this sense will then appear over the water as Nature in its most Schopenhauerian guise. This in turn will feed back to the metropolitan nation as an image of the Darwinism which is just about to shake them to their ideological core: Nature as random and purposeless, as a shattered landscape lurking as a terrifying possibility at the root of their own civility. Ireland and *Wuthering Heights* are names for that civility's sickening precariousness; for it had in its time to be wrested inch by inch from the soil, and is thus permanently capable of sliding back into it. (*Heathcliff and The Great Hunger*, p. 11)

England tended to define itself as 'culture' in opposition to Ireland's mere 'nature'.

34 S. Lysaght, 'Contrasting Natures: The Issue of Names', in Foster (ed.), *Nature in Ireland*, pp. 442–3.

35 T. O'Neill provides statistics on the numbers of evictions during and after the Famine, and claims that it was the sheer 'brutality of many evictions, even in the pre-Famine period, [that] destablised rural society' ('Famine Evictions', in C. King [ed.], *Famine, Land and Culture in Ireland* [Dublin: University College Dublin Press, 2000], p. 29).

36 Darwin, whose influence was felt almost immediately on English writers and scholars like Arnold, took longer to reach Ireland except through the indirect impact of essays like Arnold's. Perhaps because the Irish were in recovery from the most severe experience of the chance of nature's ways, because of a committed Catholicism, and because of the anti-Catholic politics of the mostly Anglo-Irish Protestants who were the Irish supporters of such science as Lyell, Darwin and Tyndall produced, evolution was rejected by most people. If the debate that took place in Belfast is any indication of the way in which the Irish responded to Darwin's ideas, resistance would have been fervent. Tyndall's appearance at an 1874 meeting resulted in a split between the scientific community that Tyndall represented and the clergy: 'In the aftermath of Tyndall's offensive, the Belfast religious community found it virtually impossible for at least a generation to find any rapprochement with Darwinian biology' (D.N. Livingstone, 'Darwin in Belfast: The Evolution Debate', in Foster [ed.], *Nature in Ireland*, p. 403).

   Any chance that Darwin's theories had of immediately rooting themselves in Ireland was further diminished by the frequent representation of the Irish by the English, in magazines like *Punch*, as monkeys and apes. The presentation of the Irish as primitive, undeveloped and non-human would severely limit the acceptance of Darwin's theories in Victorian Ireland. See also J.W. Foster's 'Darwin in Ireland: John Tyndall and the Irish Churches', in *Recoveries*.

37 Arnold, *On the Study of Celtic Literature*, p. 20.

38 'I am inclined to think that the march of science – science insisting that there is no such original chasm between the Celt and the Saxon as we once popularly imagined, that they are not truly, what Lord Lyndhurst called them, *aliens in blood* from us, that they are our brothers in the great Indo-European family – has had a share, an appreciable share, in producing this changed state of feeling' (ibid., p. 27).

39 Ernest Renan's *The Poetry of the Celtic Races and Other Studies*, trans. William B. Hutchinson (London: Kennikat Press, 1970 [1859]).

40 Arnold, *On the Study of Celtic Literature*, p. 82.

41 In attempting to classify a national character he is not, of course, unique to his time, or, indeed to previous ones – generations of writers, including such figures

as Kant, despite all his practicality and sophistication of thought, attempted to do just the same.

42 It also, Tymoczko notes, disallows 'the possibility of acknowledging the central importance of comic elements in Irish literature' (*Translation in a Postcolonial Context*, p. 207), defining what was 'Irish' in a narrow way that would eventually be absorbed by the Revival as well, when 'The pious expectation of solemnity in all things Irish' (ibid.) contributed to the uproar about Synge's *Playboy*. This colonial stereotype is eventually adopted by the Irish, in other words, in a denial of another stereotype, that of the stage Irishman.

43 Gibbons, *Transformations*, p. 9.

44 Arnold, *On the Study of Celtic Literature*, p. 95; see also p. 86.

45 Ibid., p. 120. Arnold differentiates between 'conventional' nature writing (in which the eye is not on the object, where the natural world simply serves as a backdrop to the poetic action), 'faithful' nature writing (in which the eye is on the object and attempts to detail a realism about the natural world), 'Greek' nature writing (in which the eye is on the object as in 'faithful' writing, but a certain 'radiancy' is added that is the product of poetic adornment), and 'magical' nature writing, the category that Arnold assigns to the Celt.

46 Within four years, O'Grady published a series of books that were to become of great importance to figures like Yeats: *History of Ireland: Heroic Period* (1878); *Early Bardic Literature, Ireland* (1879); *History of Ireland: Cuchulain and his Contemporaries* (1880); *History of Ireland: Critical and Philosophical*, Vol. I (1881); and *Cuchulain: An Epic* (1882). These works formed the cornerstone of O'Grady's reputation, which continued to be bolstered by his publication of essays, criticisms, historical enquiries, fiction and children's stories.

47 See S.J. O'Grady, *History of Ireland: Critical and Philosophical*, Vol. I (London: Sampson, Low & Co., 1881 [Dublin: E. Ponsonby]), pp. 425–64, for an example of O'Grady's analysis of his sources.

48 S.J. O'Grady, *Early Bardic Literature, Ireland* (London: Sampson, Low, Searle, Marston, & Rivington, 1879) p. 39.

49 Ibid., p. 14.

50 Ibid., pp. 17–18.

51 O'Grady's emphasis on the 'heroic' and 'aristocratic' past of the Irish meshed with his position as a member of the Ascendancy class who believed that the Ascendancy could still lead the Irish, and, indeed, could save them from themselves, as it were. These sentiments, while not in line with the nationalism of some of the Revivalists that were to follow him, were very much in line with the aristocratic thinking of a Yeats.

52 A.T. Seaman, 'Celtic Myth as Perceived in Eighteenth and Nineteenth-Century Literature in English', in Cyril J. Byrne *et al.* (eds), *Celtic Languages and Celtic Peoples: Proceedings of the Second North American Congress of Celtic Studies* (Halifax, Nova Scotia: D'Arcy McGee Chair of Irish Studies, St Mary's University, 1992), p. 453.

53 As Leerssen puts it, 'The popular, often illustrated stories/histories of Ireland which were published in great numbers in the closing decades of the nineteenth century, were . . . all of them stories and none of them histories proper' (*Remembrance and Imagination: Patterns in the Historical and Literary Representation of Ireland in the Nineteenth Century* [Cork: Cork University Press, 1997], p. 153). Ironically, this is in line with the medieval Irish tradition of 'pseudohistory'.

54 O'Grady, *Early Bardic Literature*, p. 31.

55 On O'Grady's translations as a 'quest for a national identity within the larger process of colonization and decolonisation', see Tymoczko, *Translation in a Postcolonial Context*, p. 178.

56 Seaman, 'Celtic Myth', p. 456.
57 O'Grady, *Early Bardic Literature*, p. 11.
58 Gibbons, *Transformations*, p. 120.
59 Largely because of O'Grady's influential shapings of the Irish past, 'the most quoted poets of the revival were [to become] Ó Rathaille and Ó Bruadair, both of whom outdid O'Grady in their eloquent contempt for churls and upstarts' (D. Kiberd, 'The Perils of Nostalgia: A Critique of the Revival', in P. Connolly [ed.], *Literature and the Changing Ireland* [Gerrards Cross: Colin Smythe, 1982], p. 19).
60 J.W. Foster, 'The Artifice of Eternity: Medieval Aspects of Modern Irish Literature', in R. Wall (ed.), *Medieval and Modern Ireland* (Totowa, NJ: Barnes & Noble Books, 1988), p. 125.
61 S. Deane, 'Introduction', in *Nationalism, Colonialism and Literature* (Minneapolis, MN: University of Minnesota Press, 1990), pp. 12–13.
62 For an analysis of the idea, see J. Genet (ed.), *Rural Ireland, Real Ireland?* (Gerrards Cross: Colin Smythe, 1996); and D. Kiberd's *Inventing Ireland* (London: Jonathan Cape, 1995), particularly p. 492.
63 On Collins see, for example, Kiberd, *Inventing Ireland*, p. 487. N. Corcoran describes de Valera's famous 1943 St Patrick's Day speech as 'comic-book Homeric pastoral' (*After Yeats and Joyce: Reading Modern Irish Literature* [Oxford: Oxford University Press, 1997], p. 59).
64 P. Bull, in his most useful study *Land, Politics and Nationalism: A Study of the Irish Land Question* (Dublin: Gill & Macmillan Ltd, 1996), describes Butt's contribution to the land question as linking land to nationalism directly. 'His attempt to create a political movement which drew its sustenance from a range of issues and embodied a distinctly Irish polity had lifted the land question out of the context of liberal reform and restated it not only in terms of its indigenous attributes as an issue, but also as a symbol and token of a distinctive Irish identity' (p. 67).
65 Ibid., p. 97.
66 See T. Reeves-Smyth, 'The Natural History of Demesnes', in J.W. Foster (ed.), *Nature in Ireland*, p. 551; and Bull, *Land, Politics and Nationalism*, pp. 152–8.
67 In Ireland, S. Lysaght has written,

> there is a particular obstacle to our relationship with nature which has to do with the fact that the old Gaelic vernacular has been lost to most of the country – and with it a range of names for plants and animals, the key to the old Gaelic's community with the natural world. The decline of that primitive relationship with land and sea, and the extinction of its vocabulary, has given rise to a powerful nostalgia. It is as if the loss of the language carried with it the loss of the objects themselves ('Contrasting Natures', in J.W. Foster (ed.), *Nature In Ireland*, pp. 440–1).

68 The Land League, for example, was founded at an O'Connell Street, Dublin meeting. Only one member of the executive was a farmer, and he was also a politician. Three of the seven executives were Members of Parliament, and four were active Fenians. 'From the beginning the Land League was in the control of a national, political and urban leadership rather than a local, agrarian and rural one' (D. McCartney, 'Parnell, Davitt and the Land Question' in C. King [ed.], *Famine, Land and Culture in Ireland* [Dublin: University College Dublin Press, 2000], p. 73).
69 Bull, *Land, Politics and Nationalism*, p. 176.
70 Although not Synge: Synge's ability to both speak and read the Irish language differentiated him from his peers, as D. Kiberd's *Synge and the Irish Language* (London: Macmillan, 1993 [2nd edn]) documents.

71 This has been increasingly claimed of Lady Gregory's translations. See the introduction to *Lady Gregory: Selected Writings* ed. by L. McDiarmid and M. Waters (London: Penguin, 1995), pp. xi–xlv.

72 K. Meyer's description of early Irish nature poetry has become familiar to students of the period and resembles arguments by Arnold and O'Grady as well as demonstrating the influence of Macpherson's creative reworkings of medieval tales:

> In Nature poetry the Gaelic muse may vie with that of any other nation. Indeed, these poems occupy a unique position in the literature of the world. To seek out and watch and love Nature, in its tiniest phenomena as in its grandest, was given to no people so early and so fully as to the Celt . . . It is characteristic of these poems that in none of them do we get an elaborate or sustained description of any scene or scenery, but rather a succession of pictures and images which the poet, like an impressionist, calls up before us by light and skillful touches. ('Find Mac Umaill', *Revue Celtique*, XXXII [1911], pp. xii–xiii)

To ascribe early nature poetry to a racially inherent ability or skill immediately imposes a system of interpretation, popular after the Romantic movement, that wants to believe in earlier cultures as truly pastoral.

73 Neither was this tendency to look backwards limited to Irish sources. Yeats, for example, looked to many cultures' pasts for inspiration and for parallels with Ireland; India and Byzantium are solid examples.

74 G. Bachelard, *The Poetics of Reverie*, trans. Daniel Russell (Boston, MA: Beacon Press, 1969), p. 119.

75 E. Burke, *A Philosophical Inquiry into the Origins of Our Ideas of the Sublime and the Beautiful,* ed. David Womersley (New York: Penguin, 1999 [London: Dodsley, 1757]), p. 17.

76 Bachelard, *The Poetics of Reverie*, p. 122.

77 Davis, *Yearning for Yesterday*, p. 18.

78 Ibid., p. 21.

79 Ibid., p. 24.

CHAPTER THREE

1 Thompson's 'The Postcolonial Tourist' notes that the notion of 'Yeats' Country' began in earnest in the 1960s as a tourism push (p. 201).

2 R. Ellmann's *Yeats: The Man and the Masks* (New York: W.W. Norton & Company, Inc., 1979 [1948]) and R.F. Foster's first volume of the two-volume biography of Yeats, *W.B. Yeats: A life I: The Apprentice Mage 1865–1914* (Oxford: Oxford University Press, 1998) do not, of course, simply romanticize their subject.

3 This phrase, coincidentally, appears in J. Hassell's *Tour to the Isle of Wight* (1790), in Andrews (ed.), *The Picturesque*, Vol. I, p. 21.

4 For Davis's definitions, see the end of the previous chapter, p. 56.

5 In a different context, N.A. Miller argues that while critics have traditionally seen Yeats as 'memorializing' and Joyce as 'counter-memorializing', Yeats is more profitably viewed as 'maintaining a place within his writing for . . . the "counter-memorial" function . . .' (*Modern Ireland*, p. 147).

6 W.B. Yeats, *Autobiographies* (London: Macmillan & Co. Ltd., 1955), p. 66.

7 H. Bloom notes that 'Yeats, in later life, writing about Shelley, said that a man's mind at twenty contains everything of importance it will ever possess. Whatever

we think of this as a general principle, it does seem relevant to Yeats himself. *The Island of the Statues* [one of Yeats's first poems] takes its Circe-like enchantress from Spenser, and most of its verse-texture from Shelley, yet its decadent and savage theme is curiously Yeats's own, holding in embryo much that is to come' (*Yeats* [New York: Oxford University Press, 1970], p. 53).

8   For an assessement of the characteristics of 'seasonal poetry', see Chapter One p. 13.

9   W.B. Yeats, 'Edmund Spenser', in *Essays and Introductions* (London: Macmillan & Co. Ltd., 1961), p. 372.

10 All quotations of Yeats's poems are from Daniel Albright's edition, *W.B. Yeats: The Poems* (London: J.M. Dent & Sons Ltd, 1990). Line and verse numbers are provided in-text to accommodate the use of other editions.

11 'I did not deceive myself; I knew how often they wrote a cold and abstract language, and yet I who had never wanted to see the houses where Keats and Shelley lived would ask everybody what sort of place Inchedony was, because Callanan had named after it a bad poem in the manner of *Childe Harold*' (Yeats, *Autobiographies*, p. 101).

12 E. Said, 'Yeats and Decolonialism', in *Nationalism, Colonialism, and Literature* (Minneapolis, MN: University of Minnesota Press, 1990), p. 69.

13 Ibid., pp. 76–7.

14 Ibid., p. 79.

15 Bloom, *Yeats*, p. 87.

16 And this attitude has survived into the present day, with studies of Celtic mysticism and the like, which insist that 'pure' Irish culture is to be found in the pre-Christian era, despite the impossibility of establishing just what that culture might have been like.

17 See, for example, K. Meyer and A. Nutt, eds and trans., *The Voyage of Bran/ Immram Brain* (London: David Nutt, 1897) and H.P. Oskamp, ed. and trans, *The Voyage of Mael Duin: A Study in Early Irish Voyage Literature* (Groningen: Wolters-Noordhoff Publishing, 1970), two secular voyage tales.

18 G. Bornstein, 'Yeats and the Greater Romantic Lyric', in R.J. Finneran (ed.), *Critical Essays on W.B. Yeats* (Boston, MA: G.K. Hall & Co., 1986), p. 206.

19 See, for example, D. Daiches' analysis in 'The Earlier Poems: Some Themes and Patterns', in N.A. Jeffares and K.G.W. Cross (eds), *In Excited Reverie: A Centenary Tribute to William Butler Yeats* (New York: St Martin's Press, 1965): 'One might say that [Yeats's early] poems, for all their use of some traditional romantic properties, contain implicit criticisms of the falsity and sentimentality of at least one romantic attitude to nature' (p. 55); 'Again and again in Yeats's early poetry we find Irish folklore, Irish heroic story, Irish history and even Irish landscape working in his imagination to mitigate the excesses of a self-indulgent romanticism, of mere dreaminess and decorativeness' (p. 63).

20 Ibid.

21 Yeats, *Autobiographies*, p. 116.

22 Ibid.

23 Cited in Foster, *The Apprentice Mage*, p. 32. While Yeats was an enthusiastic naturalist as a young man and read Darwin, Tyndall and Huxley, by the 1890s he had repudiated all of this reading and turned away from the purely scientific. As J.W. Foster notes, however, the influence of scientific advances upon Yeats's work is still present, since he 'retained the methods of science, applying them to non-scientific, or even anti-scientific, subject-matter. For example, he classified Irish fairies and fairy tales in an almost Linnean system, made claims for the "scientific utility" of the study of fairy belief, and lectured to the Belfast Naturalists' Field Club in 1893 on the subject' ('The Culture of Nature', in J.W.

Foster [ed.], *Nature In Ireland* [Dublin: The Lilliput Press, 1997] p. 606). Foster goes on to point out that *A Vision* is also a scientifically systematized text.

24 I am not the first to point out the thematic connection between Yeats's 'King Goll' and *Buile Suibhne*. See R. Fallis, *The Irish Renaissance* (Syracuse, NY: Syracuse University Press, 1977), p. 53; P. Marcus, *Yeats and the Beginning of the Irish Renaissance* (Ithaca, NY: Cornell University Press, 1970), p. 242; and Brian Foley 'Yeats's "King Goll": Sources, Revision, and Revisions', in R.J. Finneran (ed.), *Yeats: An Annual of Critical and Textual Studies*, Volume IV (Ann Arbor, MI: UMI Research Press, 1986), pp. 17–32. Foley argues that Yeats's Goll is a 'composite of Goll Mac Morna, the Gall of the *Cath Finntrágha*, and Finn Mac Cumhaill' (p. 18), but does admit that Goll also 'exhibits certain affinities to Suibhne Geilt' (p. 21). If Eugene O'Curry was, as is believed, Yeats's 'source' for the Irish sources, his version of Goll too, Foley claims, seems to be confused with Sweeney's tale.

25 R.F. Foster, *The Apprentice Mage*, p. 186.

26 Yeats, *Autobiographies*, pp. 71–2.

27 Besides the well known time he spent a night in jail for refusal to pay a tax supporting the Mexican War and a government that allowed the institution of slavery to remain intact, Thoreau's activism, as Paul Friedrich so neatly summarizes it, extended to lectures 'on environmentalism and ecology, the abolition of slavery, resistance to colonialism and imperialism, the defense of civil liberties and the respect of individual conscience, the dangers of autocracy and mob rule. An awesome catalogue of engagement for a man who was primarily and most of the time a poetic writer and a naturalist' (p. 25). Friedrich points out, however, that this intellectual activism was very much balanced by a physical activism: via protest, the helping of former slaves to escape detection, and numerous other rebellions (pp. 25–7). I am grateful to Paul Friedrich for permission to cite this unpublished essay and for a correspondence that influenced my thinking on Thoreau's influence on Yeats.

28 P.J. Mathews' *Revival: The Abbey Theatre, Sinn Féin, The Gaelic League and the Co-operative Movement* (Cork: Cork University Press, 2003) convincingly demonstrates the interconnectedness of Yeats's – and indeed other Revival figures' – activities in many realms.

29 Yeats, *Autobiographies*, p. 153.

30 Ibid., p. 150.

31 See Bull, *Land, Politics and Nationalism*.

32 Letter to Sturge Moore cited in Ellmann, *The Man and the Masks*, p. 271. Early in his relationship with Katherine Tynan, Ellmann notes, Yeats had written in a similar vein to her 'that they both needed to substitute the landscape of nature for the landscape of art' (p. 165).

33 K. Raine, 'Preface', to J.P. McGarry's *Place Names in the Writing of William Butler Yeats* (London: Colin Smythe, 1976), pp. 6–7.

34 Kiberd, *Inventing Ireland*, p. 107.

35 Yeats, *Autobiographies*, pp. 193–4.

36 Yeats, 'The Celtic Element in Literature', in *Essays and Introductions*, pp. 175–6.

37 Ibid., p. 180.

38 Ibid., p. 178.

39 An example appears when he describes his first meeting with Maud Gonne: '. . . in that day she seemed a classical impersonation of the Spring, the Virgilian commendation "She walks like a goddess" made for her alone. Her complexion was luminous, like that of apple-blossom through which the light falls, and I remember her standing that first day by a great heap of such blossoms in the window' (Yeats, *Autobiographies*, p. 123). Such a description, made as it was in

retrospection, is full of an implicit nostalgia, but also contains explicitly pastoral nostalgia, referring to Virgil directly. Maud Gonne becomes, for Yeats, a pastoral ideal, one from which he is inevitably distanced, as he is from other pastoral ideals.

40 *Walden*, of course, offers its own form of pastoral, since the text is a compression of materials into the necessary shape of narrative: Thoreau does not include references to each journey into town or evenings spent there with friends, since that would mar the atmosphere and illusion of the pastoral 'reality' of his life at Walden Pond.

41 In 'Yeats' (1940) in J. Unterecker (ed.), *Yeats: A Collection of Critical Essays* (Englewood Cliffs, NJ: Prentice-Hall, Inc., 1963), T.S. Eliot, recognizing Yeats's backward-looking tendencies, believed that Yeats 'had to wait for a later maturity to find expression of early experience' (p. 57). R.F. Foster notes that Yeats realized, as a young man, how his experiences would be the 'stuff of future memories . . . This early, he was preternaturally conscious of the need to impose a shape on his life, and able to anticipate the way it would look in retrospect' (*The Apprentice Mage*, p. 45). Yeats thus seems to have a sense of pre-formed nostalgia that is evident in many autobiographical passages.

42 In his autobiography, Yeats professes this love of, and attachment to, place that creates, inevitably, a nostalgia; and, indeed, in writing an autobiography, he is already exercising a form of nostalgia that centres around place. Yeats is not alone in the exercise of writing an autobiography; in fact, he was to write his only after other autobiographies of figures of the period had been written: Lady Gregory's, Katherine Tynan's and George Moore's. The publication of memoirs and autobiographies at this point in time offers further evidence that Revivalists were conscious of the role of nostalgia in their work. R.F. Foster points out too that Yeats thought of memoirs as a way of exerting influence on a younger generation (*W.B. Yeats: A Life II: The Arch-Poet 1915–1939* [Oxford: Oxford University Press, 2003], p. 225).

43 Cited in R.F. Foster, *The Apprentice Mage*, p. 73.

44 Yeats, *Autobiographies*, p. 378.

45 Yeats, 'The Celtic Element in Literature', in *Essays and Introductions*, p. 187.

46 In 'The Man Who Dreamed of Fairy Land' (1891), for example, the man who receives those visions is ill at ease, disturbed by the image of 'faeryland', much as Suibhne is disturbed by his appreciation of nature's beauty.

47   We say, then, that the phrase 'Romantic Ireland' denotes an idea, but that the idea is compounded mostly of desire and loss. So when we ask what the idea means, we are asking still more persistently what desires are appeased by speaking the phrase, uttering its syllables. We might interrogate with equal force such phrases as 'Merrie England' and 'The Golden Age': the chief character of these phrases is that they are uttered when England is felt to be no longer merry, the age no longer golden, Ireland no longer romantic. (D. Donoghue, 'Romantic Ireland' in A. Norman Jeffares [ed.], *Yeats, Sligo and Ireland* [Gerrards Cross: Colin Smythe Ltd, 1980], p. 17)

48 Ibid., p. 27.

49 Ibid., p. 28.

50 Ibid., p. 30.

51 Most critics have pointed to the Easter Rising as the major turning point; at least one critic, however, points to 'The Playboy Riots' in an essay of that title: 'The protest', R.M. Kain writes, 'marked the defeat of Yeats's noble dream of an Ireland spiritually united by an inherited nobility of outlook and richness of imagination' (in S.B. Bushrui [ed.], *Sunshine and the Moon's Delight: A Centenary Tribute to John Millington Synge* [Gerrards Cross: Colin Smythe Ltd, 1972], p. 177).

52 Cited in R.F. Foster, *The Arch-Poet*, p. 156.
53 I am not alone in interpreting Byzantium as a pastoral space. See, for example, A. Tate: 'Byzantium is a new pastoral symbol and will be taken as that by anybody who sees more in the pastoral tradition than ideal shepherds and abstract sheep' ('Yeats' Romanticism', in Unterecker, *Yeats: A Collection of Critical Essays*, p. 157).
54 Bornstein, 'Yeats and the Greater Romantic Lyric', p. 201.
55 D. Kiberd describes Yeats's desperation to continue to believe in paradisial existences:

> The deeper the world plunged into the chaos of imperial war and freedom struggles, the more necessary did it become for the poet to secure the Sligo idyll against accusations of naiveté, and the harder. The more he sought to recapture the dream, the more it seemed to elude him. When the much older man finally brought his newly-wed English wife on a boat-trip across Lough Gill, he failed ignominiously to locate, much less land on, the lake isle of Innisfree: a sign, perhaps, that the past in that simple-minded version was not easily recoverable. (*Inventing Ireland*, pp. 102–3)

56 'Is there', Yeats writes, 'nation-wide multiform reverie, every mind passing through a stream of suggestion, and all streams acting and reacting upon one another, no matter how distant the minds, how dumb the lips?' (*Autobiographies*, p. 263).
57 The timeless universe is marked by a recurrence of images that Denis Donoghue suggests draws upon the Nietzchean concept of eternal return (in *Yeats* [London: Fontana Paperbacks, 1971], pp. 85–6). Yeats finds images and symbols from a wide selection of a world-wide past, and draws upon them to illustrate the desire and nostalgia for a perfected, and unified, version of all pasts, created out of vision.
58 R.F. Foster, *The Arch-Poet*, p. 149.
59 Ibid., p. 303.
60 Cited in ibid., p. 179.
61 Ibid., p. 454.
62 Ibid., p. 459.

CHAPTER FOUR

1 The Synge family's estate had declined by the 1840s; after the Encumbered Estates Court sorted out the finances, the family repurchased much of the land and Glanmore Castle, so that by the 1850s the estate prospered again. During Synge's lifetime, the estate relied in part on rental income (often unforthcoming from impoverished tenants), but was in better shape than many neighbouring demesnes. See S. Clarke's *Ashford: A Journey Through Time* (Ashford, County Wicklow: Ashford Books, 2003), especially pp. 75–82.
2 N. Grene, *Synge: A Critical Study of the Plays* (London: The Macmillan Press Ltd, 1975), p. 5.
3 Mathews, *Revival*, p. 126.
4 And not merely at Yeats's recommendation, as Yeats often repeated.
5 Stocking, Jr, 'Essays on Museums and Material Culture', p. 4.
6 The first regular ferry service to the islands began only in 1891.
7 S. Cavell, *The Senses of Walden* (San Francisco CA: North Point, 1981), p. 10.

8   There is the sense that Synge is returning to his own ancestry as well as to
    ancient culture, since a relation had lived on the island some fifty years before
    as a minister. That Synge himself had once expected to become a minister is
    curious with regard to Cavell's description of Thoreau's *Walden* as a re-
    enactment of Puritian ideals. Like Thoreau's, Synge's journey becomes spiritual,
    although not religious.

9   L. Gibbons also makes this point, although in regard to image and not to the
    American literary tradition: '[T]he image of the west of Ireland elaborated in the
    Anglo-Irish contribution to the Literary Revival represents the precise opposite
    [of the American image]: an escape from individualism and the fragmentation
    of community which Synge believed to be endemic in the modernizing process'
    (*Transformations*, p. 24).

10 Ibid., p. 13.

11 Synge's brief involvement with Young Ireland ended in his resignation, which
    should not be taken as a sign of political apathy, however. W. Thornton argues
    that his resignation 'resulted not from his indifference to matters of opinion and
    principle, but from his being so concerned about them that the situation
    presented him with an unavoidable ethical choice – either compromise his
    principles or resign' (*J.M. Synge and the Western Mind* [Gerrards Cross: Colin
    Smythe Limited, 1979], p. 13).

12 J.M. Synge, *The Collected Works Volume II: Prose*, ed. A. Price (Gerrards Cross:
    Colin Smythe Ltd, 1982 [Oxford: Oxford University Press, 1966]), p. 75 n. 1.

13 'For him', D. Kiberd notes, 'Irish seemed to possess the status of a privileged
    secret language, a personal code in which he could record his feelings'. (*Synge
    and the Irish Language*, p. 29).

14 J.M. Synge, *The Aran Islands,* ed. and Intro. Tim Robinson (New York: Penguin
    Classics, 1992), p. 6.

15 Unlike Yeats, Synge did not rely upon English language versions of old Irish
    texts, but read them in the original, translating them himself. Synge was able to
    bypass the translations of O'Grady and others who had edited old Irish texts to
    a purpose; he was thus exposed to the Irish tradition as it existed in manuscript
    form, and not a modernized version of that tradition. His writings were to
    reflect that exposure, which would contribute to the often violent reactions to
    his later work.

16 'Even at this time I was a worshipper of nature. I remember that I would not
    allow my nurses to sit down on the seats by the [River] Dodder because they
    were [man-] made. If they wished to sit down they had to find a low branch of
    a tree or a bit of rock or bank' (Synge, 'Autobiographies', in *Collected Works
    Vol. II*, p. 5). Another profound love was Wordsworth, who provided an
    example of the poet connected to nature.

17 Ibid., p. 13.

18   Before I abandoned science it rendered me an important service. When I
        was about fourteen I obtained a book of Darwin's. It opened in my hands at a
        passage where he asks how we can explain the similarity between a man's
        hands and a bird's or a bat's wings except by evolution. I flung the book aside
        and rushed out into the open air – it was summer and we were in the country
        – the sky seemed to have lost its blue and the grass its green. I lay down and
        writhed in an agony of doubt. My studies showed me the force of what I read,
        [and] the more I put it from me the more it rushed back with new instances
        and power. Till then I had never doubted and never conceived that a sane and
        wise man or boy could doubt. [. . .] By the time I was sixteen or seventeen I
        had renounced Christianity after a great deal of wobbling, although I do not

think I avowed my decision quite so soon. I felt a sort of shame in being thought an infidel, a term which I have always used as a reproach. For a while I denied everything, then I took to reading Carlyle, [Leslie] Stephen and Matthew Arnold, and made myself a sort of incredulous belief that illuminated nature and lent an object to life without hampering the intellect. This story is easily told, but it was a terrible experience. (Ibid., pp. 10–11)

19 Ibid., p. 11.
20 Synge's reading was not limited to the science of his day; T. Eagleton has described Synge as the only intellectual of the Revival, 'with his impressively wide reading' (*Scholars & Rebels*, p. 33) ranging from Goethe to Herbert Spencer, from Madame Blavatsky and Swedenborg to Nietzsche and Marx. See W. Thornton's helpful list based on his study of Synge manuscripts at Trinity College Dublin (*Synge and the Western Mind*), p. 28.
21 N. Grene makes a similar point, claiming that Synge 'was right to claim that he knew the Irish countryside, but he did not know it as an Irish countryman' (*Synge*, p. 16).
22 Interestingly, many critics have also expressed an almost pastoral desire to believe wholly in Synge's Aran experience. In 'Art, Nature, and "The Prepared Personality": A Reading of *The Aran Islands* and Related Writings', in S.B. Bushrui (ed.), *Sunshine and the Moon's Delight: A Centenary Tribute to John Millington Synge* (Gerrards Cross: Colin Smythe Ltd, 1972), A. Saddlemyer, for example, argues that 'throughout [Synge] remains the *passive* but understanding *witness . . . recording accurately* and sharply the daily life of the islanders in their relationship with the natural world' (p. 107, my emphasis). 'Nothing', she continues, 'is invented, nothing is changed, but all is carefully selected and arranged to reveal further encompassing patterns' (p. 108). This of course ignores the preconceived notions that Synge brought to Aran, and dismisses some of the very art that shapes the text: for Synge's approach is, one might say, one of 'unnatural selection' that *appears* to be 'natural' in its hiding away of the mechanics of choice.
23 T. Robinson, 'Place/Person/Book: Synge's *The Aran Islands*', Introduction, in Synge, *The Aran Islands*, p. xlii.
24 Ibid.
25 Synge, *The Aran Islands*, p. 10.
26 Ibid., p. 9.
27 In *The Idea of Africa* (Indianapolis, IN: Indiana University Press, 1994), V.Y. Mudimbe describes the way that European colonizers in Africa promoted the notion of education in the colonizer's language as a privilege to be aspired to. Synge, of course, is forced to largely ignore the fact that the islanders are all fluent in English.
28 Stocking, Jr, 'Essays on Museums and Material Culture', p. 5.
29 Cited in Robinson, 'Place/Person/Book: Synge's *The Aran Islands*', p. xlii.
30 Synge, *The Aran Islands*, p. 12.
31 Synge read and annotated K. Meyer's *The Voyage of Bran* and A. Nutt's accompanying essay *Upon the Irish Vision of the Happy Otherworld and the Celtic Doctrine of Rebirth*; see Thornton, *Synge and the Western Mind*, p. 58.
32 Synge, *The Aran Islands*, p. 69.
33 Ibid., pp. 13–14.
34 Ibid., p. 84.
35 Ibid.
36 Ibid., pp. 94–5.
37 Kiberd, *Inventing Ireland*, pp. 287–8.
38 Synge, *The Aran Islands*, p. 55.

39 Ibid, p. 11.
40 Grene, *Synge*, p. 31.
41 Synge, *The Aran Islands*, p. 44.
42 Ibid., p. 21.
43 Ibid., p. 31.
44 Robinson, 'Place/Person/Book: Synge's *The Aran Islands*', p. xliv.
45 Synge, *The Aran Islands*, p. 53.
46 Ibid., p. 49.
47 Ibid., p. 118.
48 Ibid., p. 54.
49 Ibid., p. 80.
50 Ibid., p. 13.
51 Ibid., p. 33.
52 Ibid., p. 63.
53 Ibid., p. 66.
54 Ibid., p. 61.
55 Kiberd, *Synge and the Irish Language*, p. xiii.
56 Synge, *The Aran Islands*, p. 114.
57 Foster, 'The Artifice of Eternity', p. 130. Saddlemyer's 'Art, Nature and "The Prepared Personality"' makes a similar point that 'the journey to the western world was also an exploration and revaluation of his own consciousness' (p. 107).
58 Grene, *Synge*, p. 29.
59 On tourism as a commodity, see Spurgeon Thompson's unpublished Ph.D. dissertation (Notre Dame University, 2000), 'The Postcolonial Tourist'.
60 Cavell, *The Senses of Walden*, p. 78.
61 Synge, *The Aran Islands*, p. 69.
62 Ibid., p. 54.
63 Reprinted in D.H. Greene and E.M. Stephens, *John Millington Synge 1871–1909* (New York: The Macmillan Press Ltd, 1959), pp. 156–8.
64 Kiberd, *Synge and the Irish Language*, p. 109.
65 Synge, 'People and Places', *in Collected Works Volume II*, p. 199.
66 Ibid, p. 200.

CHAPTER FIVE

1 Gibbons, *Transformations*, p. 82.
2 Although up until the mid-1930s, the Irish government paid to the British government an annual sum representing the money that purchasers under the Wyndham Act had been accustomed to paying to the colonial government. This 'national mortgage' was marked paid after the de Valera government, having refused to continue the scheme, delivered a final, symbolic payment of ten million pounds. See Bull, *Land, Politics and Nationalism*.
3 Yeats, of course, was also concerned with the mapping of an interior world, but, given his preoccupation with antinomies generally, this concern is counterbalanced with another for the exterior world and the tradition he inherits as an Irish author.
4 Platt, *Joyce and the Anglo-Irish*, pp. 8–9.
5 See F. Senn's 'Clouded Friendship: A Note on "*A Little Cloud*"', in O. Frawley (ed.), *A New and Complex Sensation: Essays on Joyce's Dubliners* (Dublin: The Lilliput Press, 2004), p. 104.

6   Joyce described *Dubliners'* style as one of 'scrupulous meanness' (in R. Scholes and A. Walton Litz [eds], *Dubliners: Text and Criticism* [London: Penguin, 1996], p. 262).

7   S. Beckett, *Proust* (London: Chatto & Windus, 1931).

8   See D. Attridge and M. Howe (eds), *Semicolonial Joyce* (Cambridge: Cambridge University Press, 2000).

9   In '"*Eveline*", or the Veils of Cleaning', Wanda Balzano describes Joyce's commitment to truth in his writing as a form of redemptive cleansing away of the 'sins' of the past (in Frawley (ed.), *A New and Complex Sensation*, pp. 81–93).

10 J. Joyce, 'Gas From a Burner', in R. Ellmann *et al.* (eds), *Poems and Shorter Writings* (London: Faber & Faber, 2001), p. 104 l.53.

11 See J. Brady, 'Dublin at the Turn of the Twentieth Century' in Frawley (ed.), *A New and Complex Sensation*, p. 11.

12 See H. Ehrlich, '"Araby" in Context: The "Splendid Bazaar", Irish Orientalism and James Clarence Mangan', *James Joyce Quarterly*, 35, 2–3 (Winter/Spring 1998).

13 On Buenos Aires as a centre for slave trade, see Katherine Mullin's 'Don't Cry For Me, Argentina: "Eveline" and the Seductions of Emigration Propaganda', in Attridge and Howe (eds), *Semicolonial Joyce*.

14 See J. Fairhill, 'Big-Power Politics and Colonial Economics: The Gordon Bennett Cup Race and "After the Race"', *James Joyce Quarterly*, 28, 2 (Winter 1991).

15 Joyce, *Dubliners*, p. 39.

16 Ibid., p. 38.

17 The mood of increasing nostalgia seems to have been mirrored by Joyce's feelings in writing the story, having seemingly regretted that the collection did so little to celebrate the virtues of Dublin and its inhabitants. Of course, the revealed memories at the end of 'The Dead' show that Joyce, even when submitting to a form of personal nostalgia, refuses any idealization to be imparted to the work of art. This is not a question of paring the fingernails, perhaps – since there is no indifference in 'The Dead' – but it does certainly seem a matter of the artist remaining hidden behind his work.

18 Joyce, *Dubliners*, p. 189.

19 Ibid., pp. 188; 190.

20 Ibid., p. 189.

21 Ibid., p. 223.

22 Ibid., p. 188.

23 Ibid., p. 196.

24 Ibid., p. 213.

25 Ibid, p. 189.

26 J. Joyce, *A Portrait of the Artist as a Young Man*, ed. and Intro. Seamus Deane (London: Penguin, 1992), p. 66.

27 See Platt's *Joyce and the Anglo-Irish*, the main premise of which is that 'the antithesis between *Ulysses* and the culture of revivalism is formulated out of conflicting class and cultural identities' (p. 15). A. Gibson's *Joyce's Revenge: History, Politics, and Aesthetics in Ulysses* (Oxford: Oxford University Press, 2002) argues similarly that *Ulysses* is itself an act of 'revenge' against colonialism as well as the Revival: 'Into the formulas to which Revival historiography resorted, Joyce introduces precisely what it sought to exclude: Catholicism, the Middle Ages, the colonial past and present' (p. 117).

28 Kiberd, *Inventing Ireland*, p. 485.

29 Joyce, *Portrait*, pp. 180–1.

30 Gibson, *Joyce's Revenge*, p. 13.

31 Joyce, *Portrait*, p. 152.
32 M. Tymoczko's *The Irish Ulysses* (Berkeley, CA: Unuversity of California Press, 1994) explores the influences of medieval Irish literature upon Joyce's book.
33 Yeats does, of course, write urban poems, as well as creating the urban paradise of Byzantium, as we have seen; but his urban poems tend to be memorials to people – as in 'Easter, 1916' – rather than celebrations of the urban space as particularly Irish.
34 Following the conventions of the *James Joyce Quarterly*, all quotations from *Ulysses* are provided in-text, with episode and line numbers following H.W. Gabler's edition (London: Random House, 1986).
35 We have mention, for example, of Westmeath (1.683); Ulster (2.398); Mullingar (4.400; 16.509; 17.882); Cork (6.560; 18.365); the Sugarloaf Mountain (8.166; 18.26); the Featherbed Mountain (10.555); Lusk, Rush, Carrickmines and the M'Gillicuddy Reeks and the Shannon (12.111–2); Antrim, Limerick, Ballybough, New Ross, Wexford, Connemara, Tipperary and the Barrow and Shannon rivers (12.1244–56); Kerry, Carrantuohill, Sligo, Glendalough, Killarney, Clonmacnois, Cong Abbey, Glen Inagh, the Twelve Pins, Ireland's Eye, Tallaght, Croagh Patrick, Lough Neagh, Avoca, Cape Clear, Aherlow, Loughlinstown, Tullamore, Castleconnel, Kilballymacshonakill, Monasterboice, Maynooth, Cashel, the bog of Allen and Fingal (8.1446–61); Roscommon, Connemara and Sligo (14.614–15); Lambay Island (14.660; 682); Malahide (14.683); Wicklow (16.550; 17.164; 17.1406); Donegal and the countryside (16.550); Galway (16.965); Clare (17.622); Belfast (18.349; 18.405); Ennis (18.349); Mallow (18.357); Maryborough(18.358); and Glencree (18.417).
36 Gibraltar, its Moorish Wall, Spain and things Spanish receive the most references, with twenty-four: 2.157 (Moorish algebra); 3.149 (the Spanish Armada); 4.60 (Gibraltar); 8.25 (Spain); 11.515 (Gibraltar); 11.735 (Spain); 13.890 and 13.968 (Moorish Wall); 13.1205 (Gibraltar); 15.1730 (Gibraltar); 15.2395 (Spain); 15.3289 (Gibraltar); 15.4585 (Spain); 16.611 (Gibraltar); 16.873 (on the Spanish temper); 16.1122 (Jews in Spain); 16.1412 (Spain); 16.1433 (Madrid); 17.52 (Gibraltar); 18.136 (Gibraltar); 18.326; 18.398–400 (Spain); 18.440 (Gibraltar); 18.501(Gibraltar). Palestine, Israel and the Holy Land receive twenty mentions: 4.155–7 (the model farms); 6.819 (holy land); 7.207–10 (Jerusalem and Israel); 7.830 (Israel); 7.857 (Israel); 7.1057 (Parable of the Plums); 8.15 (Zion); 8.634 (Israel); 8.863 (Palestine); 8.1184 (Palestine); 15.982 (Agendath Netaim); 15.985 (Kinnereth); 15.1544 (Jerusalem); 15.1905 (Israel); 15.3220 (the wailing wall); 17.333 (Zion); 17.640 (Palestine); 17.750 (Israel); 17.1030 (Israel); and 17.1325 (Palestine). Egypt receives sixteen mentions: 3.178; 3.370; 7.208; 7.832; 7.838; 7.851 (Nile); 7.853; 7.858; 9.354; 14.386; 14.394 (the Nile); 14.1169; 15.947 (Pharaoh); 15.2365; 17.711; 17.770 (Egyptian alphabet); and 17.1030. Paris receives eight mentions: 1.342; 2.70; 3.164 and 179; 7.600; 9.950; 16.1181; 17.12.
37 M. Reizbaum's *James Joyce's Judaic Other* (Palo Alto, CA: Stanford University Press, 1999) points out that Joyce owned T. Herzl's *Der Judenstaat* and H. Sacher's *Sionism and the Jewish Future* (p. 21).
38 S. Bazargan, 'Mapping Gibraltar: Colonialism, Time, and Narrative in "Penelope"', in R. Pearce (ed.), *Molly Blooms: A Polylogue on 'Penelope' and Cultural Studies* (Madison, WI: University of Wisconsin Press, 1994), p. 120.
39 Gibson astutely points out that 'if an imperial discourse associated Gibraltar, above all, with a proud refusal to surrender, . . . Molly associates it with yielding and giving in' (*Joyce's Revenge*, p. 263).
40 On which see Bazargan's response to P. Herring's dismissal of Gibraltar's significance, 'Mapping Gibraltar', p. 121.

41 Ibid., p. 133.

42 Reizbaum believes that *Die Welt*, a publication of the World Zionist Organization, was 'the most likely place for Joyce to have encountered the advertisement of Agudath [sic] Netaim, the Turkish-based planting company selling land in Palestine in 1905' (*James Joyce's Judaic Other*, p. 21).

43 Reizbaum notes that 'indeed Israel was emblematized by women in some of the same ways as Ireland' (ibid., p. 22).

44 In *James Joyce and Modernism: Beyond Dublin* (Lampeter, Wales: The Edwin Mellen Press, Ltd, 2000), M.P. Levitt notes that 'The sterility of Palestine recalls the impotency of Bloom; as the fatherland of the Jews can bear no fruit, so Leopold Bloom can father no son' (p. 26). Thus Bloom's musings on Palestine are very much connected to what Leavitt calls the 'fertility echoes' throughout the novel (p. 41).

45 Gibson, *Joyce's Revenge*, p. 240.

46 With *Finnegans Wake*, Joyce went on to create the most complex of Irish literary landscapes. The *Wake* uses dream language to chart the progress of HCE through the night, but also depicts him as a giant whose body forms the landscape around Dublin, and his wife as the Liffey flowing through that landscape. The resulting novel is a memorializing mythology of Dublin and environs. In writing the *Wake*, Joyce calls upon the Irish literary tradition of memorializing place through historical-mythical figures. Any treatment of the *Wake* here would inevitably be superficial; for reasons of space, it has been left out entirely.

47 J. Marks, *English Pastoral Drama* (New York, Benjamin Blom, 1972), p. 30.

48 J. Knowlson, *Damned to Fame: The Life of Samuel Beckett* (New York: Simon & Schuster, 1996), p. 342.

49 See his *A Reader's Guide to Samuel Beckett* (London: Thames & Hudson, 1973).

50 S. Beckett, *Complete Dramatic Works* (London: Faber & Faber, 1986), p. 15.

51 S. Connor, *Samuel Beckett: Repetition, Theory and Text* (New York: Basil Blackwood Inc., 1988), p.119.

52 Beckett, *Dramatic Works*, p.17.

53 Ibid., p. 18.

54 Ibid., p. 51.

55 Ibid., p. 56.

56 Ibid., p. 57.

57 Ibid., p. 58.

58 Ibid.

59 Ibid.

60 Ibid., p. 61.

61 Ibid., p. 69.

62 Ibid., p. 87.

63 Ibid., p. 106.

64 Ibid., p. 97.

65 Ibid., p. 98.

66 Ibid., p. 100.

67 Ibid., p. 132.

68 Ibid., p. 93.

69 Ibid., p. 108.

70 Ibid., p. 111.

71 Ibid., p. 113.

72 Ibid., p. 118.

73 Ibid., p. 119.

74 Ibid., p. 215.
75 Connor, *Samuel Beckett*, p. 127.
76 Ibid., p. 130.
77 Beckett, *Dramatic Works*, p. 221.
78 Ibid., p. 223.
79 Ibid., p. 222.
80 Ibid.
81 E. O'Brien, *The Beckett Country* (London: Black Cat Press, 1986).
82 Eagleton, *Crazy John*, p. 305.

CHAPTER SIX

 1 Foster, 'The Culture of Nature', p. 618.
 2 F. O'Toole, 'Going West: The Country Versus the City in Irish Writing', *Crane Bag*, 9 (1985), p. 111.
 3 Gibbons, *Transformations*, pp. 82–93.
 4 S. Matthews, *Irish Poetry: Politics, History, Negotiation* (London: Macmillan, 1997), pp. 9–10.
 5 Corcoran, *After Yeats and Joyce*, p. 65.
 6 G. Watson's 'Landscape in Ulster Poetry' (in G. Dawe and J.W. Foster [eds], *The Poet's Place: Ulster Literature and Society* (Belfast: Institute of Irish Studies, Queen's University Belfast, 1991)) notes that 'Ulster writing has its strong relations with landscape and place, but on a somewhat more urgent level than might be suggested by the rather antiquarian flavour hanging round that definition of *dinnseanchas*' (p. 1); Watson argues that the representation of land and place in Ulster writing 'is freighted with an enormous weight of cultural codings, and at times even becomes the very emblem of the sectarian divide' (p. 2).
 7 S. Heaney, 'The Sense of Place', in *Preoccupations* (London: Faber & Faber, 1980), pp. 148–9.
 8 Heaney, 'Belfast', in *Preoccupations*, pp. 36–7.
 9 S. Burris, *The Poetry of Resistance: Seamus Heaney and the Pastoral Tradition* (Athens, OH: Ohio University Press, 1990), p. 42.
10 Heaney, 'The Sense of Place', in *Preoccupations*, p. 135.
11 Ibid., p. 132.
12 Lysaght, 'Contrasting Natures', p. 444.
13 Burris, *Poetry of Resistance*, p. 24.
14 Clare is 'liminal' in the sense of being on the sidelines of English writing traditions, but is also 'liminal' in his engagement with the horizon and the limen. On 'Clare's Horizon', see A. Fletcher, *A New Theory for American Poetry: Democracy, the Environment, and the Future of the Imagination* (Cambridge, MA: Harvard University Press, 2004), pp. 17–23 and throughout.
15 Ibid., p. 37. Burris refers here to Puttenham's *The Arte of English Poesie* (1589), which describes the pastoral as making use of 'rude speeches to insinuate and glance at greater matters' (cited in Burris, *Poetry of Resistance*, p. 1).
16 Burris, *Poetry of Resistance*, p. 51.
17 Ibid., p. 108.
18 Ibid., p. 4.
19 D. Lloyd, '"Pap for the Dispossessed": Seamus Heaney and the Poetics of Identity', in E. Andrews (ed.), *Seamus Heaney: A Collection of Critical Essays* (London: Macmillan, 1992), p. 98.
20 H. Hart, *Seamus Heaney: Poet of Contrary Progressions* (Syracuse, NY: Syracuse University Press, 1992), p. 22.

21 S. Heaney, *New Selected Poems 1966–1987* (London: Faber & Faber, 1990), p. 3.
22 J.W. Foster, *The Achievement of Seamus Heaney* (Dublin: The Lilliput Press, 1995), p. 8.
23 Burris, *Poetry of Resistance*, p. 66.
24 Heaney, 'The God in the Tree: Early Irish Nature Poetry', in *Preoccupations*, p. 185.
25 M. Allen, '"Holding Course": *The Haw Lantern* and its Place in Heaney's Development', in E. Andrews (ed.), *Seamus Heaney: A Collection of Critical Essays* (London: Macmillan, 1992), p. 194.
26 Heaney, 'The God in the Tree', in *Preoccupations*, p. 182.
27 Ibid., p. 186.
28 T. Docherty, 'Ana-; or Postmodernism, Landscape, Seamus Heaney', in M. Allen (ed.), *New Casebooks: Seamus Heaney* (London: MacMillan Ltd, 1997), p. 212.
29 Heaney, 'From Monaghan to the Grand Canal: The Poetry of Patrick Kavanagh', in *Preoccupations*, p. 122.
30 When Heaney first moved south, he lived in a cottage on the Synge family's former Wicklow estate, thus adding another layer of narrative to a particular Irish place; see 'The Glanmore Sonnets' from *Field Work in New Selected Poems*, pp. 109–18.
31 Ibid., 'Exposure' from 'Singing School', p. 90.
32 Kiberd, *Inventing Ireland*, p. 595.
33 Heaney, 'In the Country of Convention', in *Preoccupations*, p. 180.
34 'Act of Union', in *New Selected Poems*, pp. 74–5.
35 Ibid., 'North', p. 57.
36 Hart, *Seamus Heaney*, p. 24.
37 'The Seed Cutters', from 'Mossbawn: Two Poems in Dedicaton', in *New Collected Poems*, p. 51.
38 Heaney, 'The Placeless Heaven: Another Look at Kavanagh', in *Preoccupations*, p. 4.
39 See J. Allen-Randolph's useful bibliography in *Irish University Review*, 23, 1 (Spring/Summer 1993), an issue devoted to criticism of Boland's work.
40 E. Boland, 'The Future of Poetry', *The Irish Times*, 5 Feb. 1970.
41 J. Allen-Randolph, 'An Interview with Eavan Boland', *Irish University Review*, 23, 1 (Spring/Summer 1993), p. 119.
42 Ibid., p. 121.
43 Ibid., p. 123.
44 E. Boland, 'Suburban Woman', in *Collected Poems* (Manchester: Carcanet Press Ltd, 1995), pp. 50–1.
45 'Ode to Suburbia', in ibid., p. 44.
46 Ibid.
47 Allen-Randolph, 'Interview with Eavan Boland', p. 130.
48 J. Allen-Randolph, 'Private Worlds, Public Realities: Eavan Boland's Poetry 1967–1990', *Irish University Review*, 23, 1 (Spring/Summer 1993), p. 16.
49 Episode and line numbers provided in-text follow H.W. Gabler's edition of J. Joyce, *Ulysses*.
50 Allen-Randolph, 'Interview with Eavan Boland', pp. 123–4.
51 P. Haberstroh, 'Woman, Artist and Image in *Night Feed*', *Irish University Review*, 23, 1 (Spring/Summer 1993), p. 71.
52 Boland, 'The New Pastoral', in *Collected Poems*, p. 82.
53 Ibid.
54 A. Fogarty, '"The Influence of Absences": Eavan Boland and the Silenced History of Irish Women's Poetry', *Colby Quarterly* XXXV, 4 (Dec. 1999), p. 259.

55 Boland, 'Mise Eire', in *Collected Poems*, p. 102.
56 Ibid.
57 A. Martin, 'Quest and Vision: *The Journey*', *Irish University Review*, 23, 1 (Spring/Summer 1993), pp. 78–9.
58 E. Boland, *The Lost Land* (New York: W.W. Norton & Company, 1998), p. 67.

POSTSCRIPT

1 Davis, *Yearning for Yesterday*, p. 49.
2 Eagleton, *Crazy John*, p. 314.
3 H. Toliver, *Pastoral Forms and Attitudes* (Berkeley, CA: University of California Press, 1984), p. vii.

References

Allen, M. '"Holding Course": *The Haw Lantern* and its Place in Heaney's Development', in E. Andrews (ed.), *Seamus Heaney: A Collection of Critical Essays* (London: Macmillan, 1992).

Allen-Randolph, J. 'Private Worlds, Public Realities: Eavan Boland's Poetry 1967–1990', *Irish University Review*, 23, 1 (Spring/Summer 1993).

Allen-Randolph, J. 'An Interview with Eavan Boland', in A. Roche with J. Allen-Randolph (guest eds), *Irish University Review*, 23, 1 (Spring/ Summer 1993).

Anderson, A.O. and M.O. Anderson, eds. and trans., *Adomnán's Life of Columba* (Oxford: Clarendon Press, 1991).

Andrews, J.H. *A Paper Landscape* (Oxford: Oxford University Press, 1975).

Andrews, J.H. 'Paper Landscapes: Mapping Ireland's Physical Geography', in J.W. Foster (ed.), *Nature in Ireland* (Dublin: The Lilliput Press, 1997).

Andrews, M. (ed. and intro.), *The Picturesque: Literary Sources and Documents*, 3 Vols (The Banks, East Sussex: Helm Information Ltd, 1994).

Arnold, M. *On the Study of Celtic Literature and Other Essays* (London: J.M. Dent & Sons, Ltd., 1910 [1867]).

Attridge, D. and M. Howe (eds), *Semicolonial Joyce* (Cambridge: Cambridge University Press, 2000).

Bachelard, G. *The Poetics of Reverie*, trans. Daniel Russell (Boston, MA: Beacon Press, 1969).

Bachelard, G. *The Poetics of Space*, trans. Maria Jolas (Boston, MA: Beacon Press, 1994 [1964]).

Balzano, W. '"Eveline" or the Veils of Cleaning', in O. Frawley (ed.), *A New and Complex Sensation: Essays on Joyce's Dubliners* (Dublin: The Lilliput Press, 2004).

Barrell, J. *The Idea of Landscape and the Sense of Place 1730–1840: An Approach to the Poetry of John Clare* (Cambridge: Cambridge University Press, 1972).

Bazargan, S. 'Mapping Gibraltar: Colonialism, Time, and Narrative in "Penelope"', in R. Pearce (ed.), *Molly Blooms: A Polylogue on 'Penelope' and Cultural Studies* (Madison, WI; University of Wisconsin Press, 1994).

Beacon, R. *Solon His Follie*, eds and Intro. V. Carey and C. Carroll (Binghamton, NY: Medieval and Renaissance Texts and Studies, Vol. 154, 1996 [1594]).

Beckett, S. *Proust* (London: Chatto & Windus, 1931).

Beckett, S. *The Complete Dramatic Works* (London: Faber & Faber, 1986).

Bergin, O. (ed. and trans.), *Irish Bardic Poetry* (Dublin: Dublin Institute for Advanced Studies, 1970).

Bitel, L.M. *Isle of the Saints: Monastic Settlement and Christian Community in Early Ireland* (Cork: Cork University Press, 1990).

Bloom, H. *Yeats* (New York: Oxford University Press, 1970).

Boland, E. 'The Future of Poetry', *The Irish Times*, 5 Feb. 1970.

Boland, E. *Collected Poems* (Manchester: Carcanet Press Ltd, 1995).

Boland, E. *The Lost Land* (New York: W.W. Norton & Company, 1998).

Bornstein, G. 'Yeats and the Greater Romantic Lyric', in R.J. Finneran (ed.), *Critical Essays on W.B. Yeats* (Boston, MA: G.K. Hall & Co., 1986).

Brady, J. 'Dublin at the Turn of the Twentieth Century', in O. Frawley (ed.), *A New and Complex Sensation: Essays on Joyce's Dubliners* (Dublin: The Lilliput Press, 2004).

Brooke, C. *Reliques of Irish Poetry* (Dublin: G. Bonham, 1789).

Bull, P. *Land, Politics and Nationalism: A Study of the Irish Land Question* (Dublin: Gill & Macmillan Ltd, 1996).

Bunting, E. *General Collection of the Ancient Music of Ireland* (London: Preston & Sons, 1796).

Burke, E. *A Philosophical Inquiry into the Origins of Our Ideas of the Sublime and the Beautiful*, ed. David Womersley (New York: Penguin, 1999 [London: Dodsley, 1757]).

Burris, S. *The Poetry of Resistance: Seamus Heaney and the Pastoral Tradition* (Athens, OH: Ohio University Press, 1990).

Caball, M. *Poets and Politics: Reaction and Continuity in Irish Poetry, 1558–1625* (Cork: Cork University Press, 1998).

Canny, N. *The Elizabethan Conquest of Ireland* (Sussex: The Harvester Press Ltd, 1976).

Canny, N. *Making Ireland British 1580–1650* (Oxford: Oxford University Press, 2001).

Carey, J. *A New Introduction to Lebor Gabála Érenn* (Dublin: Irish Texts Society, 1993).

Carney, J. *The Irish Bardic Poet* (Dublin: Dublin Institute for Advanced Studies, 1958).

Carroll, C. *Circe's Cup: Cultural Transformations in Early Modern Ireland* (Cork: Cork University Press, 2001).

Cavell, S. *The Senses of Walden* (San Francisco, CA: North Point, 1981).

Céitinn, S. *Foras Feasa Ar Éirinn: A Complete History of Ireland Volumes I–IV*, eds and trans. D. Comyn and P.S. Dinneen (London: Irish Texts Society, 1902–14).

Chase, M. and C. Shaw 'The Dimensions of Nostalgia', in M. Chase and C. Shaw (eds), *The Imagined Past: History and Nostalgia* (Manchester: Manchester University Press, 1989).

Clarke, S. *Ashford: A Journey Through Time* (Ashford, County Wicklow: Ashford Books, 2003).

Clifford, J. 'Objects and Selves – an Afterword', in G.W. Stocking, Jr (ed.), *Objects and Others: Essays on Museums and Material Culture* (Madison, WI: University of Wisconsin Press, 1985).

Connor, S. *Samuel Beckett: Repetition, Theory and Text* (New York: Basil Blackwood Inc., 1988).

Corcoran, N. *After Yeats and Joyce: Reading Modern Irish Literature* (Oxford: Oxford University Press, 1997).

Cormack, L.B. 'The Fashioning of an Empire: Geography and the State in Elizabethan England', in A. Godlewska and N. Smith (eds), *Geography and Empire* (Oxford: Blackwell Publishers, 1994).

Coughlan, P. '"Some secret scourge which shall by her come to England": Ireland and Incivility in Spenser', in P. Coughlan (ed.), *Spenser and Ireland* (Cork: Cork University Press, 1989).

Cunningham, B. 'Native Culture and Political Change in Ireland, 1580–1640', in C. Brady and R. Gillespie (eds), *Natives and Newcomers* (Dublin: Irish Academic Press, 1986).

Daiches, D. 'The Earlier Poems: Some Themes and Patterns', in N.A. Jeffares and K.G.W. Cross, (eds), *In Excited Reverie: A Centenary Tribute to William Butler Yeats* (New York: St Martin's Press, 1965).

Darwin, C. *On The Origin of Species: A Facsimile of the First Edition*, Intro. Ernst Mayr (Cambridge, MA: Harvard University Press, 1964).

Davies, Sir J. *A Discovery of the True Causes Why Ireland was Never Entirely Subdued Nor Brought Under Obedience of the Crown of England Until the Beginning of His Majesty's Happy Reign*, in H. Morley (ed.), *Ireland Under Elizabeth and James the First* (London: Routledge, 1890 [1612]).

Davis, F. *Yearning for Yesterday: A Sociology of Nostalgia* (New York: The Free Press, 1979).

Deane, S. 'Introduction', in *Nationalism, Colonialism and Literature* (Minneapolis, MN: University of Minnesota Press, 1990).

Deane, S. (ed.), *The Field Day Anthology of Irish Writing*, 3 Vols (Derry: Field Day Publications, 1991).

Derricke, J. *Image of Ireland with a Discoverie of Woodkarne*, ed. D.B. Quinn (Dublin: Blackstaff Press, 1985 [1581]).

Docherty, T. 'Ana-; or Postmodernism, Landscape, Seamus Heaney', in M. Allen (ed.), *New Casebooks: Seamus Heaney* (London: MacMillan Ltd, 1997).

Donoghue, D. *Yeats* (London: Fontana Paperbacks, 1971).

Donoghue, D. 'Romantic Ireland', in A.N. Jeffares (ed.), *Yeats, Sligo and Ireland: Essays to Mark the 21st Yeats International Summer School* (Gerrards Cross: Colin Smythe Ltd, 1980).

Dooley, A. and H. Roe (eds and trans.), *Tales of the Elders of Ireland* (Oxford: Oxford University Press, 1999).

Dowd, M. 'Gaelic Economy and Society', in C. Brady and R. Gillespie (eds), *Natives and Newcomers* (Dublin: Irish Academic Press, 1986).

Dumville, D.N. (ed.) *Ireland's Desert Fathers* (forthcoming).

Eagleton, T. *Heathcliff and The Great Hunger: Studies in Irish Culture* (London: Verso, 1995).

Eagleton, T. *Crazy John and the Bishop and Other Essays on Irish Culture* (Cork: Cork University Press, 1998).

Eagleton, T. *Scholars & Rebels in Nineteenth-Century Ireland* (Oxford: Blackwell Publishers Ltd, 1999).

Edwards, N. *The Archeology of Early Medieval Ireland* (London: B.T. Batsford Ltd, 1990).

Ehrlich, H. '"Araby" in Context: The "Splendid Bazaar", Irish Orientalism and James Clarence Mangan', *James Joyce Quarterly*, 35, 2–3 (Winter/Spring 1998).

Eliot, T.S. 'Yeats' (1940), in J. Unterecker (ed.), *Yeats: A Collection of Critical Essays* (Englewood Cliffs, NJ: Prentice-Hall, Inc., 1963).

Ellmann, R. Yeats: *The Man and the Masks* (New York: W.W. Norton & Company, Inc., 1979 [1948]).

Emerson, R.W. *Selected Essays*, ed. Larzer Ziff (London: Penguin, 1982).

Empson, W. *Some Versions of Pastoral* (New York: New Directions Paperback, 1992 [1960]).

Fairhill, J. 'Big-Power Politics and Colonial Economics: The Gordon Bennett Cup Race and "After the Race"', *James Joyce Quarterly*, 28, 2 (Winter 1991).

Fallis, R. *The Irish Renaissance* (Syracuse, NY: Syracuse University Press, 1977).

Fletcher, A. *A New Theory for American Poetry: Democracy, the Environment, and the Future of the Imagination* (Cambridge, MA: Harvard University Press, 2004).

Flower, R. *The Irish Tradition* (Dublin: The Lilliput Press, 1994 [Oxford: Oxford University Press, 1947]).

Fogarty, A. '"The Influence of Absences": Eavan Boland and the Silenced History of Irish Women's Poetry', *Colby Quarterly*, XXXV, 4 (Dec. 1999).

Foley, B. 'Yeats's "King Goll": Sources, Revision, and Revisions', in R.J. Finneran (ed.), *Yeats: An Annual of Critical and Textual Studies*, Vol. IV (Ann Arbor, MI: UMI Research Press, 1986).

Foster, J.W. 'The Artifice of Eternity: Medieval Aspects of Modern Irish Literature', in R. Wall (ed.), *Medieval and Modern Ireland* (Totowa, NJ: Barnes & Noble Books, 1988).

Foster, J.W. *The Achievement of Seamus Heaney* (Dublin: The Lilliput Press, 1995).

Foster, J.W. (ed.) *Nature in Ireland* (Dublin: The Lilliput Press, 1997).

Foster, J.W. 'Nature and Nation in the Ninenteenth Century', in J.W. Foster (ed.), *Nature in Ireland* (Dublin: The Lilliput Press, 1997).

Foster, J.W. 'The Culture of Nature', in J.W. Foster (ed.), *Nature in Ireland* (Dublin: The Lilliput Press, 1997).

Foster, J.W. *Recoveries* (Dublin: University College Dublin Press, 2002).

Foster, R.F. *W.B. Yeats: A Life I: The Apprentice Mage 1865–1914* (Oxford: Oxford University Press, 1998).

Foster, R.F. *W.B. Yeats: A Life II: The Arch-Poet 1915–1939* (Oxford: Oxford University Press, 2003).

Friedrich, P. 'Imagination', unpublished conference paper.

Friel, B. *Translations* (London: Faber & Faber Ltd, 1981).

Genet, J. (ed), *Rural Ireland, Real Ireland?* (Gerrards Cross: Colin Smythe, 1996).

Gibbons, L. *Transformations in Irish Culture* (Cork: Cork University Press, 1996).

Gibson, A. *Joyce's Revenge: History, Politics, and Aesthetics in Ulysses* (Oxford: Oxford University Press, 2002).

Gillespie, R. 'The End of an Era: Ulster and the Outbreak of the 1641 Rising', in C. Brady and R. Gillespie (eds), *Natives and Newcomers* (Dublin: Irish Academic Press, 1986).

Gillies, W. 'The Classical Irish Poetic Tradition', in D.E. Evans *et al.* (eds), *Proceedings of the Seventh International Congress of Celtic Studies* (Oxford: Oxford University Press, 1986).

Giraldus Cambrensis. *The History and Topography of Ireland*, trans. J.J. O'Meara (New York: Penguin Books, 1982 [ca. 1188]).

Greene, D.H. and E.M. Stephens. *John Millington Synge 1871–1909* (New York: The Macmillan Press Ltd, 1959).

Gregory, Lady A. *Lady Gregory: Selected Writings*, eds and Intro. L. McDiarmuid and M. Waters (London: Penguin, 1995).

Grene, N. *Synge: A Critical Study of the Plays* (London: The Macmillan Press Ltd, 1975).

Gwynn, E. *The Metrical Dindshenchas Volumes I–V* (Dublin: The Royal Irish Academy Todd Lecture Series, Volume IX, 1903).

Haberstroh, P.B. 'Woman, Artist and Image in *Night Feed*', *Irish University Review* 23, 1 (Spring/ Summer 1993).

Haley, G.C. 'The Topography of the Táin Bó Cúailnge' (unpublished Ph.D. dissertation, Harvard University, Cambridge, MA, 1973).

Hardiman, J. *Irish Minstrelsy or Bardic Remains of Ireland*, 2 Vols, Intro. Máire Mhac an tSaoi (Shannon: Irish University Press, 1971 [London 1831]).

Hart, H. *Seamus Heaney: Poet of Contrary Progressions* (Syracuse, NY: Syracuse University Press, 1992).

Heaney, S. *Preoccupations* (London: Faber & Faber, 1980).

Heaney, S. *New Selected Poems 1966–1987* (London: Faber & Faber, 1990).

Jackson, K.H. *Studies in Early Celtic Nature Poetry* (Cambridge: Cambridge University Press, 1935 [reprinted Llanerch Publishers, Felinfach, Wales], 1995).

Jameson, F. *Postmodernism, or the Cultural Logic of Late Capitalism* (London: Verso, 1991).

Joyce, J. *Dubliners: Text and Criticism*, R. Scholes and A.W. Litz (eds) (London: Penguin, 1996 [1914]).

Joyce, J. *A Portrait of the Artist as a Young Man*, ed. and Intro. S. Deane (London: Penguin, 1992 [1918]).

Joyce, J. *Ulysses*, ed. H.W. Gabler (London: Random House, 1986 [1922]).

Joyce, J. *Finnegans Wake* (New York: Viking, 1939).

Joyce, J. *Poems and Shorter Writings*, eds R. Ellmann *et al.* (London: Faber & Faber, 2001).

Kain, R.M. 'The Playboy Riots', in S.B. Bushrui (ed.), *Sunshine and the Moon's Delight: A Centenary Tribute to John Millington Synge* (Gerrards Cross: Colin Smythe Ltd, 1972).

Kavanagh, P. *The Complete Poems*, ed. Peter Kavanagh (New York: The Peter Kavanagh Hand Press, 1972).

Kenner, H. *A Reader's Guide to Samuel Beckett* (London: Thames & Hudson, 1973).

Kenney, J.F. *The Sources for the Early History of Ireland: An Introduction and Guide. Volume I: Ecclesiastical* (New York: Columbia University Press, 1929).

Kiberd, D. 'The Perils of Nostalgia: A Critique of the Revival', in P. Connolly (ed.), *Literature and the Changing Ireland* (Gerrards Cross: Colin Smythe, 1982).

Kiberd, D. *Synge and the Irish Language* (London: Macmillan, 1993 [2nd edn]).

Kiberd, D. *Inventing Ireland* (London: Jonathan Cape, 1995).

Knowlson, J. *Damned to Fame: The Life of Samuel Beckett* (New York: Simon & Schuster, 1996).

Leerssen, J. *Mere Irish and Fíor-Ghael: Studies in the Idea of Irish Nationality, its Development and Literary Expression Prior to the Nineteenth Century* (Cork: Cork University Press, 1996).

Leerssen, J. *Remembrance and Imagination: Patterns in the Historical and Literary Representation of Ireland in the Nineteenth Century* (Cork: Cork University Press, 1997).

Lestringant, F. *Mapping the Renaissance World: The Geographical Imagination in the Age of Discovery*, trans. David Faussett (Berkeley, CA: University of California Press, 1994).

Levitt, M.P. *James Joyce and Modernism: Beyond Dublin* (Lampeter, Wales: The Edwin Mellen Press, Ltd, 2000).

Livingstone, D.N. 'Darwin in Belfast: The Evolution Debate', in J.W. Foster (ed.), *Nature in Ireland* (Dublin: The Lilliput Press, 1997).

Lloyd, D. '"Pap for the Dispossessed": Seamus Heaney and the Poetics of Identity', in E. Andrews (ed.), *Seamus Heaney: A Collection of Critical Essays* (London: Macmillan, 1992).

Lupton, J.R. 'Mapping Mutability: or, Spenser's Irish Plot', in B. Bradshaw *et al.* (eds), *Representing Ireland: Literature and the Origins of Conflict, 1534–1660* (Cambridge: Cambridge University Press, 1993).

Lysaght, S. 'Contrasting Natures: The Issue of Names', in J.W. Foster (ed.), *Nature in Ireland* (Dublin: The Lilliput Press, 1997).

MacCana, P. 'Placenames and Mythology in Irish Tradition: Places, Pilgrimages and Things', in G.W. Maclennan (ed.), *Proceedings of the First North American Congress of Celtic Studies* (Ottawa: Chair of Celtic Studies, University of Ottawa Press, 1988).

MacNeill, E. (ed. and trans.) *Duanaire Finn Volumes I and II* (Dublin: Irish Texts Society, 1908).

Macpherson, J. *The Poems of Ossian and Related Works*, ed. H. Gaskill, Intro. Fiona Stafford (Edinburgh: Edinburgh University Press, 1996).

Maley, W. 'Spenser's Irish English: Language and Identity in Early Modern Ireland', in *Studies in Philology*, 91 (1994).

Marcus, P. *Yeats and the Beginning of the Irish Renaissance* (Ithaca, NY: Cornell University Press, 1970).

Marks, J. *English Pastoral Drama* (New York: Benjamin Blom, 1972).

Martin, A. 'Quest and Vision: *The Journey*', *Irish University Review*, 23, 1 (Spring/Summer 1993).

Mathews, P.J. *Revival: The Abbey Theatre, Sinn Féin, The Gaelic League and the Co-operative Movement* (Cork: Cork University Press, 2003).

Matthews, S. *Irish Poetry: Politics, History, Negotiation* (London: Macmillan, 1997).

McCartney, D. 'Parnell, Davitt and the Land Question', in C. King (ed.), *Famine, Land and Culture in Ireland* (Dublin: University College Dublin Press, 2000).

Meyer, K. 'Uath Beinne Etair', *Revue Celtique*, XI (1889).

Meyer, K. 'Two Tales About Finn', *Revue Celtique*, XIV (1899).

Meyer, K. *Fianaigecht* (Dublin: Royal Irish Academy, Todd Lecture Series Volume XVI, 1910).

Meyer, K. 'Find Mac Umaill', *Revue Celtique*, XXXII (1911).

Meyer, K., and A. Nutt (eds and trans.), *Immram Brain (The Voyage of Bran son of Febal to the Land of the Living)* (London: David Nutt, 1897).

Miller, N.A. *Modern Ireland and the Erotics of Memory* (Cambridge: Cambridge University Press, 2002).

Montgomery, W.E. *The History of Land Tenure in Ireland* (Cambridge: Cambridge University Press, 1889).

Morrogh, M.M. 'The English Presence in Early Seventeenth Century Munster', in C. Brady and R. Gillespie (eds), *Natives and Newcomers* (Dublin: Irish Academic Press, 1986).

Mudimbe, V.Y. *The Idea of Africa* (Indianapolis, IN: Indiana University Press, 1994).

Mullin, K. 'Don't Cry For Me, Argentina: "Eveline" and the Seductions of Emigration Propaganda', in D. Attridge and M. Howe (eds), *Semicolonial Joyce* (Cambridge: Cambridge University Press, 2000).

Murphy, G. 'Vergilian Influence Upon the Vernacular Literature of Medieval Ireland', *Studi Medievali*, 5 (1932).

Murphy, G. (ed. and trans.) *Early Irish Lyrics: Eighth to Twelfth Century* (Oxford: Oxford University Press, 1956).

Nagy, J. *The Wisdom of the Outlaw: The Boyhood Deeds of Finn in Gaelic Narrative Tradition* (Berkeley, CA: University of California Press, 1985).

Nicholson, M.H. *Mountain Gloom, Mountain Glory: The Development of the Aesthetics of the Infinite* (Washington, DC: University of Washington Press, 1997).

O'Brien, E. *The Beckett Country* (London: Black Cat Press, 1986).

O'Connor, F. *The Backward Look* (London: Macmillan, 1967).

Ó Corráin, D. 'Early Irish Hermit Poetry?', in D. Ó Corráin *et al.* (eds), *Sages, Saints and Storytellers: Celtic Studies in Honour of Professor James Carney* (Maynooth: Maynooth Monographs 2, 1989).

O'Curry, E. *Lectures on the Manuscript Material of Ancient Irish History* (Dublin, 1861).

O'Grady, S.J. *Early Bardic Literature, Ireland* (London: Sampson, Low, Searle, Marston, & Rivington, 1879 [Dublin: E. Ponsonby])

O'Grady, S.J. *History of Ireland: Critical and Philosophical Vol. I* (London: Sampson, Low, & Co., 1881 [Dublin: E. Ponsonby])

O'Halloran, S. *An Introduction to the Study of the History and Antiquities of Ireland* (Dublin: T. Ewing, 1772).

O'Keeffe, J.G. (ed. and trans.), *Buile Suibhne* (Irish Texts Society Vol. XI. 2nd edn, London: Irish Texts Society, 1996).

O'Neill, T.P. 'Famine Evictions', in C. King (ed.), *Famine, Land and Culture in Ireland* (Dublin: University College Dublin Press, 2000).

Ong, W.J. *Orality and Literacy: The Technologizing of the Word* (New York: Methuen & Co. Ltd, 1982).

Oskamp, H.P. (ed. and trans.), *The Voyage of Mael Duin: A Study in Early Irish Voyage Literature* (Groningen: Wolters-Noordhoff Publishing, 1970).

O'Toole, F. 'Going West: The Country Versus the City in Irish Writing', *Crane Bag*, 9 (1985).

Ó Tuama, S. 'Stability and Ambivalence: Aspects of the Sense of Place and Religion in Irish Literature', in J. Lee (ed.), *Ireland: Towards a Sense of Place* (Cork: Cork University Press, 1985).

Ó Tuama, S. 'Celebration of Place in Irish Writing', in *Repossessions* (Cork: Cork University Press, 1995).

Palmer, P. *Language and Conquest in Early Modern Ireland* (Cambridge: Cambridge University Press, 2001).

Patten, E. 'Samuel Ferguson: A Tourist in Antrim', in G. Dawe and J.W. Foster (eds), *The Poet's Place: Ulster Literature and Society* (Belfast: Institute of Irish Studies, Queen's University Belfast, 1991).

Platt, L. *Joyce and the Anglo-Irish: A Study of Joyce and the Literary Revival* (Amsterdam: Rodopi, 1998).

Raine, K. 'Preface', in J.P. McGarry *Place Names in the Writing of William Butler Yeats* (London: Colin Smythe, 1976).

Reeves-Smyth, T. 'The Natural History of Demesnes', in J.W. Foster (ed.), *Nature in Ireland* (Dublin: The Lilliput Press, 1997).

Reizbaum, M. *James Joyce's Judaic Other* (Palo Alto, CA: Stanford University Press, 1999).

Renan, E. *The Poetry of the Celtic Races and Other Studies*, trans. W.B. Hutchinson (London: Kennikat Press, 1970 [1859]).

Robinson, T. 'Place/Person/Book: Synge's *The Aran Islands*' in J.M. Synge, *The Aran Islands*, ed. T. Robinson (London: Penguin Books, 1992).

Saddlemyer, A. 'Art, Nature, and "The Prepared Personality": A Reading of *The Aran Islands* and Related Writings', in S.B. Bushrui (ed.), *Sunshine and the Moon's Delight: A Centenary Tribute to John Millington Synge* (Gerrards Cross: Colin Smythe Ltd, 1972).

Said, E. 'Yeats and Decolonialism', in *Nationalism, Colonialism, and Literature* (Minneapolis, MN: University of Minnesota Press, 1990).

Schama, S. *Landscape and Memory* (New York: Vintage Books, 1996).

Seaman, A.T. 'Celtic Myth as Perceived in Eighteenth and Nineteenth-Century Literature in English', in C.J. Byrne *et al.* (eds), *Celtic Languages and Celtic Peoples: Proceedings of the Second North American Congress of Celtic Studies* (Halifax, Nova Scotia: D'Arcy McGee Chair of Irish Studies, St Mary's University, 1992).

Senn, F. 'Clouded Friendship: A Note on "A Little Cloud"', in O. Frawley (ed.), *A New and Complex Sensation: Essays on Joyce's Dubliners* (Dublin: The Lilliput Press, 2004).

Sigerson, G. *Bards of the Gael and Gall: Examples of the Poetic Literature of Erinn* 2nd edn (London: T. Fisher Unwin, 1907 [1897]).

Simms, K. *From Kings to Warlords: The Changing Political Structure of Gaelic Ireland in the Later Middle Ages* (London: The Boydell Press, 1987).

Smyth, W.J. 'Explorations of Place', in J. Lee (ed.), *Ireland: Towards a Sense of Place* (Cork: Cork University Press, 1985).

Spenser, E. *The Works of Edmund Spenser: A Variorum Edition*, ed. Edwin Greenlaw *et al.* (Oxford: Oxford University Press, 1943).

Spenser, E. 'Colin Clouts Come Home Againe', in *The Works of Edmund Spenser: A Variorum Edition: Vol. 7: The Minor Poems*. ed. Edwin Greenlaw *et al.* (Oxford: Oxford University Press, 1943 [1595]).

Spenser, E. *The Faerie Queene* (London: Penguin, 1978; reprinted 1987 [1590–96]).

Spenser, E. *A View of the Present State of Ireland*, A. Hadfield and W. Maley (eds) (Oxford: Blackwell Publishers, 1997 [1633]).

Stewart, S. *On Longing: Narratives of the Miniature, the Gigantic, the Souvenir, the Collection* (Durham, NC, and London: Duke University Press, 1993).

Stocking Jr, G.W. 'Essays on Museums and Material Culture', in G.W. Stocking, Jr. (ed.), *Objects and Others: Essays on Museums and Material Culture* (Madison, WI: University of Wisconsin Press, 1985).

Stokes, W. (ed. and trans.), 'Finn and the Phantoms', *Revue Celtique*, VII (1896).

Synge, J.M. *The Collected Works Volume II: Prose*, ed. A. Price (Gerrards Cross: Colin Smythe Ltd, 1982 [Oxford: Oxford University Press 1966]).

Synge, J.M. *Collected Works III and IV: Plays*, ed. A. Saddlemyer (Gerrards Cross: Colin Smythe Ltd, 1982 [Oxford: Oxford University Press, 1968]).

Synge, J.M. *The Aran Islands*, ed. and Intro. T. Robinson (New York: Penguin Classics, 1992).

Tate, A. 'Yeats' Romanticism', in J. Unterecker (ed.), *Yeats: A Collection of Critical Essays* (Englewood Cliffs, NJ: Prentice-Hall, Inc., 1963).

Theocritus. *The Idylls*, trans. R. Wells (London: Penuin, 1989).

Thompson, S. 'The Postcolonial Tourist: Irish Tourism and Decolonization Since 1850' (Unpublished Ph.D. dissertation, Notre Dame University, 2000).

Thoreau, H.D. *Walden*, ed. J. Wood Krutch (London: Bantam, 1962 [1854]).

Thornton, W. *J.M. Synge and the Western Mind* (Gerrards Cross: Colin Smythe Ltd, 1979).

Thrower, N.J.W. *Maps and Man: An Examination of Cartography in Relation to Culture and Civilization* (Englewood Cliffs, NJ: Prentice-Hall, Inc., 1972).

Toliver, H. *Pastoral Forms and Attitudes* (Berkeley, CA: Uniiversity of California Press, 1984).

Tymoczko, M. *The Irish Ulysses* (Berkeley, CA: University of California Press, 1994).

Tymoczko, M. 'A Poetry of Masks: The Poet's Persona in Early Celtic Poetry', in K.A. Klar *et al.* (eds), *A Celtic Florilegium: Studies in Memory of Brendan O Hehir* (Lawrence, MA: Celtic Studies Publications, 1996).

Tymoczko, M. *Translation in a Postcolonial Context* (Manchester: St Jerome Publishing, 1999).

Van Gennep, A. *The Rites of Passage* and *The Ritual Process: Structure and Anti-Structure*, trans. M.B. Vizedon and G.L. Caffee (Chicago, IL: University of Chicago Press, 1961 [Rites de passage, Paris, 1909]).

Virgil. *The Eclogues*, trans. A.G. Lee (London: Penguin, 1984).

Walker, J.C. *Historical Memoirs of the Irish Bards* (New York: Garland, 1971 [1786]).

Walsh, P. (ed. and trans.), *Beatha Aoda Ruaidh Uí Dhomhnaill (The Life of Aodh Ruadh O Domhnaill)* 2 Vols (Dublin: Irish Texts Society, 1948–49).

Watson, G. 'Landscape in Ulster Poetry' in G. Dawe and J.W. Foster (eds) *The Poet's Place: Ulster Literature and Society* (Belfast: Institute of Irish Studies, Queens University, 1991).

Watson, G.J. *Irish Identity and the Literary Revival: Synge, Yeats, Joyce and O'Casey,* 2nd edn (Washington, DC: The Catholic University of America Press, 1994 [1979]).

Williams, J.E.C. *The Court Poet in Medieval Ireland* (Oxford: Oxford University Press, 1972).

Williams, N.J.A. (ed. and trans.), *The Poems of Giolla Brighde Mac Con Midhe* (Dublin: Irish Texts Society, 1980).

Williams, R. *The Country and the City* (New York: Oxford University Press, 1973).

Yeats, W.B. *Autobiographies* (London: Macmillan & Co. Ltd, 1955).

Yeats, W.B. *Essays and Introductions* (London: Macmillan & Co. Ltd, 1961).

Yeats, W.B. *W.B. Yeats: The Poems*, ed. Daniel Albright (London: J.M. Dent & Sons Ltd, 1990).

Index